The Gospel of John in Christian History

Seven Glimpses into the Johannine Community
(Expanded Edition)

J. Louis Martyn

Edited by Paul N. Anderson
Johannine Monograph Series 8
Foreword by R. Alan Culpepper

WIPF & STOCK · Eugene, Oregon

THE GOSPEL OF JOHN IN CHRISTIAN HISTORY
Seven Glimpses Into the Johannine Community (Expanded Edition)
Johannine Monograph Series 8

By J. Louis Martyn, Paul N. Anderson, and R. Alan Culpepper

Copyright©2019 Wipf & Stock Publishers

Wipf and Stock Publishers
199 W 8th Ave, Suite 3
Eugene, OR 97401
ISBN 13: 978-1-5326-7164-7
Publication date 7/8/2019

Previously published by Paulist Press, as *The Gospel of John in Christian History: Essays for Interpreters* (New York: Paulist, 1978) plus four additional essays.

The Johannine Monograph Series

Edited by Paul N. Anderson
and R. Alan Culpepper

The vision of the Johannine Monograph Series is to make available in printed, accessible form a selection of the most influential books on the Johannine writings in the modern era for the benefit of scholars and students alike. The volumes in this series include reprints of classic English-language texts, revised editions of significant books, and translations of important international works for English-speaking audiences. A succinct foreword by one of the editors situates each book in terms of its role within the history of Johannine scholarship, suggesting also its continuing value in the field.

This series is founded upon the conviction that scholarship is diminished when it forgets it own history and loses touch with the scintillating analyses and proposals that have shaped the course of Johannine studies. It is our hope, therefore, that the continuing availability of these important works will help to keep the cutting-edge scholarship of this and coming generations of scholars engaged with the classic works of Johannine scholarship while they also chart new directions for the future of the discipline.

Volume 1: *The Gospel of John: A Commentary*
by Rudolf Bultmann

Volume 2: *The Composition and Order of the Fourth Gospel*
by D. Moody Smith

R. Alan Culpepper is Dean and Professor Emeritus at the McAfee School of Theology and Research Fellow at the University of the Free State, Bloemfontein, South Africa.

Paul N. Anderson is Professor of Biblical and Quaker Studies at George Fox University and Extraordinary Professor of Religion at the North-West University of Potchefstroom, South Africa.

CONTENTS

ABBREVIATIONS

AB	Anchor Bible
ABD	*Anchor Bible Dictionary*
ANRW	Aufstieg und Niedergang der römischen Welt
BAGD	Greek-English Lexicon of the NT
BBB	Bonner biblische Beiträge
BETL	Bibliotheca ephemeridum theologicarum lovaniensium
BEvT	Beiträge zur evangelischen Theologie
Bib	*Biblica*
BINS	Biblical Interpretation Series
BJRL	*Bulletin of the John Rylands Library*
BR	*Biblical Research*
BSac	*Bibliotheca Sacra*
BTB	*Biblical Theology Bulletin*
BZ	*Biblische Zeitschrift*
CBQ	*Catholic Biblical Quarterly*
CBR	*Currents in Biblical Research*
CH	*Church History*
CurTM	*Currents in Theology and Mission*
ECL	Early Christianity and Its Literature

ETL	*Ephemerides Theologicae Lovanienses*
ExpT	*Expository Times*
FB	*Forschung zur Bibel*
FFNNT	Foundations and Facets: New Testament
FRLANT	*Forschungen zur Religion und Literatur des Alten und Neuen Testaments*
GCS	Griechischen christlichen Schriftsteller
HNT	Handbuch zum Neuen Testament
HUCA	*Hebrew Union College Annual*
Int	*Interpretation*
IRT	Issues in Religion and Theology
JES	*Journal of Ecumenical Studies*
JBL	*Journal of Biblical Literature*
JR	*Journal of Religion*
JRT	*Journal of Religious Thought*
JSNT	*Journal for the Study of the New Testament*
JSOT	*Journal for the Study of the Old Testament*
JTS	*Journal of Theological Studies*
HTS	*Harvard Theological Studies*
Neot	*Neotestamentica*
NovTSup	Supplements to *Novum Testamentum*
NTS	*New Testament Studies*
PG	Patrologia Graeca
PRS	*Perspectives in Religious Studies*
PSTJ	*Perkins (School of Theology) Journal*

RBS	Resources for Biblical Study
ResQ	*Restoration Quarterly*
RevExp	*Review and Expositor*
RSR	*Reserches de science religieuse*
SBLDS	Society of Biblical Literature Dissertation Series
SBLMS	Society of Biblical Literature Monograph Series
SBLSymS	Society of Biblical Literature Symposium Series
SemeiaSt	Semeia Studies
SJLA	Studies in Judaism in Late Antiquity
SNTSMS	Society for New Testament Studies Monograph Series
SPAW	*Sitzungsberichte der preussischen Akademie der Wissenschaften*
TD	*Theology Digest*
TDNT	*Theological Dictionary of the New Testament*
TS	*Theological Studies*
TynBul	*Tyndale Bulletin*
TZ	*Theologische Zeitschrift*
UTSQ	*Union Theological Seminary Quarterly*
WUNT	Wissenschaftliche Untersuchungen zum Neuen Testament
WW	*Word and World*
ZNW	*Zeitschrift für die neutestamentliche Wissenschaft und die Kunde der älteren Kirche*
ZTHK	*Zeitschrift für Theologie und Kirche*

EDITOR'S PREFACE

THIS COLLECTION OF ESSAYS on John by J. Louis Martyn gathers four additional Johannine essays into a single volume, augmenting the three published earlier in *The Gospel of John in Christian History* (1978). In addition to the essays published in the third edition of *History and Theology in the Fourth Gospel* (2003), these two volumes preserve for later generations the complete set of Martyn's published works on John. In a timely way, the publication of this volume follows the 50th anniversary of the publication of *History and Theology* (1968), which John Ashton regarded as the most important single Johannine monograph since the commentary of Rudolf Bultmann. It also follows the fortieth anniversary of the publication of his second Johannine book (which actually came out in 1979), which serves as the core of the present volume. In Martyn's original Preface, he explains:

> The chapters in this book have grown in several settings geometrically, far removed from each other, and in those settings a number of people have made substantive contributions to their growth. During the remarkable sabbatical year in Jerusalem, 1974–75, colleague at the École Biblique offered themselves as generous conversation partners. In March 1975, the oral forms of chapters 1 and 2 were given as guest lectures at the Universities of Amsterdam, Groningen, Leiden, and Utrecht; it is pleasant to recall the gracious and helpfully critical discussions with my Dutch hosts and colleagues, and with their students. The lecture form of chapter 3 was proffered at the Journées in August 1975 at Pope

Adrian College in Louvain. On that occasion, the discussion
was extraordinarily lively, and the printed form now takes
account of that discussion at several points. Similarly helpful responses were given to chapter 2 when it was presented
to colleagues at the Studiorum Novi Testamenti Societas in
Aberdeen a few days later. And there are comparable debts
to attentive auditors at the 1975 meeting of the Society of
Biblical Literature in Chicago and at the 1976 summer lectures at Assumption College in Worcester, Massachusetts.

The four essays added to the three already published in *The Gospel of
John in Christian History* display the range of thought and its development within Martyn's appraisal of the Johannine situation in the interim between 1970 and 2007, engaging critiques and responses along
the way. Within those developments, one notes Martyn's engagements
with earlier giants of New Testament studies (Baur, Harnack, Bauer,
Bultmann, Käsemann, Jeremias, Cullmann, Meeks, Borgen, Brown,
and Smith), including the engaging of such contemporary scholars as
Gaventa and Meyer. One also notes here a number of refinements and
reinforcements of his earlier views, reminding us all that "the conversation continues" on a number of levels.

Special additions to the present volume include a tribute on behalf
of Lou's former doctoral students by Martinus C. de Boer and an ex-
pansive treatment of Martyn's monumental contribution to Johannine
studies, the history of early Christianity, and biblical interpretation in
the modern era by R. Alan Culpepper. Permissions to publish the original and additional essays have been granted by the publishers, and the
original venues of publication are as follows:

"We Have Found Elijah," first published in *Jews, Greeks, and
Christians: Essays in Honor of William David Davies*, edited by R. Ham-
merton Kelly and R. Scroggs (Leiden: E. J. Brill, 1976), 181–219.

"Persecution and Martyrdom," first published in a longer and
more technical form as "Clementine Recognitions 1, 33-71, Jewish
Christianity, and the Fourth Gospel," in *God's Christ and His People:*

Essays Honoring Nils Alstrup Dahl, edited by J. Jervell and Wayne A. Meeks (Oslo: Universitetsforlaget, 1977), 265–95.

"Glimpses into the History of the Johannine Community," first published in *L'Évangile de Jean: Sources, Rédactions, Théologie*, edited by M. de Jonge, BETL 44 (Leuven: Leuven University Press, 1977), 149–75.

"Source Criticism and *Religionsgeschichte* in the Fourth Gospel," first published in *Jesus and Man's Hope*, edited by G. Buttrick (Pittsburg: Pittsburg Theological Seminary, 1970), 1:147–73.

"A Gentile Mission that Replaced an Earlier Jewish Mission?" first published in *Exploring the Gospel of John: In Honor of D. Moody Smith*, edited by R. Alan Culpepper and C. Clifton Black (Louisville: Westminster John Knox, 1996), 124–44.

"The Johannine Community among Jewish and Other Early Christian Communities," first published in *What We Have Heard From the Beginning*, edited by Tom Thatcher (Waco: Baylor University Press, 2007), 183–90.

"Listening to John and Paul on the Subject of Gospel and Scripture," first published in *Word and World* 12.2 (1992) 68–81; also published in J. Louis Martyn, *Theological Issues in the Letters of Paul*, Studies of the New Testament and its World (Edinburgh: T. & T. Clark, 1997), 209–30.

Paul N. Anderson

J. Louis Martyn

A Brief Tribute from a Former Doctoral Student

MARTINUS C. DE BOER

THE LATE 1970S AND early 1980s were an exciting time to be a doctoral student at Union Theological Seminary in New York. In those years, J. Louis Martyn and his colleague Raymond E. Brown were bringing to fruition a profound change in Johannine studies, a change that they themselves had inaugurated with their work on John in the late 1960s when Brown published his two-volume Anchor Bible commentary on the Gospel of John (1966, 1970)[1] and Martyn his revolutionary monograph, *History and Theology in the Fourth Gospel* (1968).[2] During my time as a doctoral student at Union, Martyn published a second, revised edition of his monograph in 1979. That year also saw Martyn's publication of a collection of three recent essays on John, including "Glimpses into the History of the Johannine Community," as well as Brown's publication of *The Community of the Beloved Disciple*, which was heavily indebted to Martyn's work.[3] Brown would subsequently publish his magisterial Anchor Bible commentary on the Epistles of

1. *The Gospel According to John*, AB 29 and 29A (Garden City: Doubleday, 1966, 1970).

2. Full bibliographical information for Martyn's publications may be found in the introduction by R. Alan Culpepper.

3. New York: Paulist, 1979.

John in 1982.[4] Their work from this period profoundly shaped scholarship on the Johannine literature in the decades that followed. It was a great learning experience to be right there on the ground when these groundbreaking works were being written, published, and intensively discussed.

Lou's first doctoral student was Robert T. Fortna, and his dissertation, published in 1970 as *The Gospel of Signs: A Reconstruction of the Narrative Source Underlying the Fourth Gospel,*[5] had considerable impact on Lou's thinking and on Johannine studies generally. His subsequent doctoral students, however, appear to have chosen other areas of study for their dissertation projects, at least during the years that I was there.[6] As is now well-known, Lou Martyn's interest also extended to Paul. He began his work on his Anchor Bible commentary on Galatians already in the late 1970s,[7] and after 1980 he devoted most of his time to this commentary, which was eventually published in 1997 and would itself become a landmark in Pauline studies.[8] Of course, Lou had already written on Paul earlier in his career. His essay, "Epistemology at the Turn of the Ages," written in 1967, made a considerable impact on me and many other doctoral students.[9] Through my participation in

4. *The Epistles of John*, AB 30 (Garden City: Doubleday, 1982).

5. SNTSMS 11 (Cambridge: Cambridge University Press, 1970).

6. For example, Richard Sturm (Paul and apocalyptic), Joel Marcus (Gospel of Mark), Cain Felder (Epistle of James).

7. A perusal of the catalogues of Union Seminary from the years 1975–82 indicates that Martyn offered a seminar on the Gospel of John three times in those years, but also a seminar on Galatians an equal number of times during the same period. In addition, he offered seminars on Colossians, Philippians, Romans, and problems in Pauline Theology, among other non-Johannine topics and works, such as the Epistle of James, the Gospel of Mark, the Parables of Jesus, and Jewish Christianity.

8. *Galatians: A New Translation with Introduction and Commentary*, AB 33A (New York: Doubleday, 1997).

9. Published in W. R. Farmer, C. F. D. Moule, and R. R. Niebuhr, eds., *Christian History and Interpretation: Studies Presented to John Knox* (Cambridge: Cambridge University Press, 1967), 269–87.

Lou's advanced seminar on Galatians, I became increasingly fascinated with Paul as an apocalyptic theologian. The result was that Lou became the supervisor of my dissertation on Paul's apocalyptic eschatology, as this came to expression in 1 Corinthians 15 and Romans 5.[10] I did eventually publish a monograph on the Gospel and Epistles of John, *Johannine Perspectives on the Death of Jesus*,[11] which uses Martyn's work on the Fourth Gospel and Brown's on the Johannine Epistles as a foundation.[12] This book had its genesis during my years at Union.

Not only as a scholar, but also as a teacher, Martyn's approach was an instructive mix of close exegetical analysis, controlled historical imagination, and intensive theological engagement. Sound method and dialogue with diverse points of view, both ancient and modern, were also part of the mix. Whenever a seminar discussion threatened to lose its way, he would pipe up and say: "Let's look at the text." That was not a command but an invitation, and it was always accompanied by a gleam of expectation in his eyes.

Martyn's remarkable capacity for listening and for empathy is evident in his scholarly publications, as both his classic monograph and the essays included in this volume amply demonstrate. That capacity was also on display in his supervision of doctoral students, for whom he was

---

10. Defended in 1983, the dissertation was eventually published in revised form as *The Defeat of Death: Apocalyptic Eschatology in 1 Corinthians 15 and Romans 5*, JSNTSS 22 (Sheffield, JSOT, 1988); reprint with corrections: LNTS 22 (London: Bloomsbury Academic, 2015).

11. CBET 17 (Kampen: Kok Pharos, 1996).

12. The reconstruction of the history of the Johannine community and its literature in part I of that volume seeks to combine the best of Martyn with the best of Brown and has now been refined and presented anew in "The Johannine Community and its Literature," in the *Oxford Handbook of Johannine Studies*, edited by Judith M. Lieu and Martinus C. de Boer (Oxford: Oxford University Press, 2018), 63–82. In these publications I build on the work of Martyn in particular, as I did in the essay "The Depiction of 'the Jews' in John's Gospel: Matters of Behavior and Identity," in *Anti-Judaism and the Fourth Gospel*, edited by Reimund Bieringer et al. (Louisville: Westminster John Knox, 2001), 141–57.

a much loved and highly respected teacher and counselor. He was not a heavy-handed supervisor who sought disciples. He let you make mistakes but then helped you to rectify them; he allowed you to lose your way in the material but then helped you find your way out. When conversing with him, you always felt as if you and your ideas really mattered, even if you could not quite articulate them, and even when they did not agree with his own. As Joel Marcus put it in an obituary: "he always conveyed the sense that, however stupid you thought yourself to be, he was learning something from you. . . . [H]e saw things in his students and, more widely, in his friends, that they didn't see in themselves."[13] I myself remember with amazement and gratitude the numerous times that, after a consultation in which Lou had pretty much demolished the latest draft of a chapter of my dissertation, I left his office feeling not discouraged or humiliated, but encouraged and uplifted by his thoughtful feedback and support. For me, as for many others, Lou Martyn remained a mentor and a friend for the rest of his life.

What Hamlet said of his father I can say of my *Doctorvater*: "I shall not look upon his like again."[14] I am sure that not only his students, but also many others who knew and experienced Lou Martyn firsthand, will agree.

13. Available at http://www.snts.international/wp-content/uploads/2016/02/ J.-LOUIS-MARTYN-Joel-Marcus.pdf.

14. Act I, Scene II.

Foreword

J. Louis Martyn's Contribution to the Understanding of the Gospel of John

R. ALAN CULPEPPER

THE PUBLICATION OF J. Louis Martyn's *History and Theology in the Fourth Gospel* (*HTFG*) fifty-one years ago opened an exciting window onto the Johannine community and quickly won widespread acceptance, at least among American Johannine scholars.[1] Responses focused on Martyn's reconstruction of the Johannine community's conflict with the synagogue and his suggestion that the claim in John 9:22, that "the Jews had already agreed that anyone who confessed Jesus to be the Messiah would be put out of the synagogue" (NRSV), is an anachronistic reference to the Twelfth Benediction, the *Birkat Haminim*.[2] Reflecting on his intent and the reception of his work for the Fourth Gospel Section at the Society of Biblical Literature meeting in Anaheim, CA, in 1989, Martyn himself commented that the hypothesis

---

1. First edition (New York: Harper & Row, 1968); second edition (Nashville: Abingdon, 1979); third edition (Louisville: Westminster John Knox, 2003). Hereafter, these editions are abbreviated: *HTFG*[1], *HTFG*[2], and *HTFG*[3].

2. Although one finds this transliterated term spelled and capitalized in various ways, this essay follows *The SBL Handbook of Style*, 2nd ed.

of a connection between the reference in John 9:22 and the *Birkat* was a "pink herring." The goal he had in mind was in fact highly theological.

HTFG was written in 1963–64 as a result of Martyn's sharp debates with Ernst Käsemann in the fifties. Martyn later reflected, "we found ourselves in considerable disagreement, but the disagreement was focused on a question we agreed to be crucial: Where does the document we are reading belong in the strains and stresses characteristic of early Christian history?"[3] This became "a truly burning question" for Martyn, but his interest was still theological: "to hear the truth with the ears of the Johannine community."[4] Although early reviewers focused primarily on Martyn's history of the community, for Martyn the crux of the drama was still primarily theological. During the discussion at the SBL meeting, he responded to two rhetorical questions: what is happening to history, and what is happening to theology? In response to the first, he observed that by 1989, "one could talk about the remarkable degree to which the work of F. C. Baur [who interpreted the New Testament writings in their historical setting] was in eclipse," while in regard to the second, what is happening to theology, "new toys threaten to take over the show."[5]

Martyn's comments on his work and its reception call us to a careful reading of the times in which he wrote *HTFG*, his multifaceted proposal, its reception and responses to it over the past half century, and its continuing importance for understanding the Fourth Gospel, its theology, and the context in which it was written.

---

3. J. Louis Martyn, "Listening to John and Paul on the Subject of Gospel and Scripture," *WW* 12 (1992) 68–81, 70.

4. From my notes on Martyn's response to the panelists at the Fourth Gospel Section, SBL Annual Meeting in Anaheim, November 19, 1989, on the tenth anniversary of the publications on John by Raymond E. Brown and J. Louis Martyn in 1978–79.

5. Ibid.

Martyn's Life and Scholarship

As significant as it is, Martyn's contribution to Johannine scholarship is only part of his legacy to New Testament scholarship, which in turn does not begin to capture his gifts to his colleagues, students, and family.[6] J. Louis Martyn (October 11, 1925—June 4, 2015) first studied electrical engineering at Texas A&M, graduating in 1946. His graduate students would later say that he approached the intricacies of New Testament texts with the analytical skills he honed as an electrical engineer![7] Turning to theological studies, Martyn completed the BD at Andover Newton Theological School in 1953 and the PhD at Yale University in 1957, with a dissertation on "The Salvation-History Perspective in the Fourth Gospel" under the supervision of Paul Schubert. A Fulbright scholarship enabled him to study with Joachim Jeremias and Ernst Käsemann in Göttingen in 1957–58. The next year, Martyn taught at Wellesley College, and then joined the faculty at Union Theological Seminary, where he became the Edward Robinson Professor of Biblical Theology in 1967, a chair he held until his retirement in 1987. Martyn spent his sabbatical leave in 1974–75 at the Ecumenical Institute for Advanced Theological Studies in Jerusalem—"an unforgettable period."[8] Beverly Gaventa aptly characterizes the first stage of Martyn's work as yielding "landmarks in Johannine studies" and the second as "landmarks in Pauline studies." The latter include the Anchor Bible commentary on Galatians (1997) and *Theological Issues in the Letters of Paul* the same year. Only Martyn's contribution to Johannine studies can be pursued here.[9]

6. See the obituary written by Beverly Roberts Gaventa: https://www.sbl-site.org/assets/pdfs/Martyn-tribute-June2015.pdf.

7. A comment shared with me by Marion L. Soards.

8. J. Louis Martyn, *The Gospel of John in Christian History: Essays for Interpreters* (New York: Paulist, 1978), 113 n. 181.

9. For assessments of Martyn's work, see: Raymond E. Brown, "A Personal Word," in *Apocalyptic and the New Testament: Essays in Honor of J. Louis Martyn*, edited by Joel

Johannine Scholarship on the
Johannine Situation before Martyn

In "The Contribution of J. Louis Martyn to the Understanding of the Gospel of John," D. Moody Smith situates Martyn's work in the context of Johannine scholarship in the decades after World War II, in the context of the seminal works of the twentieth century by Bultmann, Dodd, Hoskyns, and Käsemann.[10] Bultmann attempted to define the Gospel's sources and composition history, tracing it to circles of John the Baptist followers in Syria or Palestine and a form of heterodox Judaism, from which the Mandaean sources later emerged. Dodd surveyed the connections between the Gospel and a broad range of Hellenistic and Jewish literature and concluded that it was intended for cultured, religious readers, Jew or Greek, across the Hellenistic world. As Smith put it:

> Whether in Palestine, Athens, Alexandria, or Rome, the intended reader would understand and feel the appeal of the Gospel of John. Specific historical circumstances of the Gospel's setting are less important than general religious and cultural relevance and affinities in Dodd's view.[11]

In contrast to both Bultmann and Dodd, Hoskyns was intent on setting John squarely within early Christian tradition, the historical revelation in Jesus of Nazareth, the Synoptic tradition, and New

---

Marcus and Marion L. Soards, JSNTS 24 (Sheffield: JSOT, 1989), 9–12; John Riches, *A Century of New Testament Study* (Valley Forge: Trinity Press, 1993), 180–87; Beverly Gaventa, "J. Louis Martyn," *Dictionary of Biblical Interpretation*, edited by John H. Hayes, 2 vols. (Nashville: Abingdon, 1999), 2:133–34; D. Moody Smith, "The Contribution of J. Louis Martyn to the Understanding of the Gospel of John," in *HTFG3*, 1–23; and William Baird, *History of New Testament Research: Vol. 3* (Minneapolis: Fortress, 2013), 604–22; and *Apocalyptic and the Future of Theology: With and Beyond J. Louis Martyn*, edited by Joshua B. Davis and Douglas Harink (Eugene, OR: Wipf & Stock, 2012). The papers from the 2016 SBL panel on the legacy of J. Louis Martyn for the study of the Apostle Paul are forthcoming in *Journal of Paul and His Letters*.

10. Smith, "Contribution of J. Louis Martyn," 1–5.

11. Ibid., 2.

Testament theology generally. The Gospel's historical and theological foundations were therefore more important than the setting in which it was composed, and the former do not depend on establishing the latter. Käsemann, with whom Martyn studied in the 1950s, also situated John within the development of the theology of early Christianity, but took a radically different view of its place in this history. For Käsemann, John's naively docetic view of Jesus as "God striding over the earth" originated in an early Christian "community" or "conventicle" with gnosticizing tendencies and led to later gnostic interpretations.[12]

In response to these proposals, Martyn situated the Gospel in a Jewish context, emphasized the importance of reading the Gospel in its historical setting as a way of resisting "a kind of 'timeless and place-less' reading of the gospel,"[13] and sought to illuminate the nature of the community within which it was written. Martyn was not the first to ask about the community in which the Gospel originated, but he was arguably the first to develop a view of the community that opened compelling new readings of specific sections of the Gospel.

As early as 1835, D. F. Strauss had spoken of a "Johannine school," and this term came to define a mediating position between those who maintained and those who denied the apostolic authorship of the Gospel.[14] The school hypothesis held that the apostle gathered a group of disciples around him who wrote or assisted in the writing of the Gospel, the Epistles, and in some iterations, the Apocalypse. Dodd, for example, concluded that the author of 1 John was "quite possibly a disciple of the

12. Käsemann, *The Testament of Jesus: A Study of John in the Light of Chapter 17*, translated by G. Krodel, Johannine Monograph Series 6 (Philadelphia: Fortress, 1968; Reprint, Eugene, OR: Wipf & Stock, 2017), 70, 73.

13. Martyn, "The Salvation-History Perspective in the Fourth Gospel," unpublished PhD diss., Yale University, 1957, 87.

14. David Friedrich Strauss, *The Life of Jesus Critically Examined*, edited by Peter C. Hodgson, translated by George Elliot, Lives of Jesus Series (Philadelphia: Fortress, 1972), 330. For a survey of the development of the Johannine school hypothesis, see Culpepper, *The Johannine School*, SBLDS 26 (Missoula: Scholars, 1975; Reprint, 2007), 1–38.

Fourth Evangelist and certainly a diligent student of his work."[15] In an influential and often-cited article, Adolf von Harnack outlined the possible referents of the use of "we" in the Johannine writings. From this review, Harnack concluded that the Fourth Evangelist never introduced a "kleinasiatische Zeugengruppe," or special group of eyewitnesses of the historical Jesus, but he did maintain that the Johannine writings were related to "streitenden Kreisen," or contending circles, in Asia Minor.[16] In "the New Look on the Fourth Gospel," presented at the International Congress on "The Four Gospels in 1957," John A. T. Robinson also situated the Gospel in "the life of an on-going community."[17] Martyn broke new ground, however, by separating the question of the Johannine community from the issue of the Gospel's authorship. While the description of the community loomed large for Martyn, the question of authorship was of little concern.

Neither was Martyn the first to notice conflict with the synagogue in John. Bultmann comments in passing on "the situation of the Church reflected in the Gospel of John," saying, "its problem is the conflict with Judaism." Specifically, "the Christian congregation is already excluded from the synagogue association (9:22; 16:1–3)," and "the evangelist feels the Church's estrangement from Judaism."[18] Kenneth L. Carroll also noticed these references. Drawing on the earlier work of R. Travers

15. Dodd, "The First Epistle of John and the Fourth Gospel," *BJRL* 21 (1937) 156.

16. Adolf von Harnack, "Das 'Wir' in den johanneischen Schriften," *SPAW* 17 (1923) 112–13.

17. John A. T. Robinson, "The New Look on the Fourth Gospel," in *Studia Evangelica*, TU 73 (Berlin: Akademie-Verlag, 1959), 350; reprinted in Robinson's *Twelve New Testament Studies*, SBT 34 (Naperville, IL: Allenson, 1962), 94–106.

18. Rudolf Bultmann, *Theology of the New Testament*, 2 vols., translated by Kendrick Grobel (New York: Scribner's Sons, 1951–55), 2:5.

Herford,[19] Harris Hirschberg,[20] and James Parkes,[21] Carroll identified the *minim* as Jewish Christians, dated the composition of the *Birkat Haminim* to around 90, and affirmed Herford's contention that it represents "the official condemnation by the Rabbis of the spurious Judaism which was growing in their midst, and at the same time furnished a means of detection."[22] Carroll adds, "The purpose of this malediction was to make possible the detection of the *Minim* who would inevitably omit this particular paragraph when invited to pronounce the *Eighteen Benedictions*."[23] At the same time, Carroll also concludes "there is no direct information concerning any Jewish persecution of Christians from the time of James to the beginning of the revolt in the time of Trajan."[24] Nevertheless, the *Birkat*, which Carroll surmises was communicated to synagogues by letters, stands as evidence of a "forceful attempt on the part of the Jews to rid their synagogues of Christians."[25] Because the *aposynagōgos* passages in John refer to this later development, the evangelist "has projected this attitude and action, in reality much later than the time of Jesus, back into

19. R. Travers Herford, *Christianity in Talmud and Midrash* (London: Williams & Norgate, 1903), asserts: "The theory that the *Minim* are intended to designate Jewish Christians I regard as having been now conclusively proved" (379).

20. Harris Hirschberg, "Once Again—the Minim," *JBL* 67 (1948) 305–18.

21. James Parkes, *The Conflict of the Church and the Synagogue: A Study in the Origins of Antisemitism* (London: Soncino, 1934).

22. Herford, *Christianity in Talmud and Midrash*, 385, quoted by Kenneth L. Carroll, "The Fourth Gospel and the Exclusion of Christians from the Synagogue," *BJRL* 40 (1957) 19–32, 22. Carroll is not cited in *HTFG*[1] but is cited in *HTFG*[2], 50 n. 62. T. C. Smith, *Jesus in the Gospel of John* (Nashville: Broadman, 1959), 33–34, also situated the Gospel of John in a Jewish context and pointed to the relevance of the *Birkat Haminim* for understanding John 9:22; "the author was writing with such a decree of excommunication in mind."

23. Carroll, "Fourth Gospel and the Exclusion of Christians," 23.

24. Ibid., 30.

25. Ibid., 31, cf. 23.

the period of Christian beginnings—even having Jesus himself predict the Jewish exclusion of Christians from the synagogues."[26]

Parallel developments were occurring in Matthean studies in the work of Douglas Hare and R. Hummel,[27] and W. D. Davies made the case that Samuel's revision of the *Birkat Haminim* around 85 CE contained the reference to the Nazoreans. Therefore, "the Birkath ha Minim makes it unmistakably clear that the Sages at Jamnia regarded Jewish Christians as a menace sufficiently serious to warrant a liturgical innovation."[28] The elements of Martyn's thesis were in place, but it remained for the genius of *History and Theology in the Fourth Gospel* to draw them together in dramatic fashion.[29]

26. Ibid., 32.

27. Douglas R. A. Hare, *The Theme of Jewish Persecution of Christians in the Gospel according to Matthew*, ThD diss., Union Theological Seminary, 1965; SNTSMS 6 (Cambridge: Cambridge University Press, 1967); and R. Hummel, *Die Auseinandersetzung zwischen Kirche und Judentum im Matthäusevangelium*, BEvT 33 (Munich: Kaiser, 1963).

28. W. D. Davies, *The Setting of the Sermon on the Mount* (Cambridge: Cambridge University Press, 1966), 276.

29. Martyn's engagement with Johannine scholarship between the writing of his dissertation and the publication of HTFG1 can be seen in the book reviews he wrote during this period: Review of *Images of the Church in the New Testament* by Paul S. Minear, *JBL* 80 (1961) 195–96; Review of *Der Tod des Johannes als Schlüssel zum Verständnis der Johanneischen Schriften* by Karl A. Eckhardt, *JBL* 81 (1962) 314; Review of *Bread from Heaven* by Peder Borgen, *JBL* 86.2 (1967) 244–45. Martyn calls attention to Minear's intention to grasp "the communal processes of imagination" that gave currency to the various images of the church in the New Testament. He says of Eckhardt that "he knows both how to follow a clue and how to construct a case which is highly intriguing, if not wholly convincing." While finding much to commend in Borgen's work, Martyn departs from him on the presence of "an antidocetic tendency in John 6," saying that the problem is rather "Jews who lodge a demand based on orthodox typology," a reading of John 6 that he develops in HTFG1, 112–19, esp. 116–17.

History and Theology in the Fourth Gospel (1968)

Martyn was committed to the principle that the Gospel of John must be read in its historical context, and hence the interpreter must "seek to define the particular circumstances in response to which the Fourth Gospel was written" (xvii), and even "to take up temporary residence in the Johannine community" (xviii). As a starting point, Martyn notes that each of the three healing narratives in John (4:46–54; 5:1–9; and 9:1–7) have synoptic parallels, but the latter two are the beginning of a sequence of related scenes, a distinctive literary genre he calls a drama (xxi).

Focusing on the story in John 9, and drawing on form criticism, Martyn notes that it follows the form of a healing story, with a description of the sickness, the healing, and confirmation of the healing. The appearance of the neighbors in verses 8–9, however, introduces a "dramatic expansion" of the original story that extends through verse 41. The resulting story is a drama in seven skillfully drawn scenes. The healing story in verses 1–7, Martyn suggests, is primarily related to what he terms "an *einmalig* event" [sic, an einmaliges event]; that is, an event "back there," during Jesus' lifetime. The rest of the chapter bears witness to "Jesus' powerful presence in actual events experienced by the Johannine church" (9–10). In this way, Martyn identifies in John 9 "two levels" in the narrative, which can also be found elsewhere in "certain parts" of the Gospel. The Pharisees in John 9, Martyn argues, "probably reflect the authority of the Bet Din in Jamnia much more than they reflect an historical 'Pharisaic Sanhedrin' of Jesus' day" (12 n. 28). The Jewish authorities who investigate the healing Martyn identifies as the Gerousia, "the ruling body of Jewish elders in John's city" (12 n. 28a). The authorities question the man who was healed and his parents, but not the healer, and they demand that one must choose whether to be a disciple of Moses or of Jesus. Both of these elements of the story seem to reflect the contemporary level rather than the *einmaliges* level and invite further examination.

The second chapter engages in analysis of John 9:22, especially the verb translated "had agreed" (συνετέθειντο) and the adjective ἀποσυνάγωγος. Martyn understands the former as referring to "a formal agreement or *decision* reached by some *authoritative Jewish group*" (18 [Martyn's italics]) and translates the latter "to be put out of the synagogue" (22). *Aposynagōgos* does not occur in any earlier document, nor does it correspond to any Semitic equivalent in Jewish writings. Martyn first rules out the suggestions that it refers to (1) a Jewish ban (either the *niddui* or the *cherem*) or (2) disciplinary action such as one finds in Acts, including (3) "Luke's portrait of the parting of ways in Acts 18 and 19" (29). He then marshals the evidence that it refers to the *Birkat Haminim* revised by Simeon the cotton dealer (aka "Samuel the Small") at Jamnia under the direction of Rabban Gamaliel II around 85 CE and communicated among the enactments or *Takkanoth* (b. Rosh Hashanah 31b) "published by the Jamnia authorities" (34). Such an interpretation is supported by the reference to a change in the wording of the close "of every Benediction in the Temple" in m. Berakoth 9:5: "they *ordained* that they should say" (32 [Martyn's italics]). The function of the *Birkat Haminim* is described in b. Berakoth 28b–29a: "If a reader made a mistake in any of the other benedictions, they do not remove him, but if in the benediction of the Minim, he is removed, because we suspect him of being a Min" (35). References in the Church Fathers to "the Jewish practice of cursing Christians 'while they read the prayers'" (37 n. 70) support the interpretation of the reference to "the Nazarenes and the Minim" and the petition, "let them be blotted out of the Book of Life and not to be inscribed together with the righteous" in the *Birkat* as the Jamnian response to the danger posed by "Christians" within the synagogues. John 9:22, Martyn argues, refers to "the Heretic Benediction," which was adopted "in order formally and irretrievably to separate the church from the synagogue" (41).

Turning his attention to John 16:2a–b, "put you out of the syna-gogue" and "kill you," Martyn first reconstructs a series of stages that are reflected in the drama. It begins with Christian missionaries preaching Jesus as the Messiah (1:41, 45, 49) and gathering a "messianic commu-nity," or "circle of messianic believers," who continue to participate in the synagogue meetings while also meeting separately. Their actions raise concern among the authorities, which leads to the use of the composi-tion and promulgation of the Benediction against Heretics as a means of identifying believers within the synagogues and excommunicating them. When this act of separation does not stop the stream of converts, the authorities impose a further step, namely, the arrest and execution of those who deceive and mislead the people. This process, Martyn argues, is reflected in John 5 and 7, confirming that they too are two-level dra-mas. The efforts to arrest Jesus and put him to death (perhaps based on Deuteronomy 13:6–9) reflect the threat the authorities pose for the Chris-tian missionaries at the time of the Johannine community. Specifically, the missionaries are accused of "leading the people astray" (John 5:18; 7:47) because they lead them to worship a second god alongside God. Such a process, Martyn contends, is reflected in Justin's *Dialogue with Trypho* 69 and in b. Sanhedrin 43a and 107b.

Close examination of the terms used for the Jewish leaders in John 5 and 7 provides an additional argument for reading the attempts to arrest Jesus in these chapters as also involving a two-level drama. John 5 refers to the authorities as "the Jews," as does John 7 up to the attempted arrest. At that point, they are referred to as "the chief priests and the Pharisees," a reference Martyn finds as strange as referring to a modern seminary faculty as "the ministers and Presbyterians" (72). His explanation is that it is a reference to the authorities—the Sanhe-drin on the *einmalig* level, which was composed primarily of the chief priests, and the Gerousia on the contemporary level, the majority of whose members were Pharisees. Similarly, John appears to use "the rul-ers" (οἱ ἄρχοντες; 3:1; 7:26, 48; 12:42) to refer to "the secretly believing members of the Gerousia, while 'the Pharisees' is his term for the Loyalists who dominate that body" (75–76). The evangelist himself was probably not conscious of this two-level drama (77).

The pleas in John 10:20, "Why are you listening to him?" if read as part of the two-level drama, suggest that the conversation between John's church and the synagogue continued. Martyn cites Justin, *Dialogue* 38.1, where Trypho says that their teachers warned them not to converse with Christians. Martyn asks what the conversation would have been about and points to references in John that suggest that it would have been about the claim that Jesus was the Messiah (1:41; 4:25)—a term found only in John in the New Testament—and about his signs: "When the Christ appears, will he do more signs than this man has done?" (7:31). Pursuing the question of whether there is evidence for the expectation of a miracle-working Messiah, Martyn finds that while "Judaism expected the messianic age to be a time of miracles" (85), there was no expectation that the Davidic Messiah would be a wonderworker. Yet, John links Jesus' identity as the Messiah to his signs (20:30–31). To resolve this dilemma, Martyn observes that Jewish sources mingled the expectation of various figures, so "it is just possible that traits 'properly' belonging to another eschatological figure have 'rubbed off' on the Johannine Messiah" (88).

That figure, Martyn contends, was the expected prophet like Moses. Six affirmations drawn from John shed light on what each party in the conversation was saying about Moses, the points on which they agreed and the points at issue between them. Martyn's argument here is dense and resists being summarized briefly. Contemporary texts that developed the promise of a "prophet like Moses" in Deuteronomy 18:15 and 18 show that Jewish writers, the Qumran community (1QS), and the Samaritans held differing views of the role of the Mosaic Prophet or Mosaic Prophet-Messiah, but suggest that "the Mosaic Prophet was the middle term between Moses and the Messiah" (103). While some of "the common fold in the synagogue" accepted Jesus' signs as proof that he was the

Mosaic Prophet, the "Jamnia loyalists" demanded midrashic evidence. The author of the Signs Gospel (reconstructed by Robert T. Fortna,[30] who was Martyn's student in the mid-1960s), provided "powerful midrashic demonstration that Jesus fulfills the hope for the Prophet-Messiah like Moses" (108). The evangelist, on the other hand, denies the applicability of the criterion of midrashic proof, using midrashic argument in John 6 "in order to terminate all midrashic discussion" (119). Jesus' word, "I am the bread of life," is self-authenticating.

The last chapter deals with "the presence of the Son of Man." Continuing his pursuit of the Christology of the Gospel in light of its presentation of Jesus in a two-level drama, Martyn examines the relationship between the Mosaic Messiah and the Son of Man in John and finds that "John never allows the identification of Jesus as Mosaic Prophet-Messiah to occupy center stage" for long without moving to Jesus' role as the Son of Man (125). This title, with its roots in Daniel 7 and its apocalyptic overtones, leads Martyn to observe that "John did not create the literary form of the two-level drama" (127); it can be traced to Jewish apocalypticism, where one often finds "dramas taking place both on the heavenly stage and on the earthly stage" (127). John adapts this form, however, because in the Gospel both stages are on earth and they relate not the present and the future but the past and the present. Jesus ascended and descended as the Son of Man (John 3:13), and it is "as the Son of Man that Jesus appears on the contemporary level of the drama and thus makes known his presence" (132). The promise of the Paraclete who will continue Jesus' work is the key that makes this possible: "*It is, therefore, precisely the Paraclete who creates the two-level drama*" (140, Martyn's italics). Through the Paraclete, Jesus returns to his own, so the good news that John proclaims is Jesus present as the Son of Man, both *einmalig* and on the contemporary level (142).

---

30. Robert T. Fortna, *The Gospel of Signs: A Reconstruction of the Narrative Source Underlying the Fourth Gospel*, SNTSMS 11 (Cambridge: Cambridge University Press, 1970).

Responses to *HTFG*[1] (1968–78)

As we turn to the reception of *HTFG*[1], Martyn's responses, and later developments in his thoughts, two questions loom large: (1) why was Martyn's thesis so widely accepted? and (2) why was it so widely critiqued?

The first responses came in reviews of *HTFG*[1], and the early reviews were positive.[31] They announced that this was an important contribution to Johannine scholarship, while raising only marginal points about its main thesis. T. A. Burkill ventured that it was "an unusually important work which will surely affect the course of scholarly research," and compared it to the redactional histories of the Synoptic Gospels by Trilling, Trocmé, and Conzelmann.[32] Raymond E. Brown, in his characteristically judicious manner, noted that while elements of Martyn's thesis were not new, "Martyn makes the most thoroughgoing synthesis of these ideas yet achieved; he shows how much of the Gospel is permeated by the synagogue situation without, however, claiming exclusivity."[33] Raising a question he would later engage himself, he asked, "Do some other motifs reflect different stages in the history of the Johannine community or simply different facets of the same stage?"[34] Writing a few years later, Robert Kysar described Martyn's work as "a proposal which seems to be gaining an increasing degree of consent."[35] Others too began to take up the question of the Johan-

31. W. A. Beardslee, *Religion in Life* 38 (1969) 150; Raymond E. Brown, *USQR* 23 (1968) 392–94; T. A. Burkill, *JBL* 87 (1968) 439–42; Robert H. Gundry, *Christianity Today* 12.24 (Sept 13, 1968) 42; Robert Kysar, *Dialog* 8 (1969) 70–72; John J. O'Rourke, *CBQ* 30 (1968) 629–30; Rudolf Schnackenburg, "Zur Herkunft des Johannesevangeliums," *BZ* 14 (1970) 7–9; D. Moody Smith, *Int* 23 (1969) 220–23; David Suter, *JR* 49 (1969) 275–80.

32. Burkill, *JBL* 87 (1968) 439.

33. Brown, *USQR* 23 (1968) 393.

34. Ibid., 394.

35. Robert Kysar, *The Fourth Evangelist and His Gospel: An Examination of Contemporary Scholarship* (Minneapolis: Augsburg, 1975), 149. While Kysar adds that Martyn's analysis of the evangelist's redaction of the proposed signs source "commands my

nine community and its setting, especially Wayne A Meeks, D. Moody Smith, R. Alan Culpepper, Oscar Cullmann, Raymond E. Brown, and Rudolf Schnackenburg.[36]

During this period, Martyn extended his work on the Johannine community. In the book reviews he wrote during this period, one can see "glimpses" of his developing interests and methodological convictions. For example, he faults André Feuillet because he "never seriously pursues style criticism" in his book on the prologue.[37] In his lengthy review of Barnabas Lindars's commentary on John and monograph, *Behind the Fourth Gospel* (1971), Martyn calls for distinguishing a theory of tradition-history from a theory of literary history. He agrees that Lindars has often "grasped 'John's literary technique' (*BFG*, 42) so

---

adherence" (79), he later changed his view (see below). Kysar also notes that Marinus de Jonge "explicitly endorsed Martyn's thesis" (156).

36. Wayne A. Meeks, *The Prophet-King: Moses Traditions and the Johannine Christology*, Johannine Monograph Series 5 (NovTSupp 14, 1967; Eugene, OR: 2017); idem, "The Man from Heaven in Johannine Sectarianism," *JBL* 91 (1972) 44–72; idem, "'Am I a Jew?' Johannine Christianity and Judaism," in *Christianity, Judaism and Other Greco-Roman Cults*, edited by Jacob Neusner, SJLA 12 (Leiden: Brill, 1975), 163–86; D. Moody Smith, "Johannine Christianity: Some Reflections on Its Character and Delineation," *NTS* 21 (1974–75) 222–48; R. Alan Culpepper, *The Johannine School*, SBLDS 26 (Missoula: Scholars, 1975); Oscar Cullmann, *The Johannine Circle*, translated by John Bowden (Philadelphia: Westminster, 1976); Raymond E. Brown, "Johannine Ecclesiology—The Community's Origins," *Int* 31 (1977) 379–93; idem, "'Other Sheep not of this Fold': the Johannine Perspective on Christian Diversity in the Late First Century," *JBL* 97 (1978) 5–22; Rudolf Schnackenburg, "Die johanneische Gemeinde und ihre Geisterfahrung," in *Die Kirche des Anfangs: für Heinz Schürmann*, edited by R. Schnackenburg, J. Ernst, and J. Wanke (Leipzig: St. Benno Verlag, 1977), 277–306. See also, A. J. Mattill Jr., "Johannine Communities behind the Fourth Gospel: Georg Richter's Analysis," *TS* 38 (1977) 295–315; and C. K. Barrett, *The Gospel of John and Judaism*, translated from German (1970) by D. M. Smith (Philadelphia: Fortress, 1975), esp. 47–48, where he discusses the *Birkat Haminim* and Jewish Christian relations in the second century.

37. J. Louis Martyn, Review of *Le prologue du quatrième évangile: Étude de théologie johannique*, *JBL* 89 (1970) 497–98. See also Martyn's Review of *Martyria* by Johannes Beutler, *CBQ* 39 (1977) 273–75.

as to perceive at least a part of his intention," but he calls Lindars to task for "methodological imprecision," tracing John's creative use of tradition before clearly exposing the underlying traditions and avoiding problems presented by the text. As an example, Martyn comments on Lindars's interpretation of the verb *heuriskei* in John 1:43—a text he was working on at the time (see below). Martyn also finds it necessary to respond to Lindars's misreading of *HTFG*: the discourse in John 8:31–47 is not "*a report*" of an actual debate but "*reflects* actual experiences of the Johannine community."[38]

"Source Criticism and *Religionsgeschichte* in the Fourth Gospel"

In his paper for the Pittsburgh Festival on the Gospels in 1970, Martyn's reflections on the relationship between the recent publications on John by Robert Fortna, Wayne Meeks, and Ernst Käsemann led him to think about the interactions of *Religionsgeschichte* (Meeks), *Theologiegeschichte* (Käsemann), and source criticism (Fortna). Martyn insists there must be "mutual critique" among the three disciplines.[39] One of Käsemann's contributions, he says, was "to renew and make potent in our time the voice of F. C. Baur."[40] Following this line of thought, and "numerous data in the Gospel," Martyn observes that "John is a theologian with *opponents*."[41] Putting Fortna and Käsemann together, it becomes clear that we are dealing with three stages, not two: "the writing of SG [the Signs Gospel]; subsequent and thus chronologically intervening developments,

---

38. J. Louis Martyn, Review of *The Gospel of John* by Barnabas Lindars, *JBL* 95 (1976) 667–68, 670–71.

39. J. Louis Martyn, "Source Criticism and *Religionsgeschichte* in the Fourth Gospel," in *Jesus and Man's Hope*, 2 vols. (Pittsburgh: Pittsburgh Theological Seminary, 1970), 1:247–73, 251.

40. Ibid., 249.

41. Ibid., Martyn's italics.

including activities on the part of 'opponents;' and the writing of 4G."[42] In search of the developments between the SG and the Fourth Gospel, Martyn considers the struggles with followers of John the Baptist, the conflict between synagogue and church, and inner-church problems. The question "Who is Jesus?" seems to have elicited various responses: (1) the requirement on the part of some for midrashic examination, (2) the claim that Moses had ascended and received "heavenly secrets," and (3) the charge of ditheism. None of these are at issue in the SG, but the Fourth Gospel responds to each of them. The case is the same in regard to the question "Can one follow Moses and Jesus?" A third question, "What significance has Jesus' death?" takes us into the realm of inner-church debates. In conclusion, Martyn contends that the dialogue between these three disciplines in the recent explorations of the Johannine setting confirms that the "*religionsgeschichtlich* developments behind 4G are complex," "accepting SG as a working hypothesis promises to bring the complexity into sharper focus," and "John belongs in a dominantly Jewish-Christian milieu."[43]

During the 1970s, Martyn extended his study of the historical setting and Christology of the Gospel of John in three other essays, which he then published in *The Gospel of John in Christian History*.[44]

"We Have Found Elijah"

For his contribution to the W. D. Davies Festschrift, Martyn turned to a debated christological issue and a debated verse in John 1.[45] Argu-

---

42. Ibid., 250.

43. Ibid., 269.

44. The page numbers in the next three sections reference the reprint of these three essays in Martyn's *The Gospel of John in Christian History: Essays for Interpreters* (New York: Paulist, 1978).

45. J. Louis Martyn, "We Have Found Elijah," in *Jews, Greeks, and Christians: Essays in Honor of W. D. Davies*, edited by Robert Hamerton-Kelly and Robin Scroggs (Leiden: Brill, 1976), 181–219.

ably, none of his other essays illustrates his methodical analysis of texts and issues as clearly as this one.

The early church interpreted Jesus as the "prophet like Moses" (Deut 18:15, 18), and viewed the Baptist as Elijah, but in John 1:20–21, John denies that he is Elijah. The dominant view, represented by R. H. Fuller and F. Hahn, was that "there is no evidence that the Church interpreted Jesus as Elijah" (10–11). Cullmann demurred, suggesting that the Baptist's rejection of this title in John 1 suggests "that the writer of John *wants to reserve this title for Jesus*" (11).[46]

Martyn finds that none of the six references to Elijah in the Synoptics occurs in John. Furthermore, while John 3:13 explicitly denies a link between Jesus and Elijah, saying that no one has ascended into heaven except the Son of Man, Elijah's miracle-working seems to have provided "some of the features of the Gospel's miracle-working Jesus" (25). How, then, can we explain this "divided picture" (28), with "Elijah-like traits" in some of the miracle stories but an explicit rejection in John 3:13? Martyn suggests that source criticism provides a possible resolution, with the pre-Johannine author of the Signs Gospel shaping the accounts of the signs as positive counterparts to all three of the Baptist's denials in John 1:20–21, although the evangelist "penned 3:13 in such a way as emphatically to exclude, among other things, an explicit identification of Jesus as the eschatological Elijah" (28).

To support this thesis, Martyn turns to the problematic John 1:43. He takes note of the problems presented by the verse, including the difficulty of identifying the subject of the verb, "he wished to go," and the way it breaks the pattern of one disciple finding another (33). His proposal is that in the Signs Gospel, verses 41–42, 43, and 45–47 formed a threefold sequence in which (1) Andrew found his brother Simon and said, "we have found the Messiah"; (2) Andrew found Philip and said, "we have found Elijah"; and (3) Philip found Nathanael and

---

46. Oscar Cullmann, *The Christology of the New Testament*, translated by Shirley C. Guthrie and Charles A. M. Hall (Philadelphia: Westminster, 1959), 37. Martyn's italics.

said, "the one about whom Moses wrote . . . we have found" (38–41). The evangelist, then, added the disruptive travel notice at the beginning of verse 43 and omitted the explicit reference to Elijah.

Accordingly, at least one writer in the early church (the author of the Signs Gospel) identified Jesus as the fulfillment of the expectation of the eschatological Elijah, but the evangelist suppressed this identification for christological reasons, preferring instead the identification of Jesus as the preexistent Logos at the beginning of John 1 and the Son of Man at the end of the chapter.

"Persecution and Martyrdom"

In this essay,[47] Martyn goes hunting again for early tradition that sheds light on the experience of the Johannine community while it was still a Jewish-Christian church, and this time he turns to the Pseudo-Clementines. In particular, he asks whether there is any evidence for "the particular kind of deadly persecution reflected in John 16:2 (and 7:45–52)" in sources we know come from Jewish-Christian churches (56–57).

Working with the Pseudo-Clementine literature is difficult because our extant texts date from the fourth century but appear to draw from a romance (in two editions: the *Homilies* and the *Recognitions*) written in the third century, which in turn employed second-century sources. Martyn examines *Recognitions* 1.33–71 and accepts its identification as a form of the *Ascents of James* mentioned by Epiphanius. Parts of these chapters must also be set aside as later Christian interpolations. What remains in these chapters is "a sketch of redemptive history from Abraham to the early years of the Jerusalem church" (59) that is akin to Stephen's speech in Acts 7. Martyn assigns this source to "a Jewish-Christian writer,

---

47. Originally published in an earlier, "rather more technical form," as "Clementine Recognitions 1, 33–71, Jewish Christianity, and the Fourth Gospel," in *God's Christ and His People: Essays Honoring Nils Alstrop Dahl*, edited by J. Jervell and Wayne A. Meeks (Oslo: Universitetsfort, 1977), 265–95.

in or near second-century Pella, who is concerned to provide his church with the history which gives it its distinctive identity" (63).

This Jewish-Christian community distinguished itself from non-Christian Judaism on one side, and the Pauline mission on the other. The *Ascents of James* draws from books of the Old Testament and the Synoptic Gospels (especially Matthew) but never quotes the Gospel of John. Going further, Martyn asks, "did our Jewish-Christian author occasionally allude to the Gospel of John?" (67). As candidates for such allusions, Martyn considers the identification of Jesus as the prophet foretold by Moses, polemical references to the followers of John the Baptist, and a reference to debate with the Samaritans over the proper place of worship (Jerusalem or Mount Gerizim?), but none of these warrants the conclusion that the author of the *Ascents* was dependent on the Fourth Gospel (68). Two key passages (in chapters 62–68) warn that those who lead others astray will suffer martyrdom at the hands of Jewish authorities (72)—as does John 16:2—and portray Gamaliel as a secret believer, a characterization Martyn suggests is a conflation of the reference to Gamaliel in Acts and the references to Nicodemus in John.

These literary data might be explained either on the basis of a memory of John from someone in the Pella community, or a tradition held in common by the authors of the Fourth Gospel and the *Ascents of James*. Such a tradition, which Martyn reconstructs, reflects "the situation of a Jewish Christian being subjected to a hearing or trial before a Jewish court" (85). Accordingly, after carefully examining the possible connections, Martyn finds the corroborating evidence he was looking for: "there is good reason to believe that this piece of tradition—*in the form involving the seducer charge*—was fixed in or quite near the setting in which the Fourth Gospel was written" (87).

"Glimpses into the History of the Johannine Community"[48]

By 1977 Martyn was filling out the picture of the Johannine Community that had emerged from his work, extending his dialogue with other scholars, and constructing an integrative synthesis of his view of the history of the Johannine community. Still, Martyn reminds readers that we can say very little about the Johannine community with virtual certainty: "it would be a valuable practice for the historian to rise each morning saying to himself three times slowly and with emphasis, 'I do not know'" (92). Nevertheless, he offers the connection between John 9:22 and the *Birkat Haminim* as "one of these relatively secure points" (92). Working from it, he characterizes three periods in the history of the Johannine community.

John 1:35–49, which he treated in "We Have Found Elijah" (see above), provides the literary foundation for his view that these verses are based on a very early sermon in which Jesus is presented to Jewish hearers as the fulfillment of already "well-formed messianic expectations," namely that "he is the Mosaic prophet, the eschatological Elijah, the expected Messiah" (96). The sermon, he suggests, reflects "the Gospel for the circumcised" (Gal 2:7), for which we have very little remaining evidence, and hence it offers us rare insight into the early period of the Johannine community and more generally into this early period of Jewish Christianity. During this period, which probably extended into the eighties, we should speak of a "group" rather than a "community" and "Christian Jews" rather than "Jewish Christians" (102–3 n. 164). These Christian Jews were Torah-observant Jews who responded to the evangelistic preaching with a relatively simple faith.

The middle period is defined by the trauma of midrashic debates, the exercise of the *Birkat Haminim*, the resulting exclusion from the

---

48. Originally published in *L'Évangile de Jean: Sources, redaction, théologie*, edited by M. de Jonge, BETL 44 (Leuven: Leuven University Press, 1977), 149–76. The page numbers in the following section refer to *The Gospel of John in Christian History*.

synagogue, and the persecution and martyrdom of some of the community's leaders as "seducers" or "beguilers" who led other Jews to worship a second god. This social dislocation and alienation is reflected
in the Gospel's dualism, its interpretation of Jesus as an otherworldly
figure ("the stranger from above"), and its development of an insider
language.

During the middle period, the synagogue authorities "laid down
a new dictum": one was either a disciple of Moses or a disciple of Jesus
(109; cf. John 9:28). One excluded the other. In the late period, the Christian Jews in the synagogue reacted in different ways to this new dictum,
and some determined to remain Christian Jews, even if they had to do so
in secret. Martyn argues that "the Jews who had believed in him" (8:31)
were secret believers, who in the final analysis remain Jews. To this trilateral social configuration Martyn adds a fourth element: "the other sheep"
mentioned in John 10:16. Marshalling arguments from a close reading of
John 10, where the "sheep" stand for the Johannine community, whose
members follow Jesus' voice and reject the Jewish authorities, Martyn argues against the dominant view that the "other sheep" are gentile believers. On the contrary, these who have been "scattered" (11:52) are "Jewish
Christians belonging to conventicles known to but separate from the
Johannine community" (117). Therefore, "the history of the Johannine
community from its origin through the period of its life in which the
Fourth Gospel was composed forms to no small extent a chapter in the
history of *Jewish* Christianity" (120–21, Martyn's italics).

*HTFG*² (1978)

In the changes in the "revised and enlarged" second edition,[49] Martyn is
frequently in dialogue with Brown, Meeks, and Fortna,[50] but takes into

---

49. Page numbers in the footnotes in this section refer to the second edition.

50. See for example references to Brown on pp. 20 n. 5, 33 n. 37, 134 n. 193; Meeks
55 n. 69, 103 n. 149, and 104 n. 153, 109 n. 161, 127 n. 188, 131 nn. 190–91, 142; Fortna

account the recent work of others as well.[51] He identifies "the skilled dramatist" who wrote chapters 5 and 9 as the evangelist, and assigns 9:22 to the evangelist (27, 33 n. 37). Martyn nuances and adds additional arguments for his interpretation of John 9:22 as a reference to the *Birkat Haminim.* While the picture of the academy at Jamnia may be idealized, that does not affect the data on which his argument is based (52 n. 67), and Jamnia was not "the sole locus of rabbinical activity and authority" (53 n. 68). The relationship between John 9:22 and Berakoth 28 is based on three considerations: the language in John 9:22 referring to a formal agreement; the "remarkable" correspondence between John 16:2 and Justin, *Dialogue* 16, 95, and 110; and the relationship between the second element in John 16:2 (execution) and "the rabbinical tradition about the nature of the charges that led to Jesus' death" (55 n. 69). A lengthy addition, reflecting conversations with Meeks and Morton Smith, discusses the date of the *Birkat Haminim* (56–57). Whereas Martyn dated the *Birkat* to 85 CE in *HTFG*[1], he concedes that it may be dated any time between 85 and 115 CE, but inclines toward the earlier part of that period. Smith argued for a date in the second century, but allowed an indirect connection with John, namely, that "Gamaliel is likely to have instituted the *Birkat Haminim* after similar moves had been taken against Christian Jews in numerous communities, and perhaps the Jewish community known to the Fourth Evangelist was one of these" (57 n. 75).

In response to an article by Charles Talbert, Martyn revised his view that John 5:1—7:52 is a distinct literary cycle.[52] *HTFG*[2] also omits his claim that John 4:44 refers to Judea/Jerusalem as Jesus' *patris* on the *eimalig* level and the Jewish quarter of the city on the contemporary level (see *HTFG*[1], 58). Meeks's work led Martyn to see evidence in

---

65 n. 85, 95 n. 136, 165–66. The Modern Authors index is unfortunately incomplete and inaccurate.

51. See, e.g., 50 n. 62; 64 n. 84; 121 nn. 181–82; 127 n. 188; 140 n. 209; 144 n. 217.

52. Charles Talbert, "Artistry and Theology: An Analysis of the Architecture of John 1:19-5:47," *CBQ* 32 (1970) 341–66. As a result, he omitted pages 49–52 and 58–61 of *HTFG*[1]. See *HTFG*[2], 68 nn. 91 and 92, and 73–74.

John of "the Jewish claims that Moses himself ascended on Sinai and was granted visions, and the Johannine polemic directed toward these claims" (104–5). An additional Excursus (E) gathers and discusses "Bibliography Pertinent to the Hypothesis of a Signs Source" (164–68).

Responses to Martyn (1978–96)

The publication of $HTFG^2$ at the same time as the collection of Martyn's essays in *The Gospel of John in Christian History* and Raymond E. Brown's *The Community of the Beloved Disciple* elicited a second wave of reviews, some of which treated these volumes together.[53] Brown's endorsement and his reconstruction of the history of the Johannine community added further significant support for the growing consensus that the outlines of this history could be known, even if the two differed at points such as the factors that led to the expulsion, the number of groups related to the community that can be identified, the influx of Samaritans, and the question of whether the Gospel contains allusions to a gentile mission.[54]

53. Reviews of *HTFG*2: Harold W. Attridge, *PSTJ* 33 (1979) 58–60; R. Alan Culpepper, *RevExp* 76 (1979) 573–75; W. T. Edwards, *PRS* 7 (1980) 164–67; David P. Efroymson, *JES* 19 (1982) 127–29; Lee Gallman, *Foundations* 24 (1981) 185–87; Thomas Hoyt Jr., *JRT* 37 (1980) 50–51; Benjamin J. Hubbard, *CBQ* 42 (1980) 272–73; Robert Kysar, *Religion in Life* 48 (1979) 384–85; Allan McNicol, *ResQ* 23 (1980) 126–28; D. Moody Smith, *Duke Divinity School Review* 45 (1980) 67–69; Robert Smith, *CurTM* 8 (1981) 41–44. Reviews of *The Gospel of John in Christian History*: Harold W. Attridge, *PSTJ* 33 (1979) 58–60; David E. Aune, *CBQ* 43 (1981) 137–39; David P. Efroymson, *JES* 19 (1982) 127–29; Franz Neirynck, *ETL* 58 (1982) 163–64; Robert F. O'Toole, *TS* 41 (1980) 231; Howard Rhys, *Saint Luke's Journal of Theology* 24 (1981) 236–37; B. Van Voorst, *RefR* 33 (1980) 172–73; Craig R. Koester, "R. E. Brown and J. L. Martyn: Johannine Studies in Retrospect," *BTB* 21 (1991) 51–55.

54. See Raymond E. Brown, "Johannine Ecclesiology—The Community's Origins," *Int* 21 (1977) 379–93; "'Other Sheep Not of This Fold': The Johannine Perspective on Christian Diversity in the Late First Century," *JBL* 97 (1978) 5–22; *The Community of the Beloved Disciple* (New York: Paulist, 1979, esp. 22–23, 66); and his posthumously published *Introduction to the Gospel of John*, edited by Francis J. Moloney (Garden City: Doubleday, 2003), esp. 172 n. 56 and the editor's note on page 68.

By sampling the reviews of these concurrent publications, we get a good sense of the state of the hypothesis in this period.

Robert Smith set the work of Martyn and Brown in the broader context of developments in the study of the Gospels and John since about 1950: a gnostic background of the sort Bultmann proposed "is today almost everywhere discounted" and replaced by "the current consensus" that the setting of the Gospel "was primarily Palestinian, Old Testament, and Jewish."[55] Moody Smith's early support for Martyn's thesis appears in his review of the second edition of Barrett's commentary and *HTFG*[2], where Smith claimed Martyn's work is

> a most remarkable model of how New Testament data can be correlated with contemporary (in this case Jewish) sources in an imaginative and yet highly disciplined way to illuminate the historical milieu of a gospel and advance the task of exegesis. Certainly Martyn's book has done as much to alter and inform thinking about the Fourth Gospel as any comparable work.[56]

Thomas Hoyt, Jr., called for further scrutiny of the connection between the expulsion of the Johannine community and the *Birkat Haminim* and endorsed the view that because the *Birkat* "formalized a break that had begun at an early stage, it is just as reasonable to assume that the expulsion was the result of a local decision in the synagogue prior to the Jamnian decision."[57] Harold Attridge recognized the speculative nature of Martyn's "historical allegory" but found his argument that 9:22 alludes to the *Birkat Haminim* persuasive.[58] Allan McNicol challenged Martyn's use of form criticism: "one is puzzled by Martyn's insistence that an essential ingredient for the welding of past and present into the gospel narrative is some present corollary in the life of the community to a work of Jesus

---

55. Robert Smith, *CurTM* 8 (1981) 43.

56. D. Moody Smith, *Duke Divinity School Review* 45 (1980) 69.

57. Hoyt, *JRT* 37 (1980) 51.

58. Attridge, *PSTJ* 33 (1979) 59.

as related by the tradition. . . . This hypothesis cannot be derived from traditional form critical methods."[59] Robert F. O'Toole concluded his brief review of Martyn's essays by saying "M.'s theory proves enticing, but I for one remain unconvinced."[60] Turning to a broader theological issue, David P. Efroymson asked: "the Gospel emphasized the 'replacement' of Judaism by Christianity. Can we have the Fourth Gospel and, as it seems we must, reject the theology of replacement?"[61]

More trenchant critiques of Martyn's thesis began to emerge during this period: critiques of the lynchpin of Martyn's argument—the connection between John 9:22 and the *Birkat Haminim*. Adela Yarbro Collins agreed that the Gospel reflects a social setting of crisis but departed from Martyn by rejecting a connection between the expulsion in 9:22 and Jamnia and Martyn's contention that the Jewish council in the city where the Gospel was written was arresting Christian missionaries. The crisis experienced by the community was likely broader than its conflict with the synagogue; the use of "the world" in John suggests rejection by the Roman authorities and the local populace as well.[62]

A heavy barrage from specialists in rabbinic studies followed: Reuven Kimelman (1981) and Steven T. Katz (1984). Kimelman probes the purpose of the *Birkat* and the meaning of the terms *minim* and *noṣrim*. The Genizah version of the *Birkat Haminim* includes the petition, "Let the *noṣrim* and the *minim* be destroyed in a moment."[63] In

---

59. McNicol, *ResQ* 23 (1980) 128.

60. O'Toole, *TS* 41 (1980) 231; so also Aune, *CBQ* 43 (1981) 137–39.

61. Efroymson, *JES* 19 (1982) 128.

62. Adela Yarbro Collins, "Crisis and Community in the Gospel of John," *TD* 27 (1979) 313–21.

63. Reuven Kimelman, "*Birkat ha-Minim* and the Lack of Evidence for an Anti-Christian Jewish Prayer in Late Antiquity," in *Jewish and Christian Self-Definition*, 2 vols., edited by E. P. Sanders et al. (Philadelphia: Fortress, 1981), 226–44. See also Peter Schäfer, "Die sogennante Synode von Jabne," in *Studien zur Geschichte und Theologie des Rabbinischen Judentums* (Leiden: Brill, 1978), 45–55, reprinted from *Judaica* 31 (1975); and Daniel Boyarin, "Justin Martyr Invents Judaism," *CH* 70 (2001) 427–61.

Tannaitic and Amoraic literature *minim* denotes deviant Jews. It was not to refer to gentiles, but "the Palestinian prayer against the *minim* was aimed at Jewish sectarians among whom Jewish Christians figured prominently."[64] A review of the patristic literature, especially Justin, Origen, Jerome, and Epiphanius, reveals that there are "clear references to Jews, Nazoreans, and cursing *during* the prayers thrice daily" only in the latter two writers.[65] Kimelman concludes that the Genizah text quoted above was composed between the death of R. Johanan (ca. 279 CE) and Epiphanius's writing of the *Panarion* (ca. 377 CE). Moreover, *noṣrim* does not denote Christians, but rather a Jewish Christian sect known as Nazoreans. These texts also reveal a different picture of relations between church and synagogue, namely that Jews were receptive to Christians seeking their assistance, and Christian leaders warned Christians to stay away from the synagogue. In short, "there never was a single edict which caused the so-called irreparable separation between Judaism and Christianity."[66]

Steven Katz reached similar conclusions, although his interest is in the change in relations between 70 and 135 CE.[67] In the fourth section of his essay, which focuses on the promulgation of the *Birkat Haminim*, he too weighs the evidence for regarding the reference to *noṣrim* to be a later addition and agrees with Kimelman against W. D. Davies and others who maintained that it was included in the original version of the *Birkat*.[68]

---

64. Ibid., 232.

65. Ibid., 237.

66. Ibid., 244. In the same volume, Lawrence H. Schiffman, "At the Crossroads: Tannaitic Perspectives on the Jewish-Christian Schism," 115–56, agrees that the reference to *noṣrim* is a later addition, suggesting that it was a reference to gentile Christians, in distinction from the *minim*, who were Jewish Christians (151).

67. Steven Katz, "Issues in the Separation of Judaism and Christianity after 70 CE: A Reconsideration," *JBL* 103 (1984) 43–76.

68. Ibid., 68–72; contra Davies, *The Setting of the Sermon on the Mount*, 275–76, who argued that the inclusion of *noṣrim* gives Samuel the Small's addition to the *Birkat* "a balanced form." Cf. Katz, 64 n. 81, for other scholars who support the inclusion of the term.

Noṣrim appears to be a later insertion, he argues, because: (1) it does not appear in early Christian sources until the fourth century, and (2) if it had been in the original version, since it precedes *minim*, the *Birkat* would have been known as the *Birkat Hanoṣrim*. In regard to the meaning of *minim*, Katz endorses a broad definition; it covered "all types of Jewish heretics," including (after 135 CE) gentiles.[69] Therefore, "the *Birkat ha-Minim* was not directed solely at Jewish Christians when promulgated (or revised) after 70,"[70] and "there was no official anti-Christian policy at Yavneh or elsewhere before the Bar Kochba revolt."[71]

About the same time, William Horbury published an extensive article on the *Birkat* and its history in Judaism that maintained the general reliability of Martyn's interpretation of the Jamnian *Birkat.* Horbury concluded that Justin "was right in supposing that Christians, both Jewish and Gentile, were cursed in synagogue," but "the wording of the benediction was variable, and no surviving text can be assumed to reproduce the specimen form of the Jamnian prayer."[72] The Jamnian ordinance "probably reinforced an earlier exclusion attested in John," although "these two measures may be contemporaneous."[73]

In 1986 and repeated in 1991, John Ashton lent his support to Martyn's thesis, claiming that *HTFG* "for all its brevity is probably the most important single work on the Gospel since Bultmann's commentary."[74]

69. Katz, 72–73.

70. Ibid., 73.

71. Ibid., 76.

72. William Horbury, "The Benediction of the Minim and Early Jewish-Christian Controversy," *JTS* 33 (1982) 19–61, 59.

73. Ibid., 60. See also Horbury's *Jews and Christians in Contact and Controversy* (Edinburgh: T. & T. Clark, 1998); Pieter W. van der Horst, "The Birkat Ha-Minim in Recent Research," *ExpT* 105.12 (1994) 363–68; and M. Eugene Boring, Klaus Berger, and Carsten Colpe, eds., *Hellenistic Commentary to the New Testament* (Nashville: Abingdon, 1995), 301–2.

74. John Ashton, *The Interpretation of John* (London: SPCK 1986), 5; cited from idem, *Understanding the Fourth Gospel* (Oxford: Clarendon Press, 1991), 107.

Indeed, "it is largely because of his [Martyn's] work that one can say that this area of Johannine research (that is, the one concerned with audience and situation) has been roughly mapped out. What remains is a matter of adjusting a few details and filling in some gaps."[75] Ashton proceeded to build his own view of the Gospel and the community it reflects around Martyn's outline of the early, middle, and late periods in the history of the Johannine community, quibbling only at a few points, such as Ashton's view that the charge of ditheism preceded and precipitated the expulsion from the synagogue.[76] Along these lines, Anderson too followed Martyn and Brown in outlining an early, middle, and late view of the Johannine situation, but he sided with Meeks, Brown, Borgen, Cassidy, and Käsemann in seeing a number of dialectical engagements within the Johannine situation, rather than a single Jewish engagement. Following Lindars in viewing John 6 as a later addition, Anderson suggests that a two-level reading of that chapter elucidates at least four crises in the Johannine situation, corroborated by the Johannine Epistles.[77]

75. Ibid., 109. Ashton (109 n. 105) cites David Rensberger's *Overcoming the World: Politics and Community in the Gospel of John* (London: SPCK, 1989), as "the latest and best of the many attempts to follow up Martyn's insights by combining theological and sociological analysis." From this period, see also Wayne O. McCready, "Johannine Self-Understanding and the Synagogue Episode of John 9," in *Self-Definition and Self-Discovery in Early Christianity*, edited by David J. Hawkin and Tom Robinson (Lewiston: Edwin Mellen, 1990), 147–66; and Judith Lieu, "Parting of the Ways: Theological Construct or Historical Reality?" *JSNT* 56 (1994) 101–19.

76. Ashton, *Understanding the Fourth Gospel*, 167.

77. In *The Christology of the Fourth Gospel: Its Unity and Disunity in the Light of John 6* (WUNT 2.78, 1996; 3rd expanded edition, Eugene, OR: Wipf & Stock, 2010), Paul N. Anderson sees the Johannine Jesus as engaging several crises within the Johannine situation, not simply one, and he challenges Martyn's divorcing the Johannine Gospel from the Epistles in seeking to ascertain the socioreligious ethos of Johannine Christianity (195–265). Attempting with John 6 what Martyn achieved with John 9, in his essay on "The *Sitz im Leben* of the Johannine Bread of Life Discourse and its Evolving Context," *Critical Readings of John 6*, edited by R. Alan Culpepper, BINS 22 (Leiden: Brill, 1997), 1–59, Anderson (24–57) connects four crises in the Johannine dialectical situation with John's presentation of actants in the narrative: the crowd (with Brown—representing engagements with Synoptic valuations of the feeding), the Jews

"A Gentile Mission?"

After Martyn had already turned to Paul and Galatians, he again wrote on John for the volume of essays in honor of D. Moody Smith.[78] Martyn's consistent claim that the Fourth Gospel can be situated in a Jewish Christian context (with some contact with Samaritans) through the period of the composition of the Gospel departed from the view of other interpreters who saw evidence for a gentile mission in the Gospel.

In this essay, Martyn responds by reading closely the verses most often cited in support of a gentile mission and concludes that they in fact provide little support for proponents of a Johannine gentile mission prior to the writing of the Gospel. The explanations of Jewish holy times (John 5:1; 6:4; 7:2, etc.) he takes to be, like the references to "the Jews," locutions in the Johannine idiom that refer to "a group of former Jews, not of Gentiles" (126). The translations of Jewish terms and names (such as "Rabbi," "Messiah," "Siloam," and "Rabbouni"), which would be needed only by gentiles, are, as John Painter suggested,[79] glosses added by the redactor responsible for John 21. Parenthetically, we may note that this argument implies that the work of the redactor is to be dated after Martyn's "late period" in the history of the Johannine community. The "rather opaque" reference to teaching "Greeks" in 7:32–36 he reads as saying, "does he

(with Martyn—representing engagements with contemporary Jewish leaders—cf. 1 John 2:18–25), the disciples (with Borgen—representing engagements with docetizing and assimilating traveling ministers—cf. 1 John 4:1–3; 2 John 7), and Peter (with Käsemann—representing institutionalizing developments within the early Church—cf. 3 John 9–10). For a fuller appraisal of the Johannine situation, see idem, "Bakhtin's Dialogism and the Corrective Rhetoric of the Johannine Misunderstanding Dialogue: Exposing Seven Crises in the Johannine Situation," in *Bakhtin and Genre Theory in Biblical Studies*, edited by Roland Boer, SemeiaSt 63 (Atlanta: SBL Press, 2007), 133–59.

78. J. Louis Martyn, "A Gentile Mission that Replaced an Earlier Jewish Mission?" in *Exploring the Gospel of John: In Honor of D. Moody Smith*, edited by R. Alan Culpepper and C. Clifton Black (Louisville: Westminster John Knox Press, 1996), 124–44. Page numbers in parentheses in this section refer to this essay.

79. John Painter, *The Quest for the Messiah: The History, Literature and Theology of the Johannine Community*, 2nd ed. (Nashville: Abingdon, 1993), 131.

intend to go to the Diaspora of Jews who live among the (numerous) God-fearers and there teach the God-fearers?" (126). Martyn reproduces his argument regarding the interpretation of the "other sheep" in John 10:16 (see above) in an expanded form, reasserting his conclusion that the reference is to other Jewish-Christian communities. The prophecy of Caiaphas, in which the high priest says that Jesus will die "not for the nation only, but to gather into one the dispersed children of God," (11:49–52) refers, similarly, to other Christians (cf. 1:12), scattered in other Jewish-Christian conventicles. It does not reflect a gentile mission. Similarly, the "Greeks" who came to worship at the feast (12:20–24) are not typical gentiles because they "*regularly* come to Jerusalem in order to worship at the time of Passover" (131, Martyn's italics). In fact, no stories in the Gospel represent "persons being brought into the Johannine community from the pagan Gentile world" (133).

The conclusive argument against a gentile mission, Martyn claims, is found in the conclusion to Jesus' public ministry at the end of John 12. The evangelist leaves no indications that "faced with Jewish unbelief, his community has substituted a Gentile mission for its earlier mission to its fellow Jews" (134). Acts ends with a turning to the gentiles (Acts 28:25–29), but there is no such scene in John. Taken together, Martyn claims, his reading of the pertinent verses reveals that "the community's sense of mission—at the time of the Gospel—was significantly different from the sense of mission characteristic of the Great Church" (135, Brown's term for the apostolic church of the late first century).

Readers should also note that this essay includes more extensive endnotes than Martyn's other essays. In these notes, Martyn engages both scholars who support his arguments and those who advance other readings of these texts, so one can follow the debates at a deeper level in the endnotes.

*HTFG*³ (2003)

The third edition of *HTFG* contained the revised text of the second edition, Moody Smith's essay, "The Contribution of J. Louis Martyn to the Understanding of the Gospel of John," and a "Postscript" in which Smith responds to the challenges to Martyn's theory posed by the articles on the *Birkat Haminim* summarized above.[80] Smith notes that some of Martyn's critics have caricatured Martyn's understanding of the role of the Jamnian authorities as taking action "to expel from synagogues everywhere Jews who believed that Jesus was the messiah," but this caricature "is not a falsification" of Martyn's thesis: "it is conceivable that expulsions from the synagogue occurred (or were threatened), but were prior to, and perhaps even unrelated to, the formulation of the Twelfth Benediction."[81]

Critique, Support, and Continuing Dialogue

In 2005, Robert Kysar, abandoning his earlier endorsement of Martyn's work (see above), reflected on the rise and decline of the expulsion theory. By the 1990s, he observes, "in many circles, it was often a foregone conclusion that this was the setting for the writing of the Gospel of John."[82] Charting the theory's progressive decline and abandonment by many, he cites the challenges in the early 1980s to Martyn's use of the *Birkat Haminim*, Adele Reinhartz's persistent challenges to the efficacy of reading John as a two-level drama, literary critical challenges to reading the text as a "window" on the past, and consequently the legiti-

---

80. D. Moody Smith, "The Contribution of J. Louis Martyn to the Understanding of the Gospel of John," originally published in *The Conversation Continues: Studies in Paul & John in Honor of J. Louis Martyn*, edited by Robert T. Fortna and Beverly R. Gaventa (Nashville: Abingdon, 1990), 275–94; reprinted in *HTFG*³ 1–19 along with a postscript, 19–23. See also the reviews of *HTFG*³: Otis Coutsoumpos, *BTB* 34 (2004) 130; and *TD* 51 (2004) 177.

81. Smith, "Postscript," *HTFG*³, 20–21.

82. Robert Kysar, *Voyages with John: Charting the Fourth Gospel* (Waco: Baylor University Press, 2005), 237–45, 238.

macy of the historical-critical enterprise in general. The "new history" (exemplified by Colleen M. Conway's article in which she suggests "that we think of interpretations as *productions* of the drama") may portend an era in which "the reign of history as the key to interpretation may be brought to an end."[83]

In the last sixteen years, the volume of literature referencing and engaging Martyn's work has mushroomed beyond any possibility of an adequate summary here, as work has continued on a number of related subjects: the parting(s) of the ways,[84] expulsion from the synagogue,[85]

---

83. Ibid., 242.

84. James D. G. Dunn, *Jews and Christians: The Parting of the Ways, A.D. 70 to 135* (Grand Rapids: Eerdmans, 1999); Stanley E. Porter and B. W. R. Pearson, eds. *Christian-Jewish Relations through the Centuries* (Sheffield: Sheffield Academic, 2000); Daniel Boyarin, *Border Lines: The Partition of Judaeo-Christianity* (Philadelphia: University of Pennsylvania Press, 2004); Adele Reinhartz, "A Fork in the Road or a Multi-Lane Highway? New Perspectives on the 'Parting of the Ways' between Judaism and Christianity," in *Changing Face of Judaism, Christianity, and Other Greco-Roman Religions in Antiquity,* edited by Ian Henderson and Gerbern Oegema, (Gütersloh: Gütersloher, 2006), 280–95; Adam H. Becker and Annette Yoshiko Reed, *The Ways That Never Parted: Jews and Christians in Late Antiquity and the Early Middle Ages* (Minneapolis: Fortress, 2007); Tobias Nicklas, *Jews and Christians: Second-Century "Christian" Perspectives on the "Parting of the Ways,"* Annual Deichmann Lectures 2013 (Tübingen: Mohr Siebeck, 2014); Jörg Frey, "Toward Reconfiguring Our Views on the 'Parting of the Ways': Ephesus as a Test Case," in *John and Judaism: A Contested Relationship in Context,* edited by R. Alan Culpepper and Paul N. Anderson, RBS 87 (Atlanta: SBL, 2017), 221–39.

85. Larry W. Hurtado, "Pre-70 CE Jewish Opposition to Christ-Devotion," *JTS* 50 (1999) 35–58; Edward W. Klink, III, "Expulsion from the Synagogue? Rethinking a Johannine Anachronism," *TynBul* 59 (2008) 99–118; idem, "The Overrealized Expulsion in the Gospel of John," in *John, Jesus, and History,* vol. 2: *Aspects of Historicity in the Fourth Gospel,* edited by Paul N. Anderson, Felix Just, S.J., and Tom Thatcher, ECL 2 (Atlanta: SBL, 2009), 175–84; John S. Kloppenborg, "Disaffiliation in Associations and the Ἀποσυναγωγός of John," *HTS Teologiese Studies / Theological Studies* 67 (June 6, 2011), https://doi.org/10.4102/hts.v67i1.962; Jonathan Bernier, *Aposynagōgos and the Historical Jesus in John: Rethinking the Historicity of the Johannine Expulsion Passages,* BINS 122 (Leiden: Brill, 2013).

the *Birkat Haminim*,[86] Jamnia,[87] the role of synagogues in the first century[88], John's audience[89], the Johannine community[90], "the Jews" in

86. Uri Ehrlich and Ruth Langer, "The Earliest Texts of the Birkat Haminim," *HUCA* 77 (2005) 63–112; Ruth Langer, *Cursing the Christians? A History of the Birkat Haminim* (New York: Oxford University Press, 2012).

87. Shaye J. D. Cohen, "The Significance of Yavneh: Pharisees, Rabbis, and the End of Jewish Sectarianism," *HUCA* 55 (1984) 27–53; Daniel Boyarin, "A Tale of Two Synods: Nicaea, Yavneh, and Rabbinic Ecclesiology," *Exemplaria* 12.1 (2000) 21–62.

88. L. Michael White, "Synagogue and Society in Imperial Ostia: Archaeological and Epigraphic Evidence," in *Judaism and Christianity in First-Century Rome*, edited by Karl P. Donfried and Peter Richardson (Grand Rapids: Eerdmans, 1998), 30–68; Lee I. Levine, "The Nature and Origin of the Palestinian Synagogue Reconsidered," *JBL* 115 (1996) 425–48, https://doi.org/10.2307/3266895; idem, *The Ancient Synagogue: The First Thousand Years* (New Haven: Yale University Press, 2000); Stephen K. Cato, *Reconstructing the First-Century Synagogue: A Critical Analysis of Current Research* (New York: T. & T. Clark, 2007); Anders Runesson, Donald D. Binder, and Birger Olsson, *The Ancient Synagogue from Its Origins to 200 C.E.: A Source Book* (Leiden: Brill, 2008); Anne Fitzpatrick-McKinley, "Synagogue Communities in the Graeco-Roman Cities," in *Jews in the Hellenistic and Roman Cities*, edited by John R. Bartlett (New York: Routledge, 2012), 55–87; Jordan J. Ryan, *The Role of the Synagogue in the Aims of Jesus* (Minneapolis: Fortress, 2017).

89. Edward W. Klink, *The Sheep of the Fold: The Audience and Origin of the Gospel of John*, SNTSMS 141 (Cambridge: Cambridge University Press, 2007).

90. Jerome H. Neyrey, *An Ideology of Revolt: John's Christology in Social-Science Perspective* (Eugene, OR: Wipf & Stock, 2007); idem, *The Gospel of John in Cultural and Rhetorical Perspective* (Grand Rapids: Eerdmans, 2009); David A. Lamb, *Text, Context and the Johannine Community: A Sociolinguistic Analysis of the Johannine Writings* (London: Bloomsbury, 2014); Wally V. Cirafesi, "The Johannine Community Hypothesis (1968–Present): Past and Present Approaches and a New Way Forward," *CBR* 12 (2014) 173–93; idem, "The 'Johannine Community' in (More) Current Research: A Critical Appraisal of Recent Methods and Models," *Neot* 48 (2014) 341–64; Adele Reinhartz, "Torah Reading in the Johannine Community," *Journal of Early Christian History* 5 (2016) 111–16; idem, "Story and History: John, Judaism, and the Historical Imagination," in *John and Judaism*, 113–26; Martinus C. de Boer, "The Johannine Community under Attack in Recent Scholarship," in *The Ways that Often Parted: Essays in Honor of Joel Marcus*, edited by Lori Baron, Jill Hicks-Keeton, and Matthew Thiessen, ECL 24 (Atlanta: SBL Press, 2018), 211–42.

John[91], John 9[92], and John's anti-Judaism.[93] Although much of this work

91. Stephen Motyer, *Your Father the Devil? A New Approach to John and "the Jews"* (Carlisle: Paternoster, 1997); Daniel Boyarin, "The IOUDAIOI of John and the Prehistory of Judaism," in *Pauline Conversations in Context: Essays in Honor of Calvin J. Roetzel*, edited by Janice Capel Anderson, Philip Sellew, and Claudia Setzer (London: Sheffield Academic Press, 2002), 216–39; Raimo Hakola, *Identity Matters: John, the Jews, and Jewishness* (Leiden: Brill, 2005); idem, *Reconsidering Johannine Christianity: A Social Identity Approach* (New York: Routledge, 2015); Johannes Beutler, *Judaism and the Jews in the Gospel of John* (Rome: Pontificio Istituto Biblico, 2006); Lars Kierspel, *The Jews and the World in the Fourth Gospel: Parallelism, Function, and Context*, WUNT 220 (Tübingen: Mohr Siebeck, 2006); Michael Theobald, "Das Johannesevangeliums—Zeugnis eines synagogalen 'Judenchristentums'?," in *Paulus und Johannes: Exegetische Studien zur paulinischen und johanneischen Theologie und Literatur*, edited by Dieter Sänger and Ulrich Mell, WUNT 198 (Tübingen: Mohr Siebeck, 2006); Philip F. Esler, "From *Ioudaioi* to Children of God: The Development of a Non-Ethnic Group Identity in the Gospel of John," in *In Other Words: Essays on Social Science Methods and the New Testament in Honor of Jerome H. Neyrey*, edited by Jerome H. Neyrey et al. (Sheffield: Sheffield Phoenix Press, 2007), 106–36; Ruth Sheridan, "Issues in the Translation of Οι Ιουδαιοι in the Fourth Gospel," *JBL* 132 (2013) 671–95; Ruben Zimmermann, "'The Jews': Unreliable Figures or Unreliable Narration?" in *Character Studies in the Fourth Gospel: Narrative Approaches to Seventy Figures in John*, edited by Steven A. Hunt, D. F. Tolmie, and Ruben Zimmermann (Grand Rapids: Eerdmans, 2016), 71–109; Alicia D. Myers, "Just Opponents? Ambiguity, Empathy, and the Jews in the Gospel of John," in *Johannine Ethics: The Moral World of the Gospel and Epistles of John*, edited by Sherri Brown and Christopher W. Skinner (Minneapolis: Fortress, 2017), 159–76; Tom Thatcher, "John and the Jews: Recent Research and Future Questions," in *John and Judaism*, 3–38; Paul N. Anderson, "Anti-Semitism and Religious Violence as Flawed Interpretations of the Gospel of John," in *John and Judaism*, 265–311; Urban C. von Wahlde, "Narrative Criticism of the Religious Authorities as a Group Character in the Gospel of John: Some Problems," *NTS* 63 (2017) 222–45.

92. William M. Wright IV, *Rhetoric and Theology: Figural Reading of John 9* (Berlin: de Gruyter, 2009); Stephen S. Kim, "The Significance of Jesus' Healing the Blind Man in John 9," *BSac* 167 (2010) 307–18; Kobus Kok, "The Healing of the Blind Man in John," *Journal of Early Christian History* 2 (2012) 36–62.

93. Reimund Bieringer, D. Pollefeyt, and F. Vandecasteele-Vanneuville, eds., *Anti-Judaism and the Fourth Gospel: Papers of the Leuven Colloquium, 2000* Assen: Royal van Gorcum, 2001); and Terrence L. Donaldson, *Jews and Anti-Judaism in the New Testament* (London: SPCK, 2010); Jonathan Dale Numada, "Interpreting Johannine Anti-Judaism in Light of Hellenistic Diaspora Jewish Social Identity and Cultural Memory,"

takes issue with Martyn, the engagement itself is testimony to the influence of his work upon current scholarship.

For example, Tobias Hägerland finds no evidence of two-level drama comparable to that proposed by Martyn in other contemporary works or in the Gospel itself.[94] Richard Bauckham has spearheaded a reconsideration of the widely accepted assumption that John and the other Gospels were written for particular communities.[95] Advancing the perspectives of "new historicism," Colleen M. Conway challenged the imperative of reading the Gospel in its historical context: "Rather than making the meaning of the text dependent on the specific circumstances in which it was written, one would investigate the ways in which various productions of the Gospel participate and contribute to particular historical/cultural circumstances."[96] Accordingly, Martyn's "most widely accepted idea [the notion of a particular Johannine community] may be more fundamentally wrong." His reading of the Gospel, like others, should be seen as a cultural production, and "instead of seeking *the* meaning of the text, one would examine how particular readings of the Gospel are generated by and participate in the complex 'textualized universe' at any given moment, thereby contributing to the management of reality."[97]

In a suggestive and illuminating essay, Jason Ripley turned attention to the generally neglected reference in John 16:2 to "those who kill you will think that by doing so they are offering worship to God" (NRSV).[98] The belief that piety warranted killing of those who led the

PhD diss., McMaster Divinity College, 2016.

94. Tobias Hägerland, "John's Gospel: A Two-Level Drama?" *JSNT* 25.3 (2003) 309–22.

95. Richard Bauckham, ed., *The Gospel for All Christians: Rethinking the Gospel Audiences* (Grand Rapids: Eerdmans, 1998).

96. Colleen M. Conway, "The Production of the Johannine Community: A New Historicist Perspective," *JBL* 121 (2002) 479–95.

97. Ibid., 491, 494.

98. Jason J. Ripley, "Killing as Piety? Exploring Ideological Contexts Shaping the Gospel of John," *JBL* 134 (2015) 605–35.

people to worship other gods can be traced to scriptural texts such as Deuteronomy 13:1–11; 18:20; Exodus 32:25–29; and especially Numbers 25:1–13. Because "the theme of capital punishment for religious offenses does arise in John's narrative," Ripley sees the possibility that by exploring this ideological context "we may be able to identify in a general sense some of the crucial issues shaping the content and structure of the evangelist's narrative, yet without the historically problematic invocation of the Birkat Haminim and Yavneh as the proximate cause."[99] His reading of John 8:31–59 and other parts of the Gospel advances his interpretation of John as "ideological rejection of religiously justified killing of either Roman oppressor or fellow Jew."[100]

At the end of this review of the reception of Martyn's work, we may single out Joel Marcus and Adele Reinhartz as spokespersons for Martyn's thesis (in general) and for replacing it with an alternative view of the Gospel's life setting, respectively. In defense of Martyn's thesis, Marcus revisited the origins and text of the *Birkat*, citing the work of Ehrlich and Langer on the eighty-six manuscripts of the *Birkat Haminim* found in the Cairo Genizah, from which they identified six versions.[101] It is therefore simplistic to speak of "the Genizah Version" or equate it with "the Palestinian recension."[102]

Marcus observes that while some of the criticism of Martyn's thesis may be fueled by concern over anti-Semitism, much of the criticism is based on "substantive issues of scholarly method."[103] He cites recent work that supports an early date for the *Birkat*, the existence of synagogues, and their use for worship.[104] Justin's *Dialogue with Trypho* provides

99. Ibid., 610.

100. Ibid., 635.

101. Joel Marcus, "*Birkat Ha-Minim* Revisited," *NTS* 55 (2009) 523-51; Uri Ehrlich and Ruth Langer, "The Earliest Texts of the *Birkat Haminim*," *HUCA* 77 (2005) 63-112.

102. Marcus, 524.

103. Ibid., 527.

104. Ibid., 529-30, citing Uri Ehrlich, "On the Early Texts of the Blessings 'Who Builds Jerusalem' and the 'Blessing of David' in the Liturgy," *Pe'amim* 78 (1999) 16-41

evidence for an anti-Christian version of *Birkat Haminim*, and "Ehrlich and Langer conclude that attestation for נצרים is as old as that for מינים."[105] Given the consonance between the NT passages and the rabbinic traditions, John's *aposynagōgos* references are entirely credible. After considering the other groups who might have been referred to as *minim*, Marcus concludes, "by process of elimination . . . the Jewish Christians emerge as the most prominent candidates for *min* status in the earliest strata of rabbinic literature," and "they are also people whom the rabbis consider to be fundamentally mistaken about central matters such as the unity of God."[106] Marcus offers as the most likely interpretation of "the *noṣrim* and the *minim*" the translation, "the Christians and the other heretics."[107] Moreover, there is reason to trace the *Birkat Haminim* back even earlier than the Tannaitic period; its original form probably cursed neither the "separatists" nor the "heretics" but the "arrogant," that is, the Romans. Marcus tentatively endorses David Flusser's suggestion that the cursing of the "separatists" designated not the Pharisees but the Qumran sect,[108] and that "the blessing of the separatists" may have carried a double sense: namely, the curse of the separatists and the curse that came from the separatists, which would mean that the rabbis at Yavneh revised a blessing/curse that came from the Qumran sect. His understanding of the work of the rabbis at Yavneh is:

(Hebrew); and Pieter W. Van der Horst, "Was the Synagogue a Place of Sabbath Worship Before 70 CE?" in *Japheth in the Tents of Shem: Studies on Jewish Hellenism in Antiquity*, Biblical Exegesis and Theology 32 (Leuven: Peeters, 2002 [orig. 1999]), 55-82.

105. Ibid., 532.

106. Ibid., 537.

107. Ibid., 540.

108. Ibid., 546, citing David Flusser, "4QMMT and the Benediction against the Minim," *Judaism of the Second Temple Period*, Vol. 1: *Qumran and Apocalypticism* (Grand Rapids: Eerdmans; Jerusalem: Magnes, 2007 [orig. 1992]), 103–7; and Joshua Ezra Burns, "Essene Sectarianism and Social Differentiation in Judaea After 70 C.E.," *HTR* 99 (2006) 260–68.

> They were thus not creating a liturgy *ex nihilo* but ratifying and revising one that was already in use. They did not impose this liturgy on synagogues by fiat, but by putting their stamp of approval on a particular version of the developing tradition they simultaneously accepted the common consensus, moved toward fixing its form, and solidified their claim to be the people's leaders.[109]

The authorities at Yavneh were no doubt more successful in some areas than others, and the separation of Christian Jews from the synagogues probably occurred over a period of several centuries.

Thus, if a *Birkat Haminim* served as a pre-70 CE critique of the Sadducean priesthood as *minim* in the Geniza fragment, it was likely yoked into further service in the Jamnian period. Likewise, Jonathan Bernier cites evidence that a *Birkat Haminim* was used in Jerusalem synagogues in the first third of the first century CE, seeking to disparage messianic revolutionary interests after the pattern of Galilean (and Nazarene) uprisings that had been put down with violence by the Romans, as attested by Josephus.[110] Therefore, making use of this instrument of community discipline did not begin at Jamnia, and it may have served a number of purposes within Judaism long before the explicitly Christian references by Justin.

Adele Reinhartz has been in conversation with Martyn and engaged in sketching alternatives to his expulsion theory since the publication of her first book in 1992. *The Word and the World: The Cosmological Tale in the Fourth Gospel* supplements Martyn's distinction of two levels in the Johannine narrative, which she called "the historical tale" (the tale of the historical figure Jesus) and "the ecclesiological tale" (the tale of the Johannine community), with a third, "the cosmological tale" (the tale of the

---

109. Ibid., 549.

110. So argues David Instone-Brewer, "The Eighteen Benedictions and the *Minim* Before 70 CE," *JTS* 54 (2003) 25–44. Jonathan Bernier (*Aposynagōgos and the Historical Jesus in John*, 2013), however, argues that its primary use was earlier and not later.

eternal Word).[111] Reinhartz then interpreted the *paroimia* (i.e., riddle) of John 10 in terms of the cosmological tale rather than the historical tale, showing that this reading of the *paroimia* makes better sense of the role of the sheepfold.

Befriending the Beloved Disciple: A Jewish Reading of the Gospel of John advances the work Reinhartz did on John 10.[112] The heart of the book comprises four readings of each of the three "tales" or stories: a *compliant* reading, in which the reader adopts the role of one who accepts the perspective of the Beloved Disciple; a *resistant* reading, in which the reader explores the position of the opponents in the story; a *sympathetic* reading, in which the reader focuses on areas of agreement and shared values; and an *engaged* reading, in which Reinhartz both critiques the Beloved Disciple and allows the Beloved Disciple to critique her values and perspectives. The result is a probing exploration of the Gospel's anti-Judaism and the effects of its dualistic worldview. This volume also reflects a growing resistance in Reinhartz's reading of the Fourth Gospel. She is no longer convinced that there is an "ecclesiological tale" in the Gospel, at least not in the way she originally understood it. Indeed, the Gospel contains not one but "three different models of the historical relationship between the Johannine group and the Jewish community among which it lived."[113] Employing a two-level reading, she suggests that John 11:1–44 and 12:11 offer other models of Christian-Jewish relations. If one reads them as reflections of the period in which John was written, as Martyn reads John 9, John 11:1–44 shows members of the Johannine community being comforted by Jews who did not claim Jesus as the Messiah, and John 12:11 reports comments of the Jewish leadership expressing "alarm concerning those who were

111. Adele Reinhartz, *The Word in the World: The Cosmological Tale in the Fourth Gospel*, SBLMS 45 (Atlanta: Scholars Press, 1992).

112. Adele Reinhartz, *Befriending the Beloved Disciple: A Jewish Reading of the Gospel of John* (New York: Continuum, 2001).

113. Ibid., 41.

leaving the community—apparently through their own volition—in order to join the Johannine group."[114] Reinhartz therefore calls for a re-examination of Martyn's thesis that the Johannine community emerged as a result of the exclusion of believers from the synagogue.

Cast Out of the Covenant: Jews and Anti-Judaism in the Gospel of John, Reinhartz's latest book, which she dedicated to Martyn and to Gregory A. Baum, fleshes out a different view of the life setting of the Fourth Gospel on the basis of its rhetoric.[115] The Gospel "offers its audience rebirth into a new family, the family of God, using a range of strategies that together constitute a *rhetoric of affiliation*." At the same time, however, it insists, through a *rhetoric of disaffiliation*, that participation in the family of God also requires separation from the *Ioudaioi*. Moreover, "in appropriating the scriptures, the Temple, and covenantal language for its audience, the Gospel rhetorically expropri-ates, casts out, expels, the Jews from that covenant." Reinhartz proposes that the setting in which this audience, which was predominantly gen-tile, would have heard the Gospel read or recited was probably in an *agora* or marketplace. The *aposynagōgos* references in John 9:22; 12:42; and 16:2, which were part of its rhetoric of disaffiliation, warned the audience against going to a Jewish synagogue. There is no evidence for the existence of "the Johannine community" before the composition of the Gospel, Reinhartz contends; rather, through its rhetoric of affilia-tion and disaffiliation, the Gospel created the community. The Gospel is therefore open to different readings, and one can imagine more than one life setting for which its rhetoric was shaped.

---

114. Ibid.; cf. Adele Reinhartz, "The Johannine Community and Its Jewish Neigh-bors: A Reappraisal," in *What Is John*, vol. 2: *Literary and Social Readings of the Fourth Gospel*, edited by Fernando F. Segovia, SBLSymS (Atlanta: Scholars Press, 1998), 111–38.

115. Adele Reinhartz, *Cast Out of the Covenant: Jews and Anti-Judaism in the Gos-pel of John* (Lanham: Lexington Books, 2018).

"The Johannine Community among Jewish and Other Early Christian Communities"

Martyn's last essay on John dealt again with the Jewishness of the Johannine community,[116] and it seems appropriate in this context to let Martyn have the last word in our conversation with him. The first part of the essay reflects on Bultmann, American scholarship on John in the 1950s, and his choice of a dissertation topic. He found Bultmann both "enormously impressive" and "seriously inadequate" (183)—the latter because, while he often echoed Martin Heidegger, "Bultmann had a truly skimpy knowledge of Judaism" (185). Martyn found it imperative, therefore, "to wrest the Gospel out of the hands of timeless, place-less, philosophical interpreters" and read it in its original, Jewish and Jewish-Christian context.

Reflecting on his work forty years later, Martyn said he was sobered by the responses of those "having a far greater rabbinic expertise than my own" (187) but still maintained that, laying the connection with the *Birkat Haminim* aside—a pink herring (!), the *aposynagōgos* references in John are "communal references to a communal experience" that support "the larger thesis that the Fourth Gospel is a two-level drama shaped in part by the experience of a group of Christian Jews" who were "severed" from their synagogue (187). Maintaining that only the text can liberate us from our own *Tendenzen* and those of our exegetical conversation partners, especially in the sensitive area of hostilities between Jews and Christians, Martyn remained committed to the text and to the conviction that "modern relations between Jews and Christians are not helped by an anti-historical interpretation of biblical texts" (187).

---

116. J. Louis Martyn, "The Johannine Community among Jewish and Other Early Christian Communities," in *What We Have Heard from the Beginning: The Past, Present, and Future of Johannine Studies*, edited by Tom Thatcher (Waco: Baylor University Press, 2007), 183–90. The page numbers in parentheses in this paragraph refer to this essay.

Introduction

During the last decades, studies in the Gospel of John have been moving at a remarkable pace. We have seen the appearance of several truly profound commentaries and a host of scientific monographs, a number of which have proven to be genuinely perceptive.[1] Significant strides have thus been made at perhaps half a dozen points, two of which merit special attention: the study of the Gospel's view of Christ (its christology) and attempts to ascertain the Gospel's portrait of the Church (its ecclesiology). Indeed these two areas stand out, not only because important work has been done in them, but also because some of the work that has been done is of such a nature as to give strong hints regarding what the next steps might be. It is primarily for these reasons that the present volume is designed to explore both Johannine christology and Johannine ecclesiology.

CHRISTOLOGY

The reader of John's Gospel will not have proceeded eighteen verses into the first chapter without sensing the massive concentration of the author's attention on christology. It is immediately understandable that numerous interpreters have pointed to christology as the evangelist's central interest. But centrality is surely

---

[1] See the commentaries by R. E. Brown, R. Schnackenburg, B. Lindars, and (in a revised edition) C. K. Barrett. A vast number of monographs have been touched upon by Robert Kysar, *The Fourth Evangelist and His Gospel* (Augsburg, 1975). See also M. de Jonge (ed.), *L'Evangile de Jean, Sources rédaction, théologie* (Louvain, 1977), and the articles in *Interpretation* 31 (1977) no. 4

too weak an image. For in the work of this author, as Ernst Käsemann has recently put it, christology constitutes the whole of the horizon, with the result that other matters such as pneumatology, eschatology, and ecclesiology find their support- ing positions at discrete points, so to speak, along the christologi- cal horizon.[2]

As regards exegetical research directed to this remarkable christology, the scholarly clock has not been standing still. Were one to reread the pages on John's christology in Wilhelm Bous- set's justly famous *Kyrios Christos* immediately before perusing the major contributions of the last two decades, one would see that solid advances have been made on the basis of the hypothesis that to a large degree the christological formulations of this Gos- pel are derived from concepts originally at home in streams of Jewish thought. Writing almost three quarters of a century ago, Bousset concluded that the titles "Son of Man" and "Kyrios" were of Jewish and Gentile Hellenistic derivation respectively, and he assumed with many of his contemporaries that John's Gospel lay in the line of the post-Pauline Gentile Hellenistic Church, in which the latter title had all but eclipsed the former. When he turned to John's Gospel, Bousset was therefore greatly puzzled to find exactly what he did not expect: in this "Hellenis- tic Gospel" the "Gentile Christian" title "Kyrios" is virtually absent, while the "Jewish Christian" title "Son of Man" clearly stands very near the center of the proclamation about Jesus.[3] Being unable, one supposes, to question his historical scheme in a radical way, Bousset responded to the puzzle merely by formulat- ing several "explanations" which have proven to be quite unper- suasive.

---

[2]Ernst Käsemann, *The Testament of Jesus* (Fortress, 1968), p. 16.

[3]Bousset's confidence that the title "Kyrios" was first used of Jesus in the Gentile Christian Church is shared by relatively few New Testa- ment scholars today. See, e.g., R. H. Fuller, *The Foundations of New Testament Christology* (Scribner's, 1965), pp. 185f.; note also the weighty arguments of Ph. Vielhauer, "Ein Weg zur neutestamentlichen Christologie?" *EvTh* 25 (1965) 24-72, especially 28ff., and of J. A. Fitzmyer, "Der semitische Hintergrund des neutestamentlichen Kyrios- titels," G. Strecker (ed.), *Jesus Christus in Historie und Theologie*, Festschrift Conzelmann (Tübingen, 1975), pp. 267-298.

Recent interpreters, following a rather different path, have noted not only the weighty influence on John of Jewish specula-tion about the Son of Man,[4] but also the extensive signs in the Gospel of the impact of Jewish wisdom traditions,[5] and the pow-erful effect on John's christology of Jewish thought patterns fo-cused on Moses.[6] Such discoveries have gone a long way toward clarifying the conceptual background of the Gospel's christology.

It is important to notice, however, that these solid advances have not answered the whole of Bousset's puzzle. As I have just indicated, they tell us a great deal about the Gospel's *intellectual milieu*—it is far more Jewish than Bousset imagined—but they are not designed to address in a direct way the question which perplexed Bousset much more than that of the general intellectual milieu: Where does the Gospel of John belong within *the history of specifically Christian thought and life?* It follows—if one is convinced that Bousset's question remains essential for the fuller interpretative task—that Johannine exegetes cannot be satisfied indefinitely to move about in the realm of disembodied ideas— this one is quite "Jewish," that one is rather "Gnostic," etc. On the contrary, we have in fact to return to Bousset's passionate concern to fix the locus occupied by John in the history of early Christianity.

Where will such a move lead us? At the present juncture in Johannine research one would be wise to claim little more, I think, than a glimpse of the path opening up ahead. Recall that

---

[4] See the monograph of S. Schulz, *Untersuchungen zur Menschensohn-Christologie im Johannesevangelium* (Vandenhoeck und Ruprecht, 1957), the articles by S. Smalley, "The Johannine Son of Man Sayings," *NTS* 15 (1968-69), 278-301, E. Ruckstuhl, "Die johanneische Menschensohnforschung 1957-1969," *Theologische Berichte* 1 (1972) 171-284, and P. Borgen, "Some Jewish Exegetical Traditions as Back-ground for Son of Man Sayings in John's Gospel (John 3:13-14 and Context)," pp. 243-258 in M. de Jonge (ed.) *L'Évangile de Jean.*

[5] See notably R. E. Brown, *The Gospel According to John* (i-xii), The Anchor Bible, Vol. 29 (Doubleday, 1966) CXXII-CXXVII, and R. G. Hamerton-Kelly, *Pre-Existence, Wisdom, and the Son of Man* (Cambridge, 1973), pp. 197ff.

[6] W. A. Meeks, *The Prophet-King, Moses Traditions and the Johannine Christology* (Brill, 1967).

when Bousset referred to the title "Son of Man," he was speaking in the first instance not of a disembodied *Jewish idea*, but rather of a title widely employed by flesh-and-blood *Jewish Christians* in their cultic life. It may follow that in ways he never dreamed of we should reformulate Bousset's riddle by asking whether the Gospel of John could perhaps be far more closely related to Jewish Christianity than we have previously thought. In short, we may be able to make further headway by de-emphasizing for a brief period our quite legitimate concern with such conceptual adjectives as "Jewish" and "Gnostic," in order vigorously to focus our attention on such historical nouns as "Jewish Christianity" and "Gentile Christianity." The two approaches are, of course, far from being mutually exclusive. The point is simply that the former has been pursued quite productively in recent years, while the latter has been largely neglected.

It is along the path thus indicated that the initial essay in the present volume has emerged. What are we to say regarding the locus of John's christology along the multiple and complex lines of christological development in the early Church? Did the evangelist have discernible christological predecessors, and, if so, are we able with some specificity to discover the contours of their views of Christ? Assuming for the moment positive answers, we would then be in a position to ask how and why the evangelist handled the formulations of his predecessors as he did, thus arriving at the majestic christology which subsequent theologians have consistently recognized as peculiarly his own. I am quite sure that in a single essay I have not fully answered these demanding questions, but I hope to have taken a few constructive steps that may eventually help us more fully to perceive where and how John's christology fits into the history of christological patterns in early Christianity.

ECCLESIOLOGY

The second part of the book, Chapters 2 and 3, consists of two further essays also concerned with the issue of John's place in the history of early Christianity. In these I have concentrated

not on christology, but rather on ecclesiology in a manner which
is quite concrete. Here I have asked myself several questions: In
what kind of community did the evangelist live? What was it like
to experience daily life in that community? And, finally, are we
able to piece together at least a partial picture of the community's
own history?

In the first of these essays my concern with such questions
led me—for reasons I shall explain in a moment—into the
labyrinth of the Pseudo-Clementine literature. (I have given a
brief introduction to this literature early in the second chapter,
and I have provided an English translation of the pertinent part of
it in an appendix.) It may be salutary for me to say quite directly
that I was myself surprised to find my interest directed toward
those rather exotic and esoteric writings known more or less exclusively to scholars of patristics as the Clementine *Homilies* and
Recognitions. More than one scholar has disappeared into the
Pseudo-Clementine labyrinth never to be heard from again! Why
not stick to the text of John's Gospel itself, or at the very least to
the New Testament?

Again the major answer lies in the hypothesis that our Gospel
may be much more closely connected with Jewish Christianity
than we have previously thought. If so, we need for comparative
purposes to look to those few documents of Jewish Christianity
which survived the suppressive measures of orthodox censors,
with an eye to the testing of our hypothesis. In this regard, relatively little is to be found in the New Testament itself. By and
large, and with regard to the *present form*—the uppermost
layers—of its writings, the New Testament is, as H.-J. Schoeps
has remarked, a collection of the documents of the victorious
party, the emerging Great Church.[7] But there is a discrete
stratum of tradition in the fourth-century Pseudo-Clementine literature which has long been thought to preserve an extraordinarily valuable source for the study of one branch of early Jewish
Christianity, and, unlikely as it may seem, a careful reading of
this source in parallel, so to speak, with pertinent sections of the
Gospel of John leads to the suggestion that at one stage in their

---

[7] H. J. Schoeps, *Jewish Christianity* (Fortress, 1969), p. 3.

respective histories the communities behind these two documents underwent some quite similar experiences precisely as Jewish-Christian communities. Comparison of the two communities thus leads, I think, to a clearer and more nearly complete picture of the fabric of their daily life.

The final essay is designed to draw together the major threads from the other studies and, indeed, from several previous publications as well.[8] As the title indicates, the intention is to present a sketch of the history of the Johannine community from its origin through the period of its life during which the Gospel of John was composed. Here several convictions are pursued, the chief ones being: (1) there are numerous literary strata behind the text of the Gospel as we have it; (2) to some extent it is possible to differentiate these strata from one another, thus discovering significant traces of the literary history behind the Gospel; (3) this literary history reflects to a large degree the history of a single community which maintained over a period of some duration its particular and rather peculiar identity.

It follows that we may hope to draw from the Gospel's literary history certain conclusions about the community's social and theological history. Broadly put, three major periods emerge:

1. The Early Period presumably began before the Jewish revolt and lasted until some point in the eighties. Our study of some of the lines of development which lie behind the evangelist's own majestic christology (Chapter 1 of the present book) helps us find our bearings as regards this early period. We see here a *group of Christian Jews* living in a stream of relatively untroubled theological and social continuity within the synagogue.

2. The Middle Period was ushered in when the remarkable growth of this group aroused the suspicions of the Jewish authorities and led them to take severely repressive steps designed to terminate what they saw as a serious threat. Such persecution caused some members of the group, and some who had been

---

[8]*History and Theology in the Fourth Gospel* (first edition, Harper and Row, 1968; revised edition to be published by Abingdon. 1979; "Source Criticism and Religionsgeschichte in the Fourth Gospel," *Jesus and Man's Hope* (Pittsburgh Seminary, 1970) I, 247-273.

attracted to it, to turn back from an open confession in order to remain safely in the synagogue. Those who made an open confession were excommunicated and thus became a *separated community of Jewish Christians* who were then subjected to further persecution (Chapter 2). The painful events of the Middle Period had lasting effects on the community's understanding both of Christ and of itself.

3. The Late Period saw further developments in the community's christology and ecclesiology, and it is now clear that these developments were worked out to a large extent vis-à-vis not only the parent synagogue, but also other Christian groups known to the Johannine community. Thus, when the Gospel found its final form, the horizon displayed at least four discrete social and theological groups:

1. The synagogue of "the Jews";
2. Christian Jews within the synagogue who attempted secretly to maintain a dual loyalty, and toward whom the Johannine community felt enormous antipathy;
3. The Johannine community itself;
4. Other communities of Jewish Christians who had also experienced expulsion from the synagogue, and with whom the Johannine community hoped eventually to be unified.

I say that the horizon displayed *at least* these four groups because I am sure that the situation was yet more complex; and indeed recent studies have begun further to expand and qualify this picture.[9] Such studies give me reason to hope that in the chapters

---

[9] Some of the major developments are appearing in recent articles by my colleague Raymond E. Brown: "Johannine Ecclesiology—The Community's Origins," *Interpretation* 31 (1977) 379-393; " 'Other Sheep Not of this Fold': The Johannine Perspective on Christian Diversity in the Late First Century," *JBL 97* (1978), 5-22; "The Relationship to the Fourth Gospel Shared by the Author of I John and by His Opponents." Text and Interpretation: Studies Presented to Matthew Black (Cambridge, 1979). The picture which has been unfolding in these articles is

offered here an angle of vision may emerge in a way that is sufficiently constructive to be of help to other Johannine interpreters.

now brought together and further enriched in Raymond E. Brown, *The Community of the Beloved Disciple* (New York: Paulist Press, 1979). See also D. M. Smith, Jr., "Johannine Christianity: Some Reflections on Its Character and Delineation" *NTS* 21 (1974-1975) 222-248; R. A. Culpepper, *The Johannine School* (Scholars Press, 1975); O. Cullman, *The Johannine Circle* (Westminster, 1976); A. J. Mattill, "Johannine Communities Behind the Fourth Gospel: Georg Richter's Analysis," *TS* 38 (1977) 294-315; R. Schnackenburg, "Die johanneische Gemeinde und ihre Geisterfahrung," R. Schnackenburg, J. Ernst, and J. Wanke (eds.) *Die Kirche des Anfangs*, Festschrift für Heinz Schürmann zum 65, Geburtstag (Leipzig: St. Benno, 1977), pp. 277-306; F. Vouga, *Le cadre historique et l'intention théologigue de Jean* (Paris, 1977).

CHAPTER 1

"We Have Found Elijah"

A View of Christ Formulated Very Early in the Life of the Johannine Community

I. A MODERN DEBATE

It is customary for authors of New Testament christologies to comment on the roles played in patterns of Jewish expectation by "the eschatological prophet," whether or not they consider the figure to be directly pertinent to christology as such.[10] Moreover there is general agreement that in first-century Judaism such patterns of expectation were primarily focused on two dominant figures, Moses and Elijah. The remarks of Cullmann are typical:

> The Jewish belief in a returning prophet took the particular form of an expectation of the return of a particular Old Testament prophet at the end of days. This expectation arises already with the words of Deut. 18:15 . . . [pointing to] the appearance of a prophet similar to [Moses]. . . . Above all, however, the return of Elijah was expected [as is attested in Malachi, Sirach, and rabbinical texts].[11]

---

[10] Examples include O. Cullmann, *The Christology of the New Testament* (London, 1959), pp. 13-50; F. Hahn, *The Titles of Jesus in Christology* (New York, 1969), where the matter is taken up in an appendix, pp. 352-406; and Fuller, *Foundations*, pp. 46-48, 67, 125-29, 167-73.

[11] Cullmann, *Christology*, pp. 16f.; cf. Hahn, *Titles*, p. 354; and Fuller, *Foundations*, pp. 46ff.

The distinguishing of these two forms of expectation from one another is clearly presupposed in two carefully worded statements of R. H. Fuller:

> The early Aramaic speaking church interpreted Jesus' earthly ministry explicitly in terms of the Mosaic prophet servant. The primary evidence for this is . . . the Petrine speech (Acts 3:12-26). . . . [However] there is no evidence that the post-Easter church ever interpreted Jesus . . . as Elijah *redivivus*, although certain traits from the Elijah traditions were taken up into the later conception of Jesus as an eschatological prophet. Rather, in Christian tradition John the Baptist himself became Elijah *redivivus* (Mark 9:13).[12]

Essentially the same position is taken by F. Hahn:

> There is a series of indications that the idea of the eschatological prophet was carried over to Jesus and that this was apparently done very early. . . . Here we are concerned *throughout* [durchweg] with the type of expectation that bears upon it the stamp of Deut. 18:15ff. (Footnote: On the basis of Mk. 6:15; 8:18 the question could be asked whether Jesus was not actually also regarded as the eschatological Elias. . . . It may not on any account be disputed that *a whole series of traits* remind us of Elias, but this is not the prevailing conception; rather we are clearly concerned here with separate *elements which were taken up into that other view* [the Mosaic one] of Jesus as the eschatological prophet. . . . This is easy to understand for the reason that . . . the Baptist community had already taken over the Elias conception.)[13]

To put it in a single sentence: The earliest Church viewed the Baptist as Elijah; that being the case, while some Elijah-like traits attached themselves to (the Mosaic portrait of) Jesus, *there is no*

---

[12] Fuller, *Foundations*, pp. 167f., 126f.
[13] Hahn, *Titles*, pp. 372, 399 (italics added).

evidence that the Church interpreted Jesus as Elijah.[14]

In the New Testament guild, however, few opinions are held with absolute unanimity. Returning from the view of Fuller and Hahn to Cullmann's *Christology*, for example, one finds a somewhat different picture:

> The synoptic writers did not express their personal faith in Jesus by means of this conception (the Eschatological Prophet). On the other hand, it does seem to have had a certain meaning for the writer of the Fourth Gospel. His particular emphasis of the fact that the Baptist rejected for himself the title of the Prophet, *the returned Elijah*, suggests that the writer of John *wants to reserve this title for Jesus* — along with other Christological designations and concepts, of course.[15]

Cullmann continues by commenting on christological data in the early chapters of Acts, and concludes that within the New Testament only the Gospel of John and the first (Jewish Christian) part of Acts consider Jesus to be the eschatological prophet.[16] To be sure, Cullmann essentially superimposes the figures of the Mosaic prophet and Elijah *redivivus*. Yet just in this way it is clear that we have here an opinion at variance with that of Hahn and Fuller: In the Fourth Gospel and the early chapters of Acts we find literary remains from elements of the post-Easter Church which in fact did view Jesus as—among other things—the eschatological Elijah.[17] And if one desires a yet bolder and clearer

---

[14]The tendency neatly to allot the figure of Elijah to the Baptist and the figure of the Mosaic prophet to Jesus is also reflected in the learned and highly instructive article on Elijah written by J. Jeremias: 'Ηλ(ε)ίας in *TWNT*, ed. G. Kittel, II (Stuttgart, 1935), 930-43.

[15]Cullmann, *Christology*, p. 37 (italics added).

[16]*Ibid.*, p. 38.

[17]I shall adhere to this nomenclature in what follows, for it seems to me that the expression "Elijah *redivivus*," while having the advantage of common use, is quite inappropriate in light of that element which is mainly responsible for the vitality of Elijah traditions: the Tishbite did not die, but was translated to heaven. When he comes, therefore, he is "the eschatological Elijah."

statement, J. A. T. Robinson is obliging:

> According to this very primitive Christology [Acts 3:12-26],
> Jesus is quite explicitly the Prophet like Moses (as he is also
> in Stephen's speech in Acts 7:37). It should hardly therefore
> come as a shock to find that *he is equally evidently Elijah in
> all but name.* . . . Jesus was indeed to be the Christ. But *he
> was Elijah first.*[18]

The issue is joined, at least in a preliminary way, and the arena for
debate is fixed: the Fourth Gospel and Acts. To attempt a complete resifting of the data would take us, therefore, to both of
these documents. But since the arguments of Hahn and Fuller are
basically *ex silentio*, the first question is whether *either* document
reflects an early Christian identification of Jesus as Elijah. In the
compass of the present essay we shall inquire whether such an
identification may be reflected in the Fourth Gospel.

II. Elijah in the Four Gospels

Before we turn our attention directly to the Fourth Gospel, it
will be well to make a brief survey of the obviously pertinent data
in the other Gospels. Synoptic tradition preserves six major and
explicit references to Elijah: (1) Opinions among the common folk
as to Jesus' identity include—as the second of three
possibilities—the suggestion that he is Elijah (Mk. 6:14-16; Lk.

---

[18]J. A. T. Robinson, "Elijah, John and Jesus: An Essay in Detection," *NTS* IV (1958), 277 (the first set of italics added). Cf. W. D.
Davies, *The Setting of the Sermon on the Mount* (Cambridge, England,
1964), p. 160, where Davies speaks of Christians who claimed to have
had their Elijah and his interpretation of the Law, thus implying, unless I
misread him, a Christian group which identified Jesus as Elijah. For a
critique of Robinson's provocative article and of Cullmann's views given
above, see the tightly argued study by John Knox, "The 'Prophet' in
New Testament Christology," in *Lux in Lumine, Essays To Honor W.
Norman Pittenger*, ed. R. A. Norris, Jr. (New York, 1966), pp. 23-34.
Reasons for my not finding Knox's argument entirely convincing will
emerge in the course of the present essay.

9:7-9). (2) When Jesus asks his disciples who he is popularly held to be, they mention the same possibilities, again with Elijah as the second of the three (Mk. 8:27-30; Mt. 16:13-20; Lk. 9:18-21). (3) In the transfiguration Jesus talks with Elijah and Moses (Mk. 9:2-10; Mt. 17:1-9; Lk. 9:28-36). (4) Asked by his disciples why the scribes say it is necessary for Elijah to come first, Jesus affirms the saying and implicitly applies it to the Baptist (Mk. 9:11-13; Mt. 17:10-13; no Lucan parallel). (5) Jesus, speaking to the crowds about the Baptist, explicitly identifies the latter as Elijah (Mt. 11:14; no Lucan parallel). (6) Hearing Jesus' cry from the cross, some of the bystanders opine that he is calling on Elijah, and propose to wait to see whether the Tishbite will come to his aid (Mk. 15:33-36; Mt. 27:45-49; no Lucan parallel).[19]

As regards our present concern the major dimensions of these references can be grasped in two statements: (a) Some of Jesus' contemporaries are represented as holding him to be Elijah (Mark, Matthew, Luke). (b) Jesus himself holds the Baptist to be Elijah (implicitly in Mark, explicitly in Matthew).

When one turns from these Synoptic data to a rereading of the Fourth Gospel, surprises are in store. All six references are absent. Specifically, the possible identification of Jesus as Elijah is nowhere mentioned; nor does Jesus identify the Baptist as Elijah. Instead, the Tishbite emerges explicitly in only one passage, and there in a negative role, so to speak.

John 1:20f.; 1:25

John 1:18 clearly marks the end of the prologue; 1:51 promises a vision which in fact is then given in the remainder of the Gospel; and the resulting literary piece made up of 1:19-50 divides

---

[19] It is often noted that Luke seems to view Jesus somewhat in terms of Elijah and, correspondingly, that he seems to suppress the linking of Elijah to the Baptist. See, e.g., W. Wink, *John the Baptist in the Gospel Tradition* (London, 1968), pp. 42f. In both regards we see one of the numerous points at which Luke and the fourth evangelist show (or preserve) similar attitudes. On Luke 1:17, see the passage from Wink cited above and R. E. Brown, *The Birth of the Messiah* (New York, 1977), pp. 275ff.

itself into two paragraphs: The Witness of the Baptist (1:19-34), and The First Disciples (1:35-50). It is the first of these paragraphs which contains the only two explicit references to Elijah in the Gospel, 1:20f. and 1:25.

In apparent contradistinction to the Synoptic passages in which the Baptist is identified as Elijah, he is here portrayed as explicitly denying that role for himself. Indeed, he solemnly denies for himself three titles or roles: the Christ, Elijah, the (Mosaic) prophet.

"Who are you?"
And he confessed, and he did not deny, and he confessed,
"I am not the Christ."
And they asked him, "What then?
Are you Elijah?"
And he said, "I am not."
"Are you the prophet?"
And he answered, "No."

Why these solemn denials?

To many interpreters the Baptist's denials have not seemed enormously perplexing. The dominant explanation is close at hand: whether to refute Baptist sectarians known to him or simply to provide dramatic contrast, the evangelist has the Baptist deny that he is the Christ, Elijah, and the (Mosaic) prophet as a prelude to the granting of these titles or roles to Jesus.[20] As re-

---

[20] I express, of course, nothing other than my own opinion when I call this "the dominant explanation." There are at least two other hypotheses which should be mentioned. (1) The Baptist's denial that he is Elijah may be quite simply an accurate historical reminiscence, as Robinson, "Detection," and R. E. Brown are inclined to think. See Brown, *John*, for discussion. This explanation is surely possible, but it seems to me to take too little account of the striking parallelism presented by the three denials and the solemnity with which they are introduced. (2) The evangelist may cause the Baptist to deny that he is Elijah because to allow him that role would imply the Elijah—Christ patterns held by Trypho in Justin's *Dialogue*, notably that the Christ is unaware of his own mission, is dependent on Elijah for his being revealed to men, and is a mere man among men. This is the hypothesis advanced by M. de

gards the first and third this explanation has obvious merits. By tracing the titles "Christ" and "prophet" through the Gospel, one notices that the evangelist does in fact place them in dramatic relief: the Baptist is neither; Jesus is both.[21] The explanation fails, however, with respect to the second. While the Baptist is also made to deny that he is Elijah, the contrasting positive affirmation for Jesus is nowhere forthcoming. Regarding Elijah, the Evangelist is subsequently silent, even at the expense of leaving the Baptist's second denial somewhat dangling.

Returning to our initial question—does the Fourth Gospel contain evidence of an early Christian identification of Jesus as Elijah?—this silence erects a sort of roadblock, not taken with sufficient seriousness, perhaps, by Cullmann and J. A. T. Robinson. Acknowledging the roadblock, one may be led to realize that Hahn and Fuller are correct. At least as regards the Fourth Gospel,

> . . . there is no evidence that the post-Easter church ever interpreted Jesus as . . . Elijah *redivivus*. . . .

Jonge in a study, one of the virtues of which is that it takes quite seriously the Baptist's second denial ("Jewish Expectations about the 'Messiah' according to the Fourth Gospel," *NTS* 19 [1973], 246-270). De Jonge recognizes the difficulties introduced by citing a text from the mid-second century to illustrate the background of the Fourth Gospel. I myself should not judge those difficulties to be insurmountable whenever there are clear points of contact to link the two texts. It is, however, such clear points of contact that I do not find in de Jonge's presentation. To return to what I have called "the dominant explanation," let me say that for our present purposes it does not greatly matter whether one speaks of the evangelist as refuting Baptist sectarians or as simply providing dramatic contrast, although the Syriac text of the Pseudo-Clementine *Recognitions* I.54 must surely be allowed some weight in support of the former, as R. E. Brown seems somewhat more inclined to do in "Jesus and Elisha," *Perspective* XII (1971), 86, than he is in his commentary. We shall see below that polemic with Baptist sectarians may be at least as clearly reflected in one of the evangelist's sources as in his own work.

[21] See Martyn, *History and Theology*, pp. 110-127, and note the opinion that the evangelist shows a finely nuanced position regarding Jesus' identification with the Mosaic prophet.

Alternatively, however, reading and rereading John 1:20-21 may lead one to be somewhat perseverant. The style of the verses, the careful balancing of the three titles or roles, the steadily decreasing length of the Baptist's answers, and, not least, the solemnity with which he is made to introduce his negative responses—"and he confessed, and he did not deny, and he confessed"—are factors which combine to cause one to assume that the Baptist's three negations are intended to constitute a three-membered instance of parallelism. Thus, one may be driven to try to peer a bit beyond the roadblock. Is there, in fact, no positive role for Elijah after the Baptist's solemn denial of that role for himself?

At this point two paths may be pursued to see whether they lead beyond the impasse. First, one may comb the Gospel for possible Elijah-like traits in the portrait of Jesus. And, second, one may ask whether the absence of an explicitly positive sequel to the Baptist's second negation may be a riddle that has resulted from the evangelist's editing of one of his sources.

III. ELIJAH-LIKE TRAITS IN
THE FOURTH GOSPEL'S PORTRAIT OF JESUS

In order to read through the Fourth Gospel, alert for the possibility of Elijah-like traits in the portrait of Jesus, we must first attempt to summarize the major traditions and expectations attaching to Elijah in second-temple Judaism.

A. Major Traditions about Elijah

Interpreters commonly remark that no biblical figure so exercised the Jewish imagination of the early centuries B.C.E. and C.E. as did Elijah.[22] While the material is, therefore, un-

---

[22] P. Billerbeck, *Kommentar zum Neuen Testament*, 5 vols. (Munich, 1922-56), IV, 764; Jeremias, *TWNT*, II, 930f.; G. Molin, "Elijahu der Prophet und sein Weiterleben in den Hoffnungen des Judentums und der Christenheit," *Jud* VIII (1952), 65. See also the pertinent

commonly rich, it may not lead to oversimplification to note that three elements in the prophet's Old Testament portrait are chiefly responsible for such remarkable vitality.

1. Elijah's Translation

The story of Elijah's translation (2 Kgs. 2:1-12a) is fundamental to all subsequent speculation about him. Since he was dramatically taken up into heaven, he was considered to be alive, in heaven with the (other?) angels,[23] and available, either by being equidistant, so to speak, from every generation, or by being on the verge of coming at the end-time—a fascinating figure indeed.

2. Elijah's Miracles

The translated one had been, during his time on earth, the awesome worker of miracles, and the accounts of those mighty deeds were told and retold. Josephus, for example, repeats the stories of 1 Kings 17, Elijah's miraculous provision of meal and oil to the poor widow of Zarephath, and his restoration of her son to life (*Ant.* VIII; XIII.2-3; supplemented from Menander). Moreover, not only were the stories of the earthly Elijah repeated, but also their major accents were combined with the portrait of the translated one, producing the rich image of an Elijah who could fly down to earth in order miraculously to aid those in deep distress (cf. Mark 15:35f.). Numerous legends developed from this combination.[24]

---

sections in *Élie le Prophète*, Gustave Bardy *et al.*, eds., 2 vols. (Burges, 1956), notably M. J. Stiassny, "Le Prophète Élie dans le Judaïsme," II, 199-255, and M. E. Boismard, "Élie dans le Nouveau Testament," I, 116-28.

[23] The precise location of Elijah, given as heaven in 2 Kgs. 2:11 and in 1 *Enoch* 89:52, was a subject of some debate among the rabbis (Billerbeck, IV, 765f.).

[24] L. Ginzberg, *The Legends of the Jews*, 7 vols. (Philadelphia, 1910-39), IV, 202ff.; cf. also M. Segal, *Elijah, A Study in Jewish Folklore* (New York, 1935), *passim*.

3. Elijah's Expected Coming

Precisely at the beginning of the second-temple period, "Malachi" announced that God would send a messenger before his own final advent (Mal. 3:1); and a later hand, in all probability, identified this messenger, understandably enough, with the translated Elijah who was therefore expected to come (3:1) in order to restore the hearts of fathers to their children, and the hearts of children to their fathers (3:23f.), thus mitigating God's wrath. To this portrait Ben Sira (48:10) added an element drawn from the "Servant of Yahweh" traditions (Is. 49:6), thus viewing the coming Elijah as the one who will restore the tribes of Israel. And beyond Ben Sira numerous traditions developed, the major motif being that in preparation for God's eschatological advent—and hence as the "messianic" figure himself—Elijah would come to accomplish, often miraculously, the *restitutio in integrum* of God's people. In the traditions about his eschatological coming, Elijah is expected to do many things, such as make peace, whether within families or in the whole world; reassemble the members of the people who have been taken away; determine which are the genuine Israelites, thus re-establishing the purity of corpus Israel; restore to Israel the manna, the sprinkling water, and the anointing oil; raise the dead, thus vanquishing death as he once vanquished the prophets of Baal.[25]

---

[25] In addition to the works cited in nn. 22 and 24, see E. Schürer, *A History of the Jewish People in the Time of Christ*, 6 vols. (Edinburgh, 1890-91), index; G. H. Dalman, *Jesus-Jeshua: Studies in the Gospels* (New York, 1929), pp. 124f., 164f., 205f.; and G. F. Moore, *Judaism in the First Centuries of the Christian Era*, 3 vols. (Cambridge, 1927-30), II, 357ff. Representative references may be listed as follows: *make peace*—Mal. 3:24 (familial peace); Sir. 48:10 (restoring order to the nation); Mt. 17:11 and Mk. 9:12 (cosmic order); *Ed.* 8:7 (world peace) *Reassemble the tribe*—Sir. 48:10; *Ed.* 8:7. *Purify corpus Israel*—*Ed.* 8:7 shows debate on this subject; in any case some rabbis held that Elijah would determine whom to reject and whom to admit as true Israelites (cf. Jn. 1:47). *Restore manna*, etc.—*Mek. Exod.* 16:33. *Raise the dead*—*Sota* 9:15; *pShab.* I. 3c, 7 and I. 3c, 20; cf. Billerbeck, *Kommentar*, I, 194; Jeremias (*TWNT*, II, 934, n. 45) comments that Elijah's raising the dead is found in late texts, but see Schürer, *History*, II, 2, 157; Ginzberg, *Legends*, IV, 227f., 243, 246, n. 21, and compare the comments to Luke

In short, the first two major elements—the translation to heaven and the miracles—find their home by flowing into the third—the expected coming—producing the image of the eschatological Elijah as a miraculous helper who comes to restore the people of Israel just prior to God's own advent.[26]

7:1ff. by H. Schürmann, *Das Lukasevangelium,* Erster Teil (Fribourg, 1969), pp. 398ff. I see no good reason to doubt that the expectation of Elijah's raising the dead was alive in the first century, precisely in connection with 1 Kings 17:17ff. To the five activities of the eschatological Elijah I have listed, others could, of course, be added. See particularly Ginzberg, *Legends,* IV, 233ff. New Testament students will sense the absence from my list of a reference to the calling of Israel to "repentance," as distinct from "restoring" Israel (Mal. 3:23f.). I have omitted this item because, while it may be implied in Malachi 3:23f., and while it is explicitly mentioned in *Pirke R. Eliezer* 43, I am not at all certain that the firm and focused connection between Elijah and the call to repentance as such was made without John the Baptist serving as the middle term (cf. Ginzberg, *Legends,* IV, 233). Talmudic students, on the other hand, will note that I have not mentioned Elijah's role in clarifying obscure points of Torah. Cf. the comment of Davies, *Sermon on the Mount,* p. 160, and *Ed.* 8:7 (arrange disputes) and *B.M.* 1:8; 2.8; 3,4,5; *Shek.* 2.5. This function of Elijah would seem to belong closely to that of making peace.

[26] In light of the strong tendency to connect the eschatological Elijah with John the Baptist (and not with Jesus), it may be pertinent to mention three regards in which the Baptist would seem to fit rather poorly the dominant Elijah motifs (*pace* Jeremias: "The NT Understanding of Elijah Expectation: Fulfilled in John the Baptist," *TWNT,* II, 938): (a) The eschatological Elijah is concerned to restore the purity of corpus Israel before God's coming, holding precisely, as Jeremias says, that "blood purity alone entitles one to a share in end-time salvation" (936); the Baptist, by contrast, preaches a radical repentance, holding that blood descendancy is irrelevant to the question of salvation (Mt. 4:9f.; Lk. 3:8f.). (b) What we might call the "classic" portrait of the eschatological Elijah shows him as the forerunner not of the Messiah, as the Baptist is portrayed, but rather of God. To be sure it is obvious that in some Jewish sources Elijah came to be viewed as the forerunner of the Messiah, but one is at least entitled to wonder whether this development may not be paradoxically indebted somehow to an early Christian syllogism: Jesus is the Messiah; the Baptist was Elijah; Elijah is therefore the forerunner of the Messiah. And if that should be the case, we have a second point of discontinuity between the Elijah expectations and the Baptist. (The earliest firmly datable texts showing Elijah as the forerunner of *the Messiah* present two virtually identical comments made in

B. Elijah-Like Traits in the Fourth Gospel's Portrait of Jesus?

In the compass of a relatively brief essay there is not adequate space to explore all possibilities attaching to this question, nor is that necessary. Bearing in mind the major accents in the sketch given above, it will suffice to inquire whether they are reflected in the portrait of Jesus.

1. Elijah's Translation

We must begin on a negative note, for there is good reason to read John 3:13 as a polemic, not only against the possible identification of Jesus as Elijah, but also against the view that Elijah was translated at all: "No one has ascended into heaven but he who has descended from heaven, the Son of Man."[27] To be sure, Wayne Meeks has made a strong case that the polemic is directed against claims for Moses,[28] but Elijah traditions are probably also in the picture. Indeed Meeks himself refers in a note to H. Odeberg's view that behind the Fourth Gospel stood a polemic

---

Justin's *Dialogue* by the Jew Trypho [8:4 and 49:1], but a non-Christian Jewish origin for the pattern can scarcely be affirmed on such a slim basis. I am content to cite R. E. Brown, adding italics at only one point: "The rabbinic evidence for making Elijah the forerunner of the Messiah is later than the time of Jesus, but passages like Mark 9:11 *suggest* that this idea was current in the first century" [*Perspective* XII, 100]. It seems to be one of those matters on which certainty is not in our grasp.) (c) Recalling how pervasive in those expectations is the role of the Tishbite as miraculous helper, one must consider the absence of such a note in the Synoptic portraits of the Baptist as one who is not at all a miracle worker. (The thrust of John 10:41, especially of the clause, "John [the Baptist] did no sign," is something of a puzzle. In addition to the commentaries see E. Bammel, " 'John Did No Miracle'; John 10:41," in *Miracles*, ed. C. F. D. Moule (London, 1965), pp. 179-202, and W. Wink, *John the Baptist*, pp. 97f. The thesis to which the present study leads would suggest that this negative clause is purposely harmonious with the Baptist's negation of the role of Elijah for himself. That role and its miracles attach solely to Jesus.)

[27] The additional clause "he who is in heaven" is almost certainly secondary. See the commentaries.

[28] Meeks, *Prophet-King*, p. 301.

against "the traditions of ascensions into heaven by great saints, patriarchs, and prophets of old . . . such as Enoch, Abraham, Moses, Elijah, Isaiah. . . ."[29] And Odeberg, following Billerbeck, had cited a pertinent saying attributed to Rabbi Yose ben Halafta (ca. 150 C.E.) in which the ascensions of Moses and Elijah are alike denied:

> Never did Shekina descend on earth, nor did Moses and Elijah ascend on high. . . . How can it be maintained that Moses and Elijah did not ascend to heaven? And, lo, it is written (Exod. 19:3): "And Moses went up unto God." There was a distance of ten fingers' breadth. But, lo, it is written (II Kgs. 2:11): "And Elijah went up by a whirlwind into heaven". Even here it is to be understood that there was a distance of three fingers' breadth.[30]

Doubtless the motivation for the polemic of Rabbi ben Halafta will have been different from that which may lie behind the formulation of John 3:13. The point is simply that the rabbinic passage would seem to strengthen the possibility that the evangelist wishes to suppress the portraits of both Moses and Elijah as ones who ascended to heaven. *Only Jesus* is the ascended one, and, as regards our present concern, precisely not as Elijah, but rather as the Son of Man.

This first datum lends support to the views of Hahn and Fuller, and seems to run precisely counter to the statement by Cullmann that "the writer of John wants to reserve this title [Elijah] for Jesus."

2. Elijah's Miracles

Here we encounter data which point rather clearly in the other direction. We begin with two of John's miracle stories which

---

[29]*Ibid.*, p. 301 note, quoting from H. Odeberg, *The Fourth Gospel* (Uppsala, 1929), p. 97.

[30]*Suk. 5a*, following Odeberg's text, *Fourth Gospel*, pp. 89f.; note also *Mek.* on Exod. 19:10, cited by Meeks, *Prophet-King*, p. 205.

seem quite immediately to show just the sort of traits we might expect of the miracle-working, eschatological Elijah.

(a) The Changing of Water into Wine (2:1-11)

Commenting on this passage, R. E. Brown mentions Elijah's miraculous furnishing of meal and oil to the widow of Zarephath in 1 Kings 17:1-16. R. T. Fortna, following A. Schulz, suggests the possibility that 2:5 may show a parallel "to the claim Elijah and Elisha make on those at hand to assist in a miracle." G. Reim suggests that John 2:4a may be an allusion to 1 Kings 17:18 (but see also Gen. 41:55).[31] It would indeed seem pertinent to remark that many Jews and/or Jewish Christians of the first century would think above all of Elijah when hearing a story of a miracle which answers "an unexpected physical need that in the particular circumstances cannot be satisifed by natural means."[32] The changing of water into wine may thus paint a picture of Jesus which includes accents reminiscent of Elijah's first deed of mercy to the widow. It is numbered as the first of Jesus' signs (2:11).

(b) The Healing of the Nobleman's Son (4:46-54)

This is numbered as the second of Jesus' signs (4:54), and it may reflect in part the second of Elijah's miracles for the widow of Zarephath, the restoring of her son to life. In John 4:50 Jesus says to the nobleman, "Go, your son lives," a sentence which Reim classifies as an "obvious allusion" to Elijah's remark to the widow (1 Kgs. 17:23), "Look, your son lives."[33] We may also note

---

[31]R. E. Brown, *John*, I, 101; R. T. Fortna, *The Gospel of Signs* (London, 1970), p. 32 (see also the note on that page referring to A. Schulz, who mentions the possible parallels of 2:6 to 1 Kings 18:34 and of 2:8 to 2 Kings 4:41); G. Reim, *Studien zum alttestamentlichen Hintergrund des Johannesevangeliums* (Cambridge, 1974), p. 157. That Reim speaks of a "probable allusion" to 1 Kings 17:18 in John 2:4 may somewhat overstate the case, since the Hebraic idiom "What to me and to you?" is not infrequently encountered in the Old Testament. Above all, I do not mean to suggest that the story in 1 Kings 17 is the sole element in the background of John 2:1-11, even if I cannot say that I find the recent argument of E. Linnemann to be convincing ("Die Hochzeit zu Kana und Dionysos," *NTS* XX [1973-74], 408-418). Note especially Paul W. Meyer, "John 2:10," *JBL* LXXXVI (1967), 191-197.

[32]Brown, *John*, I, 101.

[33]Reim, *Studien*, p. 156; cf. Fortna, *Signs*, p. 42.

that the second sign is closely patterned on the first.[34] In the picture of Jesus presented by these first two signs, therefore, a Jewish reader steeped in the Elijah stories would probably sense at some level of consciousness certain traits reminiscent of the great helper; and, if we bring into our purview also material from the Elisha cycle, bearing in mind the close connection between the two figures in some patterns of Jewish thinking,[35] the number of pertinent data increases.

(c) The Feeding of the Multitude (6:1-14)

While there can be no doubt that Moses traditions lie directly in the background of this story, there are also several striking parallels with the story of Elisha's miraculous provision of bread in 2 Kings 4:42-44.[36]

	2 Kings		*John*
4:42	A man came . . . bringing twenty loaves of barley	6:9	There is a lad here who has five barley loaves[37]

---

[34] Brown, *John*, I, 194.

[35] I am inclined to think that R. E. Brown has rightly warned us against an easy confusing of "the resemblances between Jesus and Elijah with the resemblances between Jesus and Elisha," in his perceptive and provocative article, *Perspective* XII, 85-104, citation from p. 85. We should begin our research by considering the two prophets separately, not least because one was translated, whereas the other died. Yet we may also allow for a degree of coalescence in light of the extremely close connection between the two, signaled by Elisha's receiving a double portion of Elijah's spirit (cf. Luke 1:17). One notes numerous points of overlapping between the two figures in Jewish tradition (Ginzberg, *Legends*, IV, 239ff.).

[36] Reim, *Studien*, p. 157.

[37] The Synoptics have only "loaves" and thus provide in this regard a less precise parallel to the Elisha story. Indeed, remarking that the two terms "made of barley" and "young child" occur only here in the NT, Fortna (*Signs*, pp. 58f.), following C. K. Barrett (*The Gospel According to St. John* [London, 1955], p. 229), also notes the presence of the latter in the story immediately preceding the one in 2 Kings 4:42ff.

4:43a . . . his servant said, "How am I to set this before a hundred men?"	6:9 . . . but, what are they among so many?
4:43b -44 So he repeated, "Give them to the men, that they may eat, for thus says the Lord, 'They shall eat and have some left'." So he set it before them. And they ate and had some left. . . .	6:13 So they gathered them up and filled twelve baskets with fragments from the five barley loaves, left by those who had eaten.

(d) The Healing of the Man Born Blind (9:1-7)

The comparison here is, of course, with Elisha's healing of Naaman.[38]

2 Kings	*John*
5:10 Go and wash in the Jordan seven times.	9:7a Go, wash in the pool of Siloam. . . .[39]
5:14 So he went down and dipped himself seven times in the Jordan . . . and his flesh was restored. . . .	9:7b So he went and washed and came back seeing.

Doubtless other "allusions" and "parallels" could be mentioned with various degrees of probability. I shall mention only the one which arises most clearly from the argument of Reim about John 11:41f., and which brings us back to the Elijah cycle.

(e) The Raising of Lazarus (11:1-44)

At the crucial point in the highly dramatic account, Jesus relates the Father to himself and to the bystanders by means of a prayer:

Father, I thank thee that thou hast heard me. I know that

---

[38] Reim, *Studien*, pp. 157ff.

[39] Fortna's comment about "the claim Elijah and Elisha make on those at hand to assist in a miracle" (*Signs*, p. 32), is referred by him to John 6:10, 12; 9:7; 11:39; and 21:6.

thou hearest me always, but I have said this on account of the people standing by, that they may believe that thou didst send me (11:41f.).

Reim suggests a comparison with the story of Elijah's contest with the Baal prophets on Mount Carmel.[40] At the crucial point in that dramatic story Elijah prays similarly:

O Lord God of Abraham, Isaac, and Israel, let it be known this day that thou art God in Israel and that I am thy servant. . . . Hear me, O Lord, hear me, that this people may know that thou art the Lord God (1 Kgs. 18:36f.).[41]

The case for linking John 11:41f. to 1 Kings 18:37 is surely not so strong as those we have presented in the earlier instances. Reim seems clearly to recognize this, for he lists five points in support of this link, saying that he does so against possible skepticism.[42] Were this suggested link standing alone, one would scarcely speak, I think, of a "probable allusion." Yet, in light of the others, I should be inclined to grant that it is at least clearly possible. In any case, the noting of striking allusions in four of the miracle stories and the possibility of one in a fifth story will suffice to suggest that the miracle-working figures of Elijah and, secondarily, Elisha have indeed provided some of the features of the Gospel's miracle-working Jesus.

3. Elijah's Expected Coming

Since it is clear throughout the Gospel—note, for example 1:35-51—that Jesus is *the* eschatological figure, all of the data we

---

[40] Reim, *Studien*, p. 157.

[41] Note also *Ber. 9b* (cited by Ginzberg, *Legends*, IV, 199), interpreting Elijah's double exclamation (Hear me, hear me!): "He spoke: Lord of the world, thou wilt send me as a messenger at the end time, but if my words do not meet with fulfillment now, the Jews cannot be expected to believe me in the latter days," and compare with the motif of the sent messenger in John 11:41f.

[42] Reim, *Studien*, p. 219.

have just surveyed under the second category are also pertinent here. Indeed, we may consider it to be at least possible that the Elijah- (and Elisha-) like traits lie in the five miracle stories because the author(s) of these stories believed the eschatological Elijah had come in Jesus. Moreover there is the striking confession which climaxes the story of the miraculous feeding:

When the people saw the sign which he had done, they said, "This is indeed the prophet who is to come into the world" (6:14).

I have already noted that the feeding story reflects imprints from at least two traditions: the miraculous provision of bread by Elisha and the expectation of eschatological manna at the hands of the Mosaic prophet. There may also be an indication that Elijah plays a role in this climactic verse. One observes that the term "the prophet" (the Mosaic prophet) is provided with the appositional expression "who is to come, etc." Now the Mosaic prophet is regularly said to be "raised up" by God (cf. the fountain text of Deut. 18:15; also Acts 3:22, 26; 7:37),[43] rather than to be one who "comes."[44] On the other hand, "the coming one" may be some-

---

[43] The import of the verb "to arise" is one of the factors supporting the reading of p[66] and p[75] in John 7:52. One hopes that future editions of the very helpful and widely used *The Greek New Testament*, ed. Aland *et al.*, 2d ed. (New York, 1969) will at least cite this reading, and, even better, select it.

[44] There are, to be sure, a few texts which link Moses with the verb "to come," notably in the Samaritan sources; see Meeks, *Prophet-King*, pp. 246ff. Compare also the Fragmentary Targum of Palestine on Exodus 12:42, cited by *ibid.*, pp. 213f. The NT evidence, on the other hand, seems clearly to reflect a pattern: leaving John 6:14 aside, in all instances in which explicit identifications of the Mosaic prophet and of the eschatological Elijah are linked with one of our verbs, the former is said *to be raised up*, while the latter is said *to come*. For the eschatological Elijah see the data presented at the beginning of Section II above, and for the Mosaic prophet see Acts 3:22 (cf. 3:26); Acts 7:37; John 7:52; perhaps Luke 7:16. See also the preceding note.

thing close to a technical term for the eschatological Elijah.[45]
Thus John 6:14 may provide a climax for the feeding story by
referring to Jesus both as the Mosaic prophet and as the eschatological Elijah. And if that is the case, we may think of John
6:1-14 not only in connection with Elisha, but also in connection
with Elijah himself. Indeed this text may show that—however
distinct from one another the figures of John 1:20f. may be—
when it comes to the *portrait* of Jesus, the miracle stories are
penned in such a way as to allow an easy coalescence among the
figures of Moses, Elijah, and Elisha.

---

[45] R. E. Brown, *John* I, 44; a more detailed argument in Brown,
"Three Quotations from John the Baptist in the Gospel of John," *CBQ*
XXII (1960), 292-298 (esp. 297): "[1] Mal. 3, 1 has the words: 'Behold he
is coming,' seemingly applied to the messenger sent to prepare the way.
[2] When in Mt. 11, 3-14 the disciples of John the Baptist ask Jesus if he is
the one *who is to come* (*erchomenos*), he answers that John the Baptist is
'Elias, *who is to come* (*mellon erchesthai*)'. [3] And the characteristics
John the Baptist attributes to the one who is to come are amazingly
Elias-like." One will want to note, on the other hand, the opinion of
Meeks, *Prophet-King*, p. 90: "It is often supposed that 'the coming one'
was a messianic title, but this cannot be demonstrated." See also a similar
position in Hahn, *Titles*, p. 393. I am inclined to feel that, while the
general arguments against which Hahn and Meeks were reacting may be
subject to objections, a specific link between numerous occurrences of
the participial expression and some of the hopes for the eschatological
Elijah enjoys some degree of probability. Note particularly Hahn, *Titles*,
p. 380. In a forthcoming study I shall explore this matter in connection
with the expressions in John 1:15, 27, 30. Meanwhile one may be permitted at least to wonder whether the texts linking Moses with the verb "to
come" (see preceding note) may not have arisen at least in part because
Elijah-like traits were transferred to the Mosaic prophet. (To be sure, one
would strongly doubt this in connection with the Samaritan evidence,
since the Samaritans recognized only the Pentateuch.) Perhaps the bold
hypothesis of O. Bauernfeind regarding an Elijah/Moses source, which
he supposed to lie behind part of Peter's speech in Acts 3, is, *qua* literary
hypothesis, as wide of the mark as E. Haenchen believes (*The Acts of the
Apostles* [Philadelphia, 1971], pp. 210f.); yet the *religionsgeschichtliche*
dimensions of the hypothesis may have some value. Of course, it is a
coalescing of the figures of Moses and Elijah which I am suggesting for
the combined expressions in John 6:14. It may be the case, nevertheless,
that the author of the verse was to some degree aware of the coalescence,
especially in light of John 1:20f.

C. Conclusion

Reading through the Fourth Gospel while seeking to be alert for Elijah-like traits in the portrait of Jesus has not brought to our attention data which one would classify as conclusive "evidence that the post-Easter Church ever interpreted Jesus as . . . Elijah *redivivus*." We have found, rather, a divided picture. On the one side stands 3:13, which seems to say that Jesus, as the Son of Man and emphatically not as Elijah, is the only one ever to ascend to heaven. On the other side are 2:1ff., 4:43ff., 6:1ff., 11:41f. (also 9:1ff. by the inclusion of Elisha traditions), which seem clearly to bring Elijah-like traits into the portrait of Jesus. How is this divided picture to be explained?

When one observes that the negative datum lies in a Son of Man saying very probably formulated by the evangelist—note the descending-ascending pattern—whereas the positive data consistently emerge in the miracle-story tradition, a two-part hypothesis lies close at hand:

1. Perhaps the three denials placed in the Baptist's mouth (1:20f.) stem from a pre-Johannine author who also collected and shaped the miracle stories—or at least five of them—in such a way as to provide positive counterparts to all three denials. Should one be convinced of this much, he *might* conclude that he is faced with evidence of at least one theologian of the post-Easter Church who, without being explicit about it, did in fact interpret Jesus as Elijah.

2. It would follow that the evangelist, while satisfied to allow *minor* Elijah-like *traits* to remain in some of the miracle stories, penned 3:13 in such a way as emphatically to exclude, among other things, an explicit identification of Jesus as the eschatological Elijah. And if this last suggestion should recommend itself as a good possibility, one may be led to inquire whether the evangelist may not have suppressed in the materials inherited from the predecessor precisely what has thus far been missing: a direct counterpart to the Baptist's second denial, an explicit identification of Jesus as Elijah.

IV. A DIVIDED PICTURE AND SOURCE CRITICISM

We begin with an observation which in and of itself may go quite some way toward testing the initial part of this hypothesis. There is the simple fact that the Baptist's three denials and all of the data which we have discovered to show Elijah- (and Elisha-) like traits in Jesus' portrait fall in sections of the Gospel assigned by a number of critics to a pre-Johannine source.[46] To be sure, it would be unwise confidently to build extensive theories on the basis of the present state of Johannine source criticism. One needs only to mention the commentaries of R. E. Brown and Barnabas Lindars to be reminded that some leading interpreters find the labors of Johannine source critics largely unconvincing.[47] For three reasons, however, I believe that a considerable degree of confidence is warranted in the present instance.

1. The question before us involves a modest portion of the source theories—only that there was a signs source which included the Baptist's pointed denials—and, as we shall shortly see, an account of the coming of Jesus' first disciples, in addition to the traditional materials in at least five of the miracle stories. Over this much ground there is extensive, though of course not unanimous, agreement.

2. This extensive agreement has emerged in the careful work

---

[46]I shall take up the work of these critics in a moment. Here one should note some of the recent assessments of the state of source criticism in John's Gospel: D. M. Smith, "The Sources of the Gospel of John: An Assessment of the Present State of the Problem," *NTS* X (1963-64), 336-351; Barnabas Lindars, *Behind the Fourth Gospel* (London, 1971), pp. 27-42 and *passim*; R. Kysar, "The Source Analysis of the Fourth Gospel, A Growing Consensus?" *Nov.T.* XV (1973), 134-152; D. M. Smith, "Johannine Christianity: Some Reflections on Its Character and Delineation," *NTS* XXI (1974-75), 223-248, especially 229; W. A. Meeks, "'Am I a Jew?'—Johannine Christianity and Judaism." in *Christianity, Judaism and Other Greco-Roman Cults*, ed. J. Neusner (Leiden, 1975), I. 163-186. Of the four scholars mentioned here, Smith and Kysar are cautiously optimistic Lindars and Meeks rather pessimistic. One should not overlook Kysar's observations as regards the degree of consensus emerging from a variety of methods.

[47]See particularly the sharp criticism given by Lindars in his lucid booklet, *Behind the Fourth Gospel*.

of four scholars, R. Fortna, J. Becker, W. Nicol, and G. Reim, three of whom (delete Nicol) carried out their labors independently of one another.[48] It would be pertinent to remark, of course, that all of these critics have drawn on Bultmann's analysis of a signs source, but it is equally pertinent to note (a) that Fortna, in particular, worked through the materials with a degree of care and methodological thoroughness not evident in any of the previous attempts, and (b) that, independently of one another, three of the analysts have disagreed with Bultmann in respect to a matter crucial for our present concerns: they all assign to the source not only the core of each of the miracle stories which show the Elijah/Elisha traits, but also the traditional materials in the paragraph containing the Baptist's pointed denials.[49] Such independent agreement must be granted considerable weight.

3. Moreover, there is the fact—not altogether surprising—that the source-critics' labors are specifically related to our questions about the eschatological Elijah. Writing several years ago, Fortna remarked that in the source

---

[48] R. T. Fortna, *Signs*; J. Becker, "Wunder und Christologie," *NTS* XVI (1969-70), 130-148; W. Nicol, *The Sēmeia in the Fourth Gospel*, in *NovT* Sup., no. 32 (Leiden, 1972); Reim, *Studien*. The independence is quite clear in the cases of Fortna and Becker (both 1970), and I am assuming it also for the basic work done by Reim, since that work was a 1967 dissertation (Oxford). My frequent citation of Reim should not be taken to indicate complete agreement. I am afraid I must share some of the reservations noted by R. E. Brown in his review of Reim, *Theol. Studies* XXXV (1974), 558-61. One should also mention the source-critical labors of E. Bammel, *Miracles*, pp. 179-202 (reconstruction of a source he calls *Z* is given on pp. 193ff.), and in his "The Baptist in Early Christian Tradition," *NTS* XVIII (1971-72), 95-128 (esp. 109-113, 122-26). Also D. M. Smith, "The Milieu of the Johannine Miracle Source: A Proposal," R. Hamerton—Kelly and R. Scroggs (eds.) *Jews, Greeks and Christians* (Leiden, 1976), 164-180.

[49] I refer to Fortna, *Signs*, pp. 167ff., Becker *NTS* XVI, 135; and Reim, *Studien*, pp. 208f. Nicol speaks at one point (*Sēmeia*, p. 89) as though he intends to include 1:19ff. in the source, but the statements there are somewhat ambiguous, and his remarks at another juncture (pp. 39f.) even point the other way. His one explicit reference to 1:19ff. follows a statement about the source *and* the rest of John, and is therefore

. . . the parallel is strongest to the Elijah/Elisha tradition. Nowhere is Jesus explicitly identified with either of those earlier prophets, but that the identification is intended is evident in several ways: the Baptist's denial that he is Elijah, implying that Jesus in fact is; the phrase 'of whom the prophets wrote', which probably has at least Mal. 4:5 in mind; and the parallels in the source both to the diction of 1 and 2 Kings (John 4:50, 6:9, 9:7) and to the particular miracles done by Elijah and Elisha (esp. John 6 and 11).[50]

These remarks of Fortna are now made even stronger by a striking and, as I have already noted, independent confirmation in the most recently published portrait of the source, that by Reim. Particularly striking is the fact that Reim's portrait has emerged, not from a study which began as a source-critical attempt, but rather from a probing of the Gospel's Old Testament background. From this point on the compass Reim noticed, among other things,

. . . that in the Gospel of John no allusions to 1 and 2 Kings are found outside of five passages which all stand within the signs-source postulated by various scholars.

And he did not hesitate to draw a conclusion:

We see, then, that the author who assembled the signs-source had a definite interest in presenting the miracle stories of Jesus against the background of the Elijah and Elisha miracles. . . . This little book of miracles was designed to show that one cannot view the Baptist as Elijah or the Prophet— the Baptist himself refuses these roles—but rather only the wonder-working Jesus.[51]

---

of no use as regards the distinction (p. 87).

[50] Fortna, Signs, p. 232.

[51] Reim, Studien, pp. 207f. Cf. similar remarks on the part of Nicol, Sēmeia, p. 89.

In the analyses of these source-critics, one finds, then, confirmation of the first part of our hypothesis: the Baptist's denial
that he is Elijah, and the Elijah/Elisha-like traits as applied to
Jesus would seem indeed to stand in the text of John because the
evangelist inherited them from a predecessor. Contrary to Hahn
and Fuller, we have apparently encountered data indicating that
at least one early Christian theologian—yet not John himself, as
affirmed by Cullmann—did in fact view Jesus as the eschatological Elijah.

Yet some degree of doubt may remain, not only because the
source-critical analyses fail to be universally convincing, but also
because, as Fortna put it, "Nowhere [in the source] is Jesus
explicitly identified with [Elijah]."[52] If the author of the source
actually intended to grant to Jesus all three of the "titles" denied
for himself by the Baptist, why did he fail to make this intention
explicit only in the case of the second? To return to Hahn and
Fuller, we may recall that they clearly acknowledge the application to Jesus of "certain traits from the Elijah tradition," and of "a
whole series of traits [which] remind us of Elias." Yet they are
equally clear with regard to the absence of even one datum showing an explicit interpretation of Jesus as Elijah, and it is precisely
the absence of such a datum—the Baptist's second denial is still
dangling—which faces us at the end of the path we have followed.

Have we, however, really come to the end of the path?
Hardly. There is still that strikingly divided picture presented by
the Gospel as it stands, a picture which would seem to be there
because of a marked difference in attitude toward an Elijah-like
Jesus on the part of the source's author and on the part of the
evangelist. *Ex hypothesi* the evangelist is not concerned to ex-
punge minor Elijah-like traits in the miracle stories, but he is
determined to exclude as possibly pertinent to the portrait of
Jesus that element in the picture of Elijah without which the latter
has, so to speak, no vitality—the prophet's ascension to heaven.
Now, given both the absence of an explicit identification of Jesus
as Elijah and the nature of this divided picture, the question must

---

[52] Fortna, *Signs*, p. 232.

be raised whether the attitude of the source's author was so positive as to cause him to make an explicit identification of Jesus as
Elijah, and, correspondingly, whether the attitude of the evangelist
was so negative as to embolden him to suppress such an explicit
identification.

We should have to admit that it is not possible to go beyond
the mere posing of these questions, were it not the case that
shortly after the Baptist's dangling denial of his being Elijah — en
route, so to speak, from that denial to the miracle stories whose
portrait of Jesus borrows several colors from the pictures of
Elijah — we encounter a verse replete with problems which, in
turn, may indicate both the original Elijah identification by the
author of the source and its suppression at the hands of the
evangelist. The verse stands, one hastens to add, in a paragraph
beginning at John 1:35, the traditional materials of which are assigned to the source by all four source-critics mentioned above.

John 1:43 has drawn a considerable amount of comment from
interpreters precisely because of its vexing problems.[53] There is,
first, the difficulty of identifying the subject of the verb "he
wished to go." Three possibilities are regularly mentioned: One
may take as subject the last person named, Peter; or one may
elect the person who is the subject of the last finite verb, Jesus;
or. taking one's cue from an adverbial reading of "first" in verse
41, one may identify the subject as Andrew, who on this reading
found, first of all, his brother (v. 41), and then, secondly, Philip
(v. 43). As the text stands, there is little doubt that the first and
third of these possibilities are to be excluded. As R. E. Brown
comments, ". . . while John might tell us that Peter found Philip,
he would scarcely stop to tell us that Peter wanted to go to
Galilee."[54] By the same token, as the text now stands, Andrew is
to be excluded; and this leaves the subject as Jesus. It is surely

---

[53] At this point it may be pertinent for me to remark to the reader that
the present study had its origin, not in a critical assessment of the statements by Hahn and Fuller, but rather in several attempts over a period of
time to come to terms with the problems of this single verse. The reader
will find most of the problems clearly defined in Bultmann, *Das
Evangelium des Johannes* (Göttingen, 1950).

[54] R. E. Brown, *John*, I, 81.

Jesus who desires to make the journey, and it is thus Jesus who finds Philip. To make this grammatical decision is not, however, to get rid of the problem. Would an author composing his narrative in a simple and straightforward manner express himself so clumsily?

In the second place, one notes the location of the expressed subject, Jesus. To be sure, verse 43 stands in a passage replete not only with parataxis, but also with the well-known and largely Semitic pattern of placing the verb before the subject. Hence the expression "and said Jesus to him" calls for no special comment. What is striking is the supplying of the subject after the *third* of three verbs, all of which share this same subject.[55] Elsewhere in the paragraph when there is a series of such coordinated verbs, the subject is consistently supplied after the first of them (vv. 41, 45, 47), and this seems generally to be expected in such constructions.[56] To express the problem in less technical language: Would an author, composing freely, employ a finite verb to speak of an impending journey, use a second finite verb to indicate an act of finding, and, finally, use a third verb of speaking, only then providing the subject of all three verbs?

Third, there is the rather abrupt travel notice. Commentators regularly remark that it looks forward to the Cana story, but almost as regularly they express some puzzlement over its being given here.[57] Why does it not come immediately before 2:1?

---

[55] I read verse 43 as three independent clauses of a single sentence, the second and third being introduced by "and." See the note on punctuation in Aland, *Greek New Testament*. I am inclined to think that it is precisely the awkwardness of the text which has caused the majority of modern editors to place a full stop after either the first or the second clause. While that may be sound practice for a modern translator, the exegete is obliged, of course, to deal with the awkwardness.

[56] I have found in the standard handbooks no example of the subject being supplied after the third of three coordinate, finite verbs; nor have consultations with Semitic scholars produced any such instances.

[57] As Bultmann remarks, the travel notice of verse 43 makes it difficult to picture the events which follow (*Johannes*, p. 68). Interpreters also note that the dangling "first" of verse 41 and the form of Philip's claim in verse 45: "we have found," should quite possibly be reckoned as two further problems which arise from the present wording of verse 43.

Finally, and perhaps most tellingly, not a few interpreters have sensed that verse 43 breaks the chain-like character of the gathering of disciples. The remarks of M. E. Boismard are particularly cogent. Having noted that 1:6-8 and 1:9ff. emphasize the primal character of the Baptist's witness, Boismard continues:

> The first link of the chain is given in 1:35-39: two disciples of the Baptist hear him affirm that Jesus is the Messiah, and, on the basis of his word alone, they begin to follow Jesus. Both then believe in Jesus on account of the testimony of the Baptist. . . .
>
> The second link is given in 1:40-42: Andrew, one of the two disciples, leads his brother Simon to Jesus by declaring to him: "We have found the Christ." Through the agency of Andrew, the faith of Simon clearly links up with the testimony of the Baptist.
>
> The chain seems to break in 1:43ff. A new person appears, Philip, who is called directly by Christ: "Follow me!" Moreover, it is Philip, and not Andrew, who leads Nathanael to Christ (1:45-47). Neither the faith of Philip nor that of Nathanael is linked to the testimony of the Baptist, then; and that is why the chain seems broken.[58]

A partial solution proposed by Boismard is to identify the second disciple of verses 35-39 as Philip, thus achieving a balanced picture: Andrew and Philip, disciples of the Baptist, first attend to his witness, and then become themselves apostles, both to the Jewish world (to Simon, v. 41; and to Nathanael, v. 45) and to that of the Gentiles (to the Greeks of 12:20-22). It is, thus, thanks to the witness of the Baptist, as 1:7 predicts, that all—both Jews and Gentiles—come to believe in Christ.

Yet verse 43, with its breaking of the chain, still stands in the way; for here Jesus appeals directly to Philip. Facing this prob-

---

[58] M.-E. Boismard, "Les traditions johanniques concernant le Baptiste," *RB* LXX (1963), 5-42 (40).

lem, Boismard comes, finally and with admirable reserve, to the suggestion that the verse is the work of a post-Johannine redactor (who in Boismard's view is already on the scene, so to speak, being responsible for constructing the present text of 1:19-36 out of two earlier and strikingly parallel versions). Boismard remarks that his hesitancy to suggest such a solution was overcome in part when he noted that F. Spitta and W. Wilkens, without being guided by the prediction of 1:7, had already allotted verse 43 to the hand of a redactor simply on the basis of factors in that verse itself.[59] In turn, the arguments of Boismard, Spitta, and Wilkens clearly had an impact on R. Schnackenburg: "On this [redactional] hypothesis some things are easier to understand. . . ."[60] He is, nevertheless, reluctant to assign verse 43 to the redactor's hand without some indication in verse 44 that it did in fact originally follow immediately upon verses 40-42.[61]

If, now, the four problems just outlined incline one to consider the possibility of editorial activity in verse 43, yet the arguments for allotting the whole verse to the post-Johannine redactor are found inconclusive, it may be wise to ponder whether the problems did not perhaps arise at an earlier point, i.e., at the level of the evangelist's editing of his source.[62]

---

[59]*Ibid.*, p. 42, referring to F. Spitta, *Das Johannes-Evangelium* (Göttingen, 1910), p. 57 and to W. Wilkens, *Die Entstehungsgeschichte des vierten Evangeliums* (Zollikon, 1958), p. 35. The comments of both authors are well worth reading. One should also ponder Boismard's observation (thanks, apparently, to M. l'abbé Georges Roux) that the expression "Follow me" occurs in the Fourth Gospel only in 1:43 and in the redactional Chapter 21 (v. 19). Note also Boismard's more recent comments about the final redaction of the Fourth Gospel: P. Benoit and M. E. Boismard, *Synopse des Quatre Évangiles* (Paris, 1972), II, 16, 43 and *passim*.

[60]R. Schnackenburg, *The Gospel According to St. John* (London, 1968), I, 313.

[61]Presumably the case would have been acceptable to Schnackenburg if verse 44 had read somewhat as follows: "And Philip, the second of the two who had heard John, was from Bethsaida. . . ."

[62]Schnackenburg's typically sagacious comments on 1:43 form one of the points at which one wonders why, having granted some probability to the hypothesis of a signs source (*St. John* I, 67), the author does not

This is, in fact, the route elected both by Bultmann and by Fortna.[63] The latter proposes that in the source 1:43 read as follows:

> And he (Andrew) found Philip.
> And Jesus said to him:
> "Follow me!"

He then holds the evangelist responsible for the first half of the present verse—"on the morrow . . . Galilee"—which he judges to be "an artificial insertion."

Considering the possible cogency of Fortna's analysis, one must admit, I think, that the second line follows rather abruptly on the first and that the antecedent "to him" is consequently a bit awkward. One might thus entertain doubts that Fortna has in this case recovered the whole of the source's reading, and yet be inclined to consider seriously the hypothesis that at 1:43 the source did in fact read somewhat differently from the present text. Can further analysis yield a more convincing reading?

Two literary observations intersect in a way which would seem to justify an affirmative answer. First, we may reread the whole of 1:35-49, bearing firmly in mind the Baptist's three denials (1:20f.). As is well known, this paragraph abounds in the application to Jesus of christological titles, but *literarily* two of these are accented by being placed as the objects of the single verb-form "we have found," namely "the Messiah" (v. 41) and "the one of whom Moses wrote" (v. 45).[64] One notices that these

---

draw on this probability to wrestle with certain kinds of problems in the present text. The question does not arise in just the same way, of course, as one reads the commentary of Lindars, for whom the theory of two major editions largely takes the place of source criticism. One learns a great deal from Lindars' massive labors, but his specific comments on 1:43 do not seem to bring us very far forward: ". . . awkward as it is, the text can stand. . . . In any case the verse is only aimed at bringing Philip onto the stage, because of his part in what follows" (*Behind the Fourth Gospel, ad loc.*).

[63] Bultmann, *Johannes*, p. 68; Fortna, *Signs*, pp. 184f.

[64] Fortna, *Signs*, p. 188; for the subject of the verb in the first line, see p. 184.

accented titles correspond to the first and last of the three titles which the Baptist so dramatically denies for himself. When one also notices that our problematic verse lies precisely between these two, the suggestion virtually presents itself that the Baptist's second denial, otherwise left dangling, may have had its positive counterpart in the original wording of verse 43:

Three Denials	*Three (?) Affirmations*
20. I am not the Christ	41. We have found the Messiah
21. Are you Elijah? . . . I am not	43. (We have found Elijah)?
21. Are you the prophet? . . . No	45. The one of whom Moses wrote . . . we have found

Second, and rather more weighty, I think, is the observation that verses 41f. and 45-47 evidence a remarkable degree of structural similarity which may be represented as follows:[65]

---

[65] The structural similarity of verses 41f. and verses 45ff. has been frequently observed, of course, even if not always displayed in the same way. See, e.g., the analysis made by Boismard, "Les traditions," p. 41, and note the important observation by Hahn that "die Anrede ἴδε ἀληθῶς Ἰσραηλίτης ἐν ᾧ δόλος οὐκ ἔστιν in v. 47b zumindest in einer lockeren Entsprechung zu der Namensverleihung in v. 42b zu sehen [ist]" ("Die Jüngerberufung Joh. 1, 35-51," *Neues Testament und Kirche* [für Rudolf Schnackenburg], ed. J. Gnilka [Freiburg, 1974], p. 180). Strangely, however, this observation is one of the remarkably few points at which the analysis made by Hahn and that of the present essay exhibit agreement. Regarding this divergence there is space here for only four brief comments: (1) While, as always, I am instructed by several aspects of Hahn's work, (see, for example, "Der Prozess Jesu nach dem Johannesevangelium," *Evangelisch-Katholischer Kommentar zum Neuen Testament*, 3 vols. [Neukirchen, 1970], II, 23-96), I find that his analysis in this case shows the necessity to pursue in great detail the literary structure of the text before us—and hence the literary problems, including those of syntax—*before* one turns to *Formgeschichte*. This is precisely what Hahn does not do. One can only register amazement that he passes right by the vexing problems of verse 43, a procedure which is scarcely unrelated to his allotting virtually the whole of the verse as it stands to the "Grundform der Berufungserzahlung" (p. 178). (2) It is this same

vv. 41f.

(1) He (Andrew) *found* first his brother . . . Simon
(2) *and said to him*, "We have found the Messiah."[66]
(3) He led him to Jesus.
(4) Looking at him,
(5) *Jesus said*, "You are Simon. . . ."

vv. 45-47

(1) Philip *found* Nathanael
(2) *and said to him*, "The one of whom Moses wrote . . . we have found. . . ."
(3) And Nathanael said to him. . . . Philip said to him, "Come and see."
(4) *Jesus* saw Nathanael coming to him, and
(5) he *said* about him, "Behold, truly an Israelite. . . ."[67]

---

electing of *Formgeschichte* prior to a detailed literary analysis which enables Hahn to speak of verse 43 as evidencing a useful parallelism to the Synoptic *Berufungsgeschichten*. In spite of the absence of the third expected element, the *Vollzugsbericht*, Hahn locates the expected *Situationsbeschreibung* in Jesus' finding of Philip and the expected *Berufungswort* in the brief call "Follow me!" About the latter point there is no debate. The call is certainly traditional. As regards the former, however, Hahn fails to observe the facts about the verb "to find": (a) It is used in none of the Synoptic *Berufungsgeschichten*. (b) It provides one of the major characteristics of the present passage (five times in five verses). Hence this verb ties verse 43 not to the *Synoptic* form of the *Berufungsgeschichte*, but rather to its present context. The distinction is crucial to the literary analysis, and, if it is taken into account, one will scarcely identify Jesus' finding of Philip as a pre-Johannine *Situationsbeschreibung*. (3) Hahn is surely correct to point out two rather different pictures in the paragraph. In verse 43 it is Jesus who takes the initiative, making a man into his disciple by means of his authoritative word. In verses 41, 42a, and 45f. it is, on the other hand, not Jesus himself, but rather one of his disciples who issues the call. In Hahn's opinion, both of these pictures have come to John from tradition. On the face of it, that is, of course, entirely possible, especially if one leaves aside a detailed analysis of the problems presented by the present wording of verse 43. Even so, a warning signal would certainly arise from careful consideration of such passages as 5:14; 6:44, 65; 15:16; and 9:35, all of which seem clearly to come from the evangelist. In light of these passages, one could at least ask whether the picture in which Jesus takes the initiative (present form of verse 43) may not stem from the evangelist.

Now, if one recalls the four vexing problems of verse 43 as it is presently worded, if one entertains seriously the possibility that these problems may have arisen as a result of editorial activity on the part of the evangelist, if one bears in mind the suggestion that the second of the Baptist's denials may have had some kind of positive counterpart in the original wording of this problematic verse, and if, finally, the form of verses 41f. and 45-47 should lead one to credit the author of the source with a good sense for parallel structuring, it is surely no huge step to the hypothesis that in the source the verse read somewhat as follows, showing the same five-membered structure:

The fact that it contains *one* traditional clause "Follow me!" should scarcely lead one to assign it *in its present form* to pre-Johannine tradition. (4) Finally, there is the weighty theological issue of the nature of the call to discipleship. At the end of his article, Hahn has some words about this issue which seem to me both perceptive and puzzling. Since he believes that the evangelist has developed verses 45f. out of verses 41 and 42a, it is not greatly surprising that he finds the evangelist's own concern to be expressed in the *indirekte Berufung* of these verses rather than in the *direkte Berufung* of verse 43: "Er [der Evangelist] wollte damit der Situation der Jünger in einer Zeit gerecht werden, in der die *indirekte Berufung* in die Nachfolge längst an die Stelle der direkten getreten war. . . ." (p. 190, italics added). In light of 6:44, 65, etc. (see above), this statement seems to me to stand the matter exactly on its head; and I cannot avoid wondering whether Hahn does not at some level realize that; for his final words are: ". . . denn wie immer sich die Nachfolge vollzieht, *die unmittelbare Begegnung* mit dem lebendigen Herrn ist das Herzstück christlicher Jüngerschaft" (p. 190, italics added). Regarding John 4:39-42, another passage which could come under consideration, see H. Leroy, *Rätsel und Misverständnis* (Bonn, 1968), pp. 92ff., and the comment below in note 83.

[66] It would be the evangelist, of course, who provides the interpretation of the term "Messiah"; cf. Fortna, *Signs*, p. 184.

[67] Verses 45-47 paint a somewhat more detailed picture than do verses 41f., but the essential structure is strikingly similar. I have underlined "Jesus" in line 4 because it clearly goes with the verb "he said" in line 5. Note moreover "to Jesus" in line 3 of verses 41f., and compare with "to him" in line 4 of verses 45-47. Compare also "looking at" with "he saw."

v. 43

(1) He (Andrew secondly)[68] *found* Philip

(2) *and said to him*, "We have found Elijah who comes to restore all things [or some such]."

(3) He led Philip to Jesus [or some such].

(4) And, looking at him,

(5) *Jesus said*, "Follow me!"[69]

Voilà! A direct facing of the problems of verse 43, notably the break in the witness/discovery chain, and a structural analysis of the surrounding verses have led us to hypothesize that John's source for 1:19ff. and 1:35ff. and at least five of the miracle stories did in fact contain—between the Baptist's denial that he is Elijah and the Elijah-like portrait of Jesus—exactly what we have been watching for, an explicit identification of Jesus as Elijah.

It would be dishonest of me to say that I consider this hypothesis to be extremely tenuous. On the contrary, it seems to me to enjoy a considerable egree of probability.[70] Nevertheless, I am bound to face the question whether the emergence of this line of thought is a case of watching for something so intently that one finds it by hypothesizing it into existence without adequate

---

[68] I have placed these two words in parenthesis because of the difficulty of deciding whether the likelihood lies with Andrew or with Peter.

[69] One should not be greatly surprised to note that the weighty Christian interpretation of the verb "to follow" (see E. Schweizer's classic *Lordship and Discipleship* [Naperville, 1960]) emerges on all three levels in the Fourth Gospel: the signs source (1:37; 1:40; apparently 1:43), the evangelist's own composition (8:12; 13:36; etc.), and the work of the post-Johannine redactor (21:19ff.). That the verb is traditionally used in stories of Jesus' call to discipleship leads Hahn (n. 65 above) to assign 1:43 to a pre-Johannine, Synoptic-like tradition; that the formula "Follow me!" occurs in 21:19 caused Boismard (in 1963) to assign 1:43 to a post-Johannine redactor; the presence of the verb in the context of 1:43, in verses assigned by Fortna to the source, inclines me to think that it was used by the author of the source in his form of 1:43.

[70] Not least because, as I have indicated above (n. 43), the present study began not at all as a quest for a confession of Jesus as Elijah, but rather as an attempt to solve the syntactical problems of 1:43.

grounds. Beyond one's judgment of the arguments advanced thus far, the answer given will depend to some degree on the results of two final questions: (1) whether the hypothetical reading of 1:43 helps us to recover a section of the source which offers a picture of the author that is coherent and both *religionsgeschichtlich* and *theologiegeschichtlich* convincing, and (2) whether, beginning with the hypothesis, one sees compelling theological reasons for thinking that the evangelist, faced with such a reading in his source, would probably have altered the text to the present wording.

V. THE ELIJAH COMPONENT IN THE SOURCE'S CHRISTOLOGY

Following Haenchen and Fortna, I find it quite plausible to think that the source in question served as a kind of rudimentary Gospel in John's church prior to his own literary activity.[71]

---

[71] E. Haenchen, "Johanneische Probleme," *ZTK* LVI (1959), 53f. No aspect of Fortna's work has been more hotly debated than his conclusion that a single document lies behind most of John's narrative sections, including the passion, and that it should properly be termed, therefore, the Signs *Gospel*. See, e.g., J. M. Robinson's comments in J. M. Robinson and H. Köster, *Trajectories Through Early Christianity* (Philadelphia, 1971), pp. 247-249. It would be foolish for me to think that in a footnote I can add anything significant to the debate. I do want, however, to make three brief comments for clarification: (1) D. M. Smith's recent discussion of this question seems to me to warrant serious consideration (*NTS* XXI, 24f.), and one will want to attend to Fortna's latest word on the issue in "Christology in the Fourth Gospel: Redaction-Critical Perspectives," *NTS* XXI (1974-75), 17ff. (2) While I am inclined to accept Fortna's thesis in general outline, I must point out that for the present study it is a matter of inconsequence whether one links the source material behind 1:19-49 to a signs source or to a signs Gospel. (3) This last point could be questioned, to be sure, precisely in light of the present thesis that for the author of the source Jesus was the eschatological Elijah. Would an author be likely, so the counter-argument could run, to ask his readers to think that the Elijah who escaped death, being translated to heaven, had returned to earth in Jesus, not only miraculously to help the needy, but also to suffer and die? Hence, if one is convinced that

Whether one agrees or not, however, it seems quite clear that there is no passage allotted to the source which is more transparent to the author's intention than the one which has just drawn our attention: the traditional elements behind 1:35-49.[72] For here we find not only an amazing richness in christological titles— Lamb of God, Messiah, *ex hypothesi* Elijah, Mosaic prophet, Son of God, and King of Israel—reflecting, no doubt, the author's concentrated attention to christology, but also a *line* of christological *movement* constructed in a way which would seem to show that the author presupposes on the part of his readers certain patterns of thought not very difficult to reconstruct. To be specific, he seems to take for granted that his readers are persons who already have messianic expectations. These already-had expectations form a sort of launching pad from which issues a christological trajectory, so to speak, which finds its goal, according to the author, in Jesus of Nazareth.[73] One of the central verbs is "to find" (twice in v. 41, once and *ex hypothesi* twice in v. 43, and twice in v. 45). To the centrality of this verb it corresponds that the portrait of Jesus in this paragraph is remarkably passive. He *walks* by (v. 36); he *responds* to persons who themselves are responding not to him, but to the words and acts of others (vv. 38, 42, 43 [as reconstructed], 47); these others speak and act *not because Jesus has himself commissioned them to do so*, but

---

John 1:43 originally made the Elijah identification, would it not follow that it was most likely a link in a document which consisted solely of miracle stories? This is a point at which the Coptic Elijah apocalypse emerges as pertinent, for it shows clearly that it was not ruled out, in our general period, to think of the eschatological Elijah as coming to earth only to experience suffering and death (and resurrection!). See the Coptic *Apocalypse of Elijah*, paragraph 42 (Akhmimic); G. Steindorff, "Die Apokalypse des Elias," *TU* XVII, no. 3a (1899), 169, kindly translated for me by Holland Hendrix.

[72] For reasons which cannot be developed here, I believe the evangelist authored 1:50 as a transition from the source to the Son of Man *logion* of 1:51.

[73] For what Robinson and Köster have called "trajectory," with qualifications (*Trajectories*, p. 14), Fortna helpfully proposes "direction of flow" (*NTS* XXL, n. 4). For what I am describing in the source's christology, however, "trajectory" seems the appropriate term.

rather because they stand as links in a (Baptist) chain of witness-bearing and discovery which ties traditional christological titles to the remarkably passive figure of Jesus. As it stands in the source, this paragraph should not be titled "Jesus *Calls* the First Disciples" (although Jesus' call forms a subordinate note), but rather "Some Jews Begin To *Find* the One Pointed-To in Their Expectations." Only at the end, in verse 48, does Jesus significantly qualify the line of christological movement from traditional expectations to discoveries of fulfillment by informing Nathanael that his knowledge of him anteceded Philip's calling of him. This qualification must be given its due weight; in particular it may have special import for the evangelist. The fact remains that even here it is Philip and not Jesus who calls Nathanael.

It seems reasonable to assume, therefore, that the author of the source writes both for confirmed members of his Church and for Jews whom he views as potential converts. He presupposes that the latter are persons who have long treasured in their hearts various elements of messianic expectation. He therefore allows them first to hear the Baptist deny for himself three key titles; then he allows them to behold a chain of Jews, expectant like themselves, proceeding to discover the fulfillment of their messianic hopes not in the Baptist,[74] but rather in Jesus of Nazareth, a man who is the Messiah, the eschatological Elijah, and the Mosaic prophet.[75] As the Messiah, Jesus is also the Son of God, and is so confessed, both here—by Nathanael—and at the climactic terminus of the source preserved in 20:30f. But before the author brings his document to that climax, he presents a series of miracle stories designed to follow the confessions of 1:42, 43, and 45 by presenting to his Jewish readers a rich portrait of Jesus as

---

[74]Bammel holds, interestingly, that his source *Z* ends with John 10:41 and its emphatic note that the Baptist did no sign (*Miracles*, 193ff.).

[75]Following an oral suggestion kindly made by Fortna, I am inclined to think that the rather strange construction of 1:45b may have resulted from the evangelist's adding to his source the words "and the prophets." Assuming that he suppressed the identification with Elijah in 1:43, one may guess that he felt it appropriate to append in verse 45 these words which somehow round out the picture without reintroducing what he wants to suppress.

the one who was in fact the Mosaic prophet, the eschatological Elijah, and the Messiah. The author, far from being suspicious of the line of christological movement which stretches from traditional expectation to discovered fulfillment, actually considers that line of movement to be the firm foundation of the good news.

To sharpen the point, one could use one's imagination to compose a text expressive of the author's missionary horizon, in order to compare it with such a text which appears in the Pauline corpus:

> They from of old who await in hope shall see, and they who search the Scriptures shall find the Messiah. (The author of the source)

> They who have never been told of him shall see, and they who have never heard of him shall understand. (Paul quoting Is. 52:15 in Rom. 15:21)

In short, the author of the source, however clearly he may write for Christian readers, seems also to represent what Paul calls "the Gospel of the circumcision."[76] For our present concern the major point is that one would scarcely be surprised to find such an author holding to the conviction that one element in the Gospel for the circumcision is the discovery on the part of Jews that their longing for the coming of the great helper and restorer—the eschatological Elijah—finds its rest in Jesus of Nazareth.[77]

---

[76] As far as I can see, neither the literary evidence employed for the study of Jewish Christianity by such authors as J. Daniélou, H. J. Schoeps, and A. F. J. Klijn, nor the archeological data collected by B. Bagatti and P. E. Testa have shown it to be a Jewish Christian motif to identify Jesus as Elijah. Such silence certainly does not help the hypothesis being pursued here; but neither does it damage the hypothesis, if one bears in mind that our attempts to reconstruct the history and thought of Jewish Christianity are being made, thus far, on the basis of data which put us in touch with a *very* small fraction of the original picture(s)—shall we say one-tenth or one-onehundredth?

[77] Referring to the copious discussion of recent years on the question of the Gospel *Gattung* and the possible pertinence of Greco-Roman

VI. The Johannine Redaction

A full exploration of the hypothesis as regards the evangelist's redaction of the form of 1:43, which he found in the source, would take us far beyond the necessary limits of the present essay; for we would need in that case comprehensively and in

---

aretalogies, R. E. Brown aptly remarks: "If the Elijah and Elisha cycles of miracles had been composed in Greek in the second century B.C., with the name of a Greek god substituted for Yahweh, I suspect that these cycles would be classified by scholars as aretalogies and would be singled out as the closest analogues to the collected miracles of Jesus of Nazareth. But since they are eighth- and seventh-century Hebrew miracle collections, they do not enter much of this discussion about pre-Gospel aretalogies" (*Perspective* 12, 97). See also Reim, *Studien*, pp. 206ff.; and recall two pertinent remarks made by Bultmann in his commentary. Noting that some of the Baptist's disciples surely became members of the Christian Church, Bultmann continues, "That the Evangelist himself belonged to such disciples is probable, for that would make understandable his use of Baptist tradition. The paragraph of 1:35-51 would show, then, that the Evangelist had been converted through such disciples of the Baptist who themselves had become Christian before him. The source which he employs in this paragraph had its origin in the propaganda which such persons formulated in behalf of Christian faith" (*Johannes*, p. 78 and n. 6 there). Two pages later we find another comment which may be pertinent to the question of Gospel *Gattung*. Noting that two of the miracles in the pre-Johannine source are numbered, Bultmann poses a question and cites a relevant datum: "Was it already a practice in Judaism to number the Old Testament miracles and place them in a series? Compare *Yoma 29a* (Billerbeck, *Kommentar*, II, 409f.): Rabbi Asi (ca. 300) said: Esther is the conclusion of all [OT] miracles" (*Johannes*, p. 78, no. 4). It hardly needs to be added that these helpfully provocative observations of Brown and Bultmann should not be interpreted as favoring a "Jewish" milieu for the source as to a "Hellenistic" one. One hopes it will soon be common knowledge that the Judaism of New Testament times—with all of its manifold variations—was itself, to one degree or another, a Hellenistic religion. Regarding a dominant strain in the *religionsgeschichtliche* aspects of Nicol, *Sēmeia*, Meeks is, I think, fully justified in speaking sharply: " . . . Nicol is so determined to show that there is nothing 'Hellenistic' about the signs source that he falls into an incredibly wooden and confused use of the categories "Hellenistic' and 'Jewish.' Consequently the second chapter is an anachronism in research today" (" 'Am I a Jew?' Johannine Christianity and Judaism," in *Christianity, Judaism, and Other Greco-Roman Cults* I [Leiden, 1975], p. 184, n. 82).

great detail to consider the broad picture of his redactional activity in the whole of the first chapter and beyond.[78] In the present context, we must limit ourselves to a few observations which bear directly on the degree of probability one may grant to the hypothesis.

A. The Literary Dimensions

The literary dimensions of the editing required by the hypothesis may be easily grasped simply by returning to the text proposed for the source:

(1) He (Andrew secondly) found Philip
(2) and *said* to him, "We have found Elijah who comes to restore all things."
(3) He led Philip to Jesus.
(4) And, looking at him,
(5) *said* Jesus, "Follow me!"

An author concerned to suppress the identification of Jesus with Elijah would have little difficulty altering this text to that end. There are two instances of the verb "he said" (lines 2 and 5), and the Elijah identification lies between the two. It would be easy, therefore, simply to delete the intervening material by passing from the first "he said" to the second:

(1) He (Andrew secondly) found Philip
(2) and said to him . . .
(3) . . .
(4) . . .
(5) . . . Jesus, "Follow me!"

---

[78] It is obvious that the major motivation for studies such as the present one may properly lie in the possibility of employing redaction criticism in order to bring the evangelist's own theology more clearly into focus. Two qualifications, however, are in order. The first is that of time and space, already mentioned. The second is the need to broaden our understanding of lines of development in early Christian thought and life. The fact that the Church did not canonize the source with its inclusion of an "Elijah christology" cannot in itself assure us that the latter has no theological value.

An author who wanted, in addition, to provide a travel notice in preparation for the story of Chapter 2 would perhaps elect to do so at a point at which he is already making alterations. Prefixing a notice of Jesus' movement to Galilee would virtually necessitate awarding the verb "he found" to Jesus—picturing the events is difficult enough, even with Jesus as the subject of all three finite verbs. Hence:

(0) On the morrow[79] he wished to go to Galilee, and
(1) he found . . . Philip
(2) and said to him . . .
(3) . . .
(4) . . .
(5) . . . Jesus, "Follow me!"

There is, to be sure, one further change which would seem to be called for: the advancing of the subject "Jesus" into line (0), either immediately before or after "he wished." While the translator of the Peshitta, sensing the syntactical difficulty, took exactly this step,[80] it is clear from the present state of the text that the author from whose hand it has come to us was not bothered by its awkwardness. *Ex hypothesi* he was satisfied to have suppressed the Elijah identification and to have introduced the travel notice, without having to go to great lengths to do so.

B. The Major Motivational/Theological Dimensions of John's Redaction

While a comprehensive analysis of the evangelist's redaction at 1:43 must await another setting, as I have indicated above, some exploration is in order here. I have just mentioned two redactional motives: the evangelist's apparent determination to suppress the Elijah identification, and his desire to introduce a travel notice. The latter needs no further comment in the present study. The former, by contrast, calls, of course, for concentrated attention. Before we turn to it, however, there is yet another

---

[79] See Fortna, *Signs*, p. 184: ". . . the scheme of days . . . (cf. 4:3, 43; 6:1, 7:1) is an artificial insertion by John."
[80] Noted by Bultmann, *Johannes*, p. 68, n. 3.

possible motive which deserves brief discussion. The literary clue which indicates the possibility of this motive is the evangelist's replacing of Andrew by Jesus as the subject of the verb "he found" in line (1).[81]

I have suggested above that this change is mainly a matter of the evangelist's maintaining a reasonable degree of editorial coherence. Once he has introduced the travel notice, the demands of syntactical and logical clarity lead him to allow Jesus—however awkwardly—to be the subject of "he found." This may, in fact, be the whole story. On the other hand, to change the subject of *this* verb is to make an alteration of some theological import, and it would seem unlikely that such a matter would be entirely accidental on the part of one of the subtlest theologians of the early Church. There are, moreover, reasons to think that the evangelist was quite happy to make the change.

It has two major dimensions: it alters the otherwise remarkably passive portrait of Jesus, showing him in *this* instance to take the initiative in finding a disciple;[82] and it breaks the chain of witness-discovery so fundamental to the source's christological trajectory, which arches from traditional expectations to discovered fulfillment. As regards the second of these—they are virtually opposite sides of a single coin—there are passages elsewhere in the Gospel which would seem to indicate considerable reservations on the part of the evangelist toward precisely the source's traditional christological trajectory.[83] I shall mention only one.

---

[81] I have mentioned above the possibility that in the source Peter rather than Andrew was the subject. It could also have been the unnamed disciple of verse 40. One can scarcely be very confident, nor is this an instance in which confidence greatly matters.

[82] See again the discussion of Hahn (*Neues Testament und Kirche*, 172-90) in n. 65 above.

[83] See, e.g., 5:14; 6:44, 65; 9:35; 15:16. One would certainly be tempted to cite also 4:39-42, in spite of the perceptive argument made by Leroy, *Rätsel*, pp. 92ff., for viewing that text as a deposit from Samaritans who, by the claim given there, succeeded against opposition in entering the Johannine community. If Leroy is correct, the Samaritans' success could be due to the use of a confession quite harmonious with a theological point high on the evangelist's agenda.

On the day following the feeding miracle of John 6:1ff., a group of persons emerge who are represented as harboring messianic expectations on the basis of Scripture (6:25-31). Moreover, they are obviously considering the possibility—in however prejudicial a manner—that the trajectory issuing from these traditional expectations does indeed find its goal in Jesus. It would have been quite harmonious in the scene had the narrator introduced a second group coming to the first and asking whether they had "found" the expected Messiah.

As the scene actually unfolds, however, the crowd's comments create an atmosphere quite different from that of 1:35ff. For what these people propose to do is to give Jesus a *chance* to meet their messianic expectations (6:30f.), and subsequent developments show that they do not consider him to have passed *their test* (6:41f., 52). In short, the christological trajectory so positively exemplified in the source at 1:35ff. proves here to be a debatable matter. Those who *begin* with traditional expectations believe themselves competent to preside over the question whether their expectations are fulfilled in one they consider to be a prospective *candidate*.

Faced with *this* development (one supposes it is portrayed in Chapter 6 because it somehow corresponds to actual events which have transpired since the writing of the source) the evangelist sees the necessity fundamentally to qualify the christological trajectory itself. Hence he hears Jesus speak the sharp words: "Why [like the wilderness generation] do you murmur among yourselves? No one is able to come to me [cf. "find the Messiah"] unless the Father who sent me draw him" (6:43f.; cf. 6:65).[84]

---

[84]Cf. Is. 43:18ff. and particularly Ps. 78:17ff. The latter presents an especially striking pattern. First, the wilderness generation experiences God's grace in the gift of water from the rock. One supposes they gave thanks for the welcome stream. Next, however, they proceed, so to speak, to wrench God's gracious deed out of his hand (to separate it from him) and to turn it into the genesis of a trajectory of expectation on the basis of which they themselves propose to preside over the next move. They are the ones who give God the test (v. 18) and who say, "He smote the rock so that water gushed out. . . . Can he also give bread . . . ?" (v. 20).

Returning now to 1:43, one can easily see that the evangelist's making Jesus the subject of "he found" results in a verse which similarly—though, as is appropriate in this context, non-polemically—qualifies the source's christological trajectory by placing in the midst of the witness/discovery chain one instance in which the initiative (of election) lies clearly with Jesus. Because the atmosphere created in this paragraph of the source is so positive and compelling, one would scarcely suppose, to be sure, that the evangelist altered the verse primarily in order to provide this qualification. It would seem, however, that, having decided to edit the verse for other reasons, the evangelist was happy also to seize the opportunity to reveal the gracious line which finds its beginning not in traditional expectation, but rather in God's sovereign election through Jesus Christ.[85]

We come, finally, to the heart of the evangelist's editing of 1:43, the suppression of the Elijah identification. In order to see it in perspective, we need to look briefly at the literary structure achieved by the evangelist in the first chapter.

Assuming the validity of the hypothesis, it would seem that in Chapter 1 the evangelist has taken four major steps in regard to the source: (1) he has prefixed a hymn (vv. 1ff.), which finds its focus in statements about the pre-existent logos, now become incarnate in Jesus; (2) he has completed his prologue by immediately providing on the basis of the hymn an exegesis, the climax of which includes a polemically formulated denial that anyone other than the Incarnate One has ever seen God (v. 18);

---

[85] Even in the positive and compelling atmosphere of 1:35ff., the evangelist may have qualified the source's traditional christological trajectory at one other point, verse 48. Above I have implied that this verse is to be assigned to the source. That may, indeed, be the best analysis; yet there are several reasons for seeing it, on the whole, as a redactional insertion by John. (a) However the literal call to discipleship may be issued, Jesus is shown to be the active and prescient Lord; (b) the question "how," while not always from the evangelist's hand, is often his; (c) the formula "he answered and said" has been judged to be a stylistic characteristic of the evangelist (E. Ruckstuhl, *Die literarische Einheit des Johannesevangeliums* [Freiburg, 1951], pp. 197f.). The last two of these observations were made by Fortna, and he therefore felt obliged to overcome them in order to assign 1:48 to the source (*Signs*, p. 186).

(3) he has employed from the source an account of the Baptist's witness, including his three denials, and an account of the coming of the first disciples in which he has suppressed the explicit identification of Jesus as Elijah;[86] and (4) he has provided as a climax for the chapter a highly impressive Son of Man logion (v. 51).[87] Without entering into detailed discussion, it is not difficult to see that these four steps are tightly interlocked. Whatever the precise relationship between hymn and Gospel, one thing is transparent: the evangelist has an extraordinary affinity for the hymn's christology; for his Christ is clearly the One who receives reverent witness from Abraham (8:56), Moses (5:39), and the prophets (12:41), while towering far above them in his eternal pre-existence: "I solemnly assure you, before Abraham was I am" (8:58). As the One who existed from eternity at the Father's side, he and he alone has seen the Father (1:18); he and he alone comes from above, having witnessed the heavenly glories (3:13, 31ff.); he and he alone can therefore impart the revelation of God (1:18; 3:31ff.). In his identity as the pre-existent Son of Man, he is the sole locus of communication between heaven and earth (1:51).

Could one identify this figure with Elijah? To ask the question is to answer it. The evangelist could leave Elijah-like traits strewn among the miracle stories, and very probably not merely out of reverence for his source. But he could scarcely allow the explicit identification and at the same time maintain the integrity of his own massive christology; for, in the frame of *his* christology, to do so would have implied that the logos experienced successive incarnations.[88] We can be very nearly certain that this

---

[86] In suggesting that the evangelist deliberately suppressed the Elijah identification, I find myself making a statement at variance with a goodly number of interpreters who hold either that all of the major literary layers in the Gospel represent the essentially unchanging views of a single theologian or school (R. E. Brown; B. Lindars), or that, while the evangelist employed a signs source, he did not at any point intend to contradict it (Fortna, *NTS* XXI, 26).

[87] These remarks should not be taken to imply that all of 1:19-50 comes from the source.

[88] It will be obvious, by contrast, that the evangelist was able to combine the identification of Jesus as the Mosaic prophet with his em-

latter idea never seriously presented itself to John as a usable scheme, not because it was *religionsgeschichtlich* inconceivable (note the successive incarnations of the "true prophet" in the Kerygmata Petrou), but because it would have diluted what for him could not be diluted: Jesus Christ the eternal Son as the sole mediator of God's revelation. In short, the Elijah christology of the source had to give way to the christology of eternal pre-existence, expressed initially in the figure of the logos, and then dominantly in the figure of the descending and ascending Son of Man.[89]

Ex hypothesi, therefore, as far as we can see, it is the fourth evangelist who bears the responsibility for the disappearance from subsequent Christian thought of the identification of Jesus as the eschatological Elijah.[90] We thus witness one of the points in history—only one of them—at which an aspect of the varied

---

phasis on Christ's pre-existence. For the major line of hope attaching itself to the Mosaic prophet looks forward to one who is *like* Moses. Hence, to identify Jesus as the Mosaic prophet is to affirm a typological relationship between two distinct figures. See Martyn, *History and Theology.*

[89] To return to the matter of the literary-theological structure of Chapter 1, we may now note that the Elijah identification is, so to speak, squeezed out of the picture between the pre-existent logos on the one side (1:18) and the pre-existent Son of Man on the other (1:51). See R. Hamerton-Kelly, *Pre-Existence, Wisdom, and the Son of Man: A Study of the Idea of Pre-Existence in the New Testament* (Cambridge, 1973), pp. 197-242. In a future study I hope to explore the implications which the Elijah identification itself may have had for the thought of pre-existence. See the comments on John 1:15, 27, and 30 in n. 45 above. Did the author of the source, having identified Jesus as. the eschatological Elijah, take the additional and rather short step to the thought of pre-existence?

[90] I say "as far as we can see" because there is, of course, no strong reason to think that the identification emerged at only one point in early Christian thought, i.e., only in the mind of the Johannine source's author. It would be strange, in fact, if numerous kinfolk of persons healed by Jesus did not identify him as Elijah, as is implied in the Synoptics (Mk. 6:15, etc.). Did none of these become "Christians"? Reim *Studien*, p. 9: "We will have to reckon with an Elijah christology *within* early Christianity."

patterns of christological thinking in Jewish Christianity was suppressed. Whether that which was put in its place justifies the
suppression is a question for the fully theological interpretation
not only of the Fourth Gospel itself, but also of the role it has
played in the subsequent history of Christian thought and life.[91]
In light of the disastrous effects of the monolithic wall which the
West erected against the Jewish Christians in the latter part of the
second century (i.e., from Irenaeus onward), one may perhaps be
permitted some degree of ambiguity, while yet recognizing the
ultimacy of that christology to which Zinzendorf bore witness in
his famous confession: "I have but one passion. That is he and
only he."[92]

---

[91] See the studies by W. von Loewenich, *Das Johannesverständnis
im zweiten Jahrhundert* (Giessen, 1932); F. M. Braun, *Jean Le Théolo-
gien et son Évangile dans l'Église ancienne* (Paris, 1959); J. N. Sanders,
The Fourth Gospel in the Early Church (Cambridge, 1943); M. F. Wiles,
The Spiritual Gospel (Cambridge, 1960); T. E. Pollard, *Johannine Chris-
tology and the Early Church* (London, 1970); E. Pagels, *The Johannine
Gospel in Gnostic Exegesis* (Nashville, 1973); C. K. Barrett, " 'The
Father Is Greater Than I (John 14:28): Subordinationist Christology in the
New Testament," in *Neues Testament und Kirche*, ed. Gnika pp. 144-59.

[92] Quoted by Käsemann, *The Testament of Jesus*, p. 38. We are
moving, I think, toward a more adequate understanding of the phenomenal christological concentration of the Johannine community and the
particular forms it took, thanks to several recent studies mentioned in the
notes; special attention is due to the masterful article by Meeks, "The
Man from Heaven in Johannine Sectarianism," *JBL* XCI (1972), 44-72.
Perhaps on the basis of these various studies it will even prove possible
to give in general terms a history of christological thinking within the
Johannine circle. c.f. U. B. Müller, *Die Geschichte der Christologie in der
Johanneishen Gemeinde* (Stuttgart, 1975).

CHAPTER 2

Persecution and Martyrdom

**A Dark and Difficult Chapter in the
History of Johannine Christianity**

I. POSING THE QUESTIONS

In the previous chapter we have seen grounds for positing a relationship between the Gospel of John and Jewish Christianity, primarily because the Gospel retains views of Christ characteristic of Jewish Christians. The fourth evangelist proves to have been the shaper of *christological formulations* which he inherited quite directly from Jewish-Christian sources.

The question now arises whether aspects of *ecclesiology* which emerge in his Gospel may also point in the direction of Jewish Christianity. In the present chapter we will pursue this question in a quite specific form: Would it perhaps be the case that certain experiences of the Johannine community indicate it to have been itself a Jewish-Christian church at one point in its history?

When one ponders this question, two strands in the Fourth Gospel come dominantly to mind. The first strand consists of those passages which announce that Jews who confess Jesus to be the Messiah are expelled from the synagogue (9:22; 12:42; 16:2). Excommunication from the synagogue for messianic confession of Jesus would clearly be an experience peculiar to Jewish Christians. In the present context I shall take for granted both that basic point and my own earlier analysis ·of the factors involved (see Chapters One and Two of *History and Theology in the Fourth Gospel,* revised and enlarged edition, Abingdon, 1979). On that ground alone we are able to answer our question in the affirmative. At the very beginning of its existence as a community

55

separate to itself, the Johannine church must have been Jewish-Christian in nature.

We may still ask, however, whether it existed as such *for some period of time*; and when we pose the question in this way, we are reminded of a second strand in the Gospel which indicates that Jews who believe in Jesus may be subjected not only to expulsion from the synagogue, but also to severe discipline and indeed to persecution which goes as far as death:

> I have told you these things (that the world will hate you) to keep you from being shaken in your faith. They are going to excommunicate you from the synagogue. Indeed the hour is coming when the man who puts you to death will believe that in doing so he is offering an act of service to God! (16:2)

We are not told much about this man who persecutes to the death, except that he understands his activity to be an act of worshipful service to God. In light of the fact that the horrible and heinous and centuries-long persecution of Jews by Christians has sometimes been "justified" by the theory that the Jews did the first persecuting, it is understandable that a number of Christian interpreters have wished to see this verse as a reference to the persecution of Christians not by Jews, but by Roman authorities. Yet the Greek word rendered "act of (worshipful) service" refers elsewhere in the New Testament to Jewish worship, and the other experience referred to in this text, excommunication from the synagogue, points to the action of Jewish authorities. Modern relations between Jews and Christians are not helped by an antihistorical interpretation of biblical texts. I have argued elsewhere that for the Johannine community this additional experience of ultimate persecution was also experienced at the hands of Jewish authorities (Chapters Three and Four of *History and Theology*). What needs now to be further pursued is the question whether we are thereby speaking of an experience of the Johannine community during a period in which it *remained a Jewish*-Christian church.

A major line of investigation could perhaps open up were we to inquire whether the particular kind of deadly persecution reflected in John 16:2 (and 7:45-52) may also be reflected in sources we know to come from Jewish-Christian churches. The posing of this question will obviously lead us to ascertain whether there are Jewish-Christian sources which reflect the same kind of persecution at the hands of Jewish authorities. One thinks first of all to ask whether the New Testament itself may contain what we need. But as a matter of fact in their *present form* the books of the New Testament are virtually without exception products of Gentile Christianity; and while there are points in them at which Jewish-Christian tradition peeks through, none of these provides a picture of persecution which is strikingly and helpfully similar to that which emerges in the pertinent Johannine passages.

There are, however, a few invaluable sources for the study of Jewish Christianity which lie outside the New Testament, and one of these contains material which may indeed provide illuminating points of comparison. This Jewish-Christian source is now embedded in the so-called Pseudo-Clementine literature. Because this literature is not widely known, it will be well to pause for a word of introduction before we study the pertinent texts.

II. A JEWISH-CHRISTIAN SOURCE IN THE PSEUDO-CLEMENTINES

The Pseudo-Clementine literature consists of a romance preserved in two parallel yet distinct editions called the *Homilies* and the *Recognitions*. Both of these received their present forms in the fourth century, but they draw on the common basis of a romance written in the third century, and it in turn was written by someone who employed sources penned in the second century.[93]

---

[93] The best overview of the history of research on the Pseudo-Clementines is given in the first chapter of G. Strecker, *Das Judenchristentum in den Pseudoklementinen* (Berlin, 1958; revised edition expected soon). In the Tübingen school the Pseudo-Clementines were judged to be the single most important document for understanding the post-apostolic age. Incorrect and tendentious as this judgment was, the seminal labors on the Pseudo-Clementines proved, in fact, to be those of F. C. Baur, who, in his characteristic way, succeeded—partly by indirection—in

The basic story is the familiar one of a promising youth who moves from one philosophy/religion to another in his quest for truth, coming finally to Christianity. In the present case the youth is represented to be Clement of Rome, and the major part of the romance is given over to his travels with Peter and in fact to lengthy and sometimes tedious disputes between Peter and Simon Magus. In most of the material which constitutes the romance itself we are faced with an obvious fiction penned, as I said above, not by Clement of Rome (fl. 95 A.D.), but by an unknown literary figure of the third century who drew on a number of earlier sources and who wrote long passages which have caused numerous readers to lay his text aside out of sheer boredom.

---

posing the two driving questions for subsequent research: Are the Pseudo-Clementines pertinent for the study of Jewish Christianity? Is it possible carefully to distinguish literary layers, so as to recover discrete and approximately datable sources? Vis-à-vis these questions, subsequent studies have tended to flow along two rather distinct lines: (1) John Chapman, "On the Date of the Clementines," ZNW 7 (1908) 21ff., 147ff., and Eduard Schwartz, "Unzeitgemässe Beobachtungen," ZNW 31 (1932), are the major interpreters who answered both of Baur's questions in the negative, and J. Irmscher has voiced a similar position in the current scene, "The Pseudo-Clementines," pp. 532-535 in Hennecke-Schneemelcher, New Testament Apocrypha II (Philadelphia, 1965). One should note also the caution represented in J. A. Fitzmyer's article, "The Qumran Schools, the Ebionites, and Their Literature," Theol. Studies 16 (1955) 335-372 (349). (2) Hans Waitz, Die Pseudoklementinen, Homilien und Rekognitionen. Eine quellenkritische Untersuchung (1904, TU 25, 4), on the other hand, answered both questions decisively in the affirmative, following to some extent A. Hilgenfeld, and while his work had some identifiable flaws, its main lines have proven widely convincing. One may see its influence, to mention two examples, in the dissertation of O. Cullmann, Le problème littéraire et historique du roman pseudo-clementin (Paris, 1930), and in the highly valuable and often aggravating study of H.-J. Schoeps, Theologie und Geschichte des Judenchristentum (Tübingen, 1949). The major heir of Waitz on the current scene is Georg Strecker, who has helpfully and creatively reviewed, refined, corrected, and extended Waitz's labors. Broad skepticism as to the possibility of Clementine source analysis seems to me to be quite unwarranted; and two of the sources resulting from such analysis do in fact prove to be quite pertinent to the study of second-century Jewish Christianity. See comments below on the Kerygmata Petrou and the Ascents of James.

One sparkling exception lies before us in the first book of the *Recognitions* (the text of R 1, 33-71 is provided in the Appendix). While the early chapters of Book One merely present the initial elements necessary for the Clementine romance, chapter 27 (R 1, 27) begins a substantial section which is unrelated to the romance and which has a kind of integrity not matched in the preceding dialogue material. This section is made up of what one might call two historical accounts. The first, that of R 1, 27-32, rests on a source which traced God's dealing with the world and man from creation through (at least) the twenty-first generation, that of Abraham. This source was surely written by a Jew who, in a quite straightforward way, referred to Abraham as the one "from whom our Hebrew nation is derived" (R 1, 32, 1). It is therefore not Jewish-Christian, but rather simply Jewish.

As to the remaining account, R 1, 33ff., it may be of significance not only that it begins precisely where the redemptive-historical sketch in Stephen's speech takes its beginning (Acts 7:2ff.), but also that it runs somewhat parallel to it: Abraham, Isaac, Jacob, the twelve patriarchs, the seventy-five (Acts) or seventy-two (R) who entered Egypt, and Moses, together with Moses' promise that God would raise up another prophet like him. Noting this degree of similarity, one also observes numerous instances of literary dependence on the text of canonical Acts. Clearly the author of R 1, 33ff. had the text of canonical Acts before him. More of that presently. If this literary piece begins at R 1, 33, where does it end?

Its terminus, as far as the piece is preserved in the Clementines, would seem clearly to lie at the end of R 1, 71, where the Clement romance once again emerges with a portrait of Peter lodging in the house of Zacchaeus in Caesarea, while readying himself for the disputation with Simon Magus. In between R 1, 33 and R 1, 71 there is clearly one sizable insertion from a later hand, but we are on solid ground in the assumption that we have before us in R 1, 33-71 (less the insertion in R 1, 44, 4—1, 53, 3) a literary piece penned by someone who desired to provide a sketch of redemptive history from Abraham to the early years of the Jerusalem church. Of course the presence of one insertion should warn us that there may be others, and indeed Georg Strecker has advanced good arguments for so considering the whole of chapter 63, as well as R 1, 69, 6-7 and some other snippets.[94] Qualified in this way, R 1, 33-71 presents us, I think, with a discrete literary piece.[95] Indeed, following a line of suggestions stretching all the way back to J. Köstlin (1849), Strecker has provided a strong case for identifying this literary piece not only as one of the basic sources for the Clementine romance, but also specifically as a form of the *Ascents of James* mentioned by Epiphanius.[96] A number of scholars expert in the study of Jewish Christianity hold this view, and its probability will be assumed as we proceed.[97] R 1, 33-71 (less R 1, 44, 4—1, 53, 3, etc.) is surely a discrete literary piece antedating the author of the romance, and very probably a form of the *Ascents of James*. The reader will follow our further explorations rather easily if he will pause here to read the text as it is given in the Appendix.

These literary conclusions enable us, now, to move a step further by asking who penned this historical sketch and in what setting.

One begins to attack this question by noting that the author of our source emphasizes two points of distinction as regards the Jerusalem church. The true line of religion, he tells his readers, extends from Abraham through Moses and Moses' greater successor to the Jerusalem church led by James. As the embodiment of true religion, that church is distinguished on the one side from the errors of non-Christian Judaism, and on the other from the falsity of Paulinism. (Small wonder that Matthew is the author's favorite Gospel.)

With regard to the first of these, the author explicitly says

---

[94] Strecker, *Judenchristentum*, pp. 42f., 223-250.

[95] One can survey its contents quite readily in Strecker, *Judenchristentum*, pp. 223-250.

[96] Epiphanius, *Panarion* 30, 16, 6-9 [A. F. J. Klijn and G. J. Reinink, *Patristic Evidence for Jewish-Christian Sects* (Leiden, 1973), p. 184]; Strecker, *Judenchristentum*, pp. 251-253. For the reasons advanced by Strecker I shall follow him in designating this source as the *Ascents*.

[97] See, for example, M. Simon, "La migration à Pella, Légende ou réalité?" *Judéo-christianisme, RSR* 60 (1972; Daniélou Festschrift) 49, and Klijn and Reinink, *Evidence*, pp. 81, 282.

that the Jerusalem church differs from "the unbelieving Jews" in one point only: the confession of Jesus as the Christ (R 1, 43, 2). With this it is harmonious that he does not speak a single word against circumcision. Indeed, it is doubtless an important clue to the character of the author's own church that he paints a picture in which Christian baptism emerges as a replacement for the sacrificial cult of the Jerusalem temple.[98] We may assume, I think, that the author belongs to a community which practices both circumcision and Christian baptism, and which is therefore made up of circumcised, baptized Jewish Christians.[99]

On the other side he is clearly concerned to distinguish the line extending through the Jerusalem church to his own community from the line represented in the development of Pauline Christianity. In all probability he included in his document a narrative of the Damascus conversion of Paul, but unfortunately that part of his work is not preserved.[100] In the material we have, Paul appears only in his pre-Christian role as the persecutor of the Church. Even here, however, two notes in particular would seem to indicate that the author intends to discredit Pauline Christianity.

1. Until Paul interferes in the temple, the mission to the Jews is enjoying phenomenal success (R 1, 69-70). By preaching for seven successive days (!), James has persuaded "all the people and the high priest" that they should be baptized (R 1, 69, 8). It is precisely at this point of unprecedented success that Paul enters and derails "what had been arranged with much labor" (R 1, 70, 4). Thus Paul is the enemy of the Jewish mission. Apart from his activity, that mission would presumably have been fantastically successful. Of course Paul is at this point not a Christian of any sort whatever. I am simply observing that our author presents

---

[98] R 1, 39, and R 1, 55; Strecker, *Judenchristentum*, pp. 228f.; cf. also pp. 141, 196ff.

[99] Vis-à-vis the mass of non-Christian Jews he seems, in fact, to use the terms "the rite of sacrifice" and "the baptism of Jesus" as equivalent expressions respectively for Judaism and Jewish Christianity; see e.g., R 1, 55.

[100] See R 1, 71; cf. Strecker, *Judenchristentum*, p. 253; Schoeps, *Theologie und Geschichte*, pp. 452f.

Paul's activity as the chief cause of a failure in the Jewish mission, and I am suggesting that he may have done this because he feels that Pauline Christianity has played exactly that role. The author would have his readers believe that had Paul and his churches never materialized, the mission of the Jewish church to its brethren would have been invincible.

2. It is doubtless significant that the author portrays Paul as the enemy, in the first instance, of James, and only in a secondary way as the enemy of Peter. For when he introduces James as the one whom the Lord ordained to be bishop over the Church of the Lord constituted in Jerusalem (R 1, 43, 3), he surely means that James represents Jewish Christianity. By the same token, he allows Paul indirectly to represent his own mission, and that mission is the enemy. To be sure, the author knows of and endorses the general mission to the Gentiles (R 1, 42, 1). It is only the specifically Pauline line which he identifies as unquestionably false.

From these two points of distinction, then, we reach a conclusion of great importance for our present concern. There is, in fact, no section of the Clementine literature about whose origin in Jewish Christianity one may be more certain.[101] The author of the *Ascents* is a Jewish Christian, a member of a church which is itself a Jewish-Christian church. On the one side stands the community of Judaism and on the other the churches of the Gentiles. Among the latter the Pauline churches stand as clearly in error as do the "unbelieving Jews." Indeed we may say something yet more specific about the author's setting, for one notes the presence of two references to the Pella story (R 1, 37, 2 and 1, 39, 3), the story which states that the Jerusalem church fled to Pella

---

[101] From the very beginning of scientific attempts at source criticism of the Clementines (Hilgenfeld), this section of R 1 has figured prominently, and it has been repeatedly recognized as being of Jewish-Christian origin. It is illuminating to compare with one another the attempts to interpret R 1 by Waitz and Strecker. Note also the all too brief remarks (pp. 256, 268) in the invaluable Appendix, "On the Problem of Jewish Christianity," which G. Strecker wrote for the revised edition of W. Bauer, *Orthodoxy and Heresy in Earliest Christianity* (Philadelphia, 1971).

in Transjordan just before or during the war of 66-70 A.D. Since that story is nowhere explicitly narrated in the New Testament (cf. Lk. 21:20ff.), we may presume that our Jewish-Christian author received it from oral tradition.[102] Moreover, since the story is of considerable importance both to him and to his readers — one notices that he can take for granted his readers' ability to understand cryptic references to it — we are surely justified in assuming that his church lies in or near Pella.[103] As to the date at which he wrote, there are good grounds for placing it near the mid-point of the second century.[104]

In studying R 1, 33-71, we are invited, therefore, to look over the shoulder, so to speak, of a Jewish-Christian writer, in or near second-century Pella, who is concerned to provide his church with the history which gives it its distinctive identity.

III. The Jewish-Christian Source called *The Ascents of James* and the Gospel of John

The material which provides illuminating parallels to the strand in John's Gospel about deadly persecution stretches from R 1, 62 to R 1, 68. We shall make a detailed analysis momentarily. It will be profitable to approach that analysis, however, via the question whether our second-century Jewish-Christian author may be literarily dependent on the Gospel of John, for the significance of the parallels would be greatly affected by an answer to that question.

We begin by recalling that our author knew and used the canonical Acts of the Apostles. He seems in fact to have had as

---

[102] For our present purposes it is not necessary to enter into the heated debate as to whether Luke 21:20ff. reflects the Pella legend. The most one can claim is an indirect reflection. See Strecker's sharp remarks in *Judenchristentum*, p. 230, drawing on comments of Eduard Schwartz. Cf. also the article of M. Simon mentioned in note 97 above, where the views of Munck, Strecker, and Brandon are summarized and criticized.

[103] Strecker, *Judenchristentum*, p. 253.

[104] Strecker, *Judenchristentum*, pp. 253f.

one of his major concerns to stand Luke's heroic portrait of Paul exactly on its head. The Pauline mission, far from being paradigmatic of God's way with all of humankind (so canonical Acts), is one of the two major paths of error, the other being Judaism *per se*. True religion has been preserved in the Jerusalem church of James and in its progeny, such as the church of Pella.[105] Thus the author of the *Ascents* certainly intended to correct canonical Acts, and perhaps even to replace it.

It is equally clear that he knew and used several books of the Old Testament, and the Gospels of Matthew, Mark, and Luke. Indeed he shares with other Jewish Christians of the early centuries a particular love for the Gospel of Matthew, citing it quite frequently. Did he also know and draw on the Gospel of John? Two degrees of possible dependence are to be distinguished in this regard:

A. Did the Jewish-Christian author of the *Ascents of James* draw quotations from the Gospel of John?

Interpreters have located five passages which come into question as possibly containing quotations drawn from John:

1. *R 1, 40, 2*

With the coming of the Mosaic prophet in Jesus,[106] the people refused to believe. Indeed they added blasphemy to their unbelief, saying that he was a gluttonous man (*voracem hominem*) and a belly slave (*ventri servientem*), and that he was

---

[105] Whether the church of Pella was historically an heir of the Jerusalem church or only understood itself to be such is a question that may remain unattended in the present context. See Strecker's arguments, *Judenchristentum*, pp. 227, 229-231, and M. Simon's article cited above in note 97. Cf. also A. Spijkerman, "An Unknown Coin-Type of Pella Decapolis, *Studii Biblici Franciscani Liber Annus* 20 (1970) 353-358, and B. Bagatti, *The Church from the Circumcision* (Jerusalem, 1971) pp. 7f.

[106] Another source behind the Pseudo-Clementines, the *Kerygmata Petrou*, speaks of the "True Prophet." See Strecker, *Judenchristentum*, pp. 223f., 145-153.

activated by a demon (*daemone agi eum*). The first two of these charges are surely drawn from Matthew 11:19 (a glutton and a drunkard; cf. Mt. 9:14). The third could stand on John 7:20 (You have a demon), as a footnote in the critical edition of the text suggests (see the Appendix). Since the first two are taken from Matthew 11:19, however, one would want to ponder whether it is not more probable that the third is drawn from the preceding verse, Matthew 11:18 (He has a demon, referring to John the Baptist), it being the case that the Synoptic tradition about Jesus' being possessed by the prince of demons (Mk. 3:22 and parallels) has enabled the author to employ both Matthew 11:18 and 11:19 as charges against Jesus himself. The very most one could say is that John 7:20 could be somewhere in the background. The slimness of that possibility is reflected, I think, in the fact that neither of the previous commentators (Waitz and Strecker) mentions it.[107]

2. *R 1, 43, 1*

This is one of the passages affirming the often repeated request of the Jewish authorities for a discussion with the apostles, the proposed topic being the question whether Jesus was the prophet whom Moses foretold, who is the eternal Christ (*qui est Christus aeternus*). The possibility of dependence on John 12:34 has been suggested in the critical edition of the text. The thought of the Messiah's eternity is, however, much too widespread to allow us to move beyond mere possibility.[108] Previous commentators have left us no guidance.

3. *R 1, 54, 5*

Describing the beliefs of the Samaritans, the author comments that from the predictions of Moses they rightly expect the prophet. The critical edition of the text mentions John 4:25, but

---

[107] Unspecified references to Waitz and Strecker pertain to their Pseudo-Clementine monographs (see note 93 above).

[108] Cf. Raymond E. Brown, *John* I, 469; Barnabas Lindars, *The Gospel of John* (London, 1972), pp. 434f.

the cited aspect of Samaritan theology was quite widely known and cannot, therefore, be used to indicate dependence on the Johannine text.[109] Again previous commentators are silent.

4. *R 1, 45, 4*

Christ was the Son of God and the beginning of all things (*initium omnium*); yet he became man (*homo factus est*). The possibility of dependence on John 1:1 and 1:14 shades over into probability, I think, but the passage falls in the large insertion made by the author of the romance (R 1, 44, 4—1, 53, 3). This tells us, in fact, something which we must bear in mind: It is probable that the author of the romance drew on the Fourth Gospel—at least this once—in editing the *Ascents*.

5. *R 1, 69, 5*

This is the crucial passage as regards the question whether our Jewish-Christian author ever quoted from John's Gospel; for it is the last, and the preceding ones have brought no more than vague possibilities. It falls in the speech made by James. After the author has given a rather full account of the speech, we find the following:

> (5) And when he had plainly taught the people concerning these things, he added this also: that unless a man is baptized in water, in the name of the threefold blessedness, as the True Prophet taught, he can neither receive remission of sins nor enter into the kingdom of heaven; and he declared that this is the prescription of the unbegotten God. (6) To which he added this also: 'Do not think that we speak of two unbegotten Gods. . . . (7) But we speak of the only-begotten Son of God . . . and in like manner we speak of the Paraclete.' (8) But when he had spoken some things also concerning baptism, through seven successive days he persuaded all the

---

[109] See particularly Meeks, *The Prophet-King*, pp. 216ff., and the bibliographical references there.

people and the high priest that they should hasten immediately to receive baptism.

I have given a detailed discussion of this text elsewhere.[110] Here I shall say only that it is literarily complex, revealing the hands of our Jewish-Christian author and perhaps two later editors. If there is dependence on John 3:5, that must be credited to one of the later editors. With this observation we are led to conclude—with Hans Waitz[111] and apparently with Georg Strecker[112]—that as far as the *Ascents* has been preserved, it does not present a single quotation from the Fourth Gospel to accompany those drawn from Matthew and Luke.

B. Did our Jewish-Christian author occasionally allude to the Gospel of John?

Even if our author did not quote from the Fourth Gospel, he may have left clues of some other sort which indicate a dependence on it. Are there perhaps motifs which are found both in the Fourth Gospel and in the *Ascents*, and which are presented in the *Ascents* in such a way as to indicate Johannine influence? Previous interpreters have weighed three arguments which would be advanced in support of this hypothesis.

1. One notices that the identification of Jesus as the prophet foretold by Moses plays a weighty role in the *Ascents* (R 1, 36, 2; 37, 2; 37, 3; 39, 1; 39, 3; 40, 4; 41, 2; 43, 1). As is well known, this motif occupies an important place in the Fourth Gospel (e.g.,

---

[110] In the original form of the present study. See notably A. J. Bellinzoni, *The Sayings of Jesus in the Writings of Justin Martyr* (Leiden, 1967), pp. 134ff.

[111] Waitz, *Pseudoklementinen*, p. 361; "The New Testament citations do not reflect even distant awareness of the Gospel of John; they contain only words and allusions which belong to the circle of the Synoptic Gospels."

[112] Strecker, *Judenchristentum*, p. 253: In discussing the literary activity of the author of the *Ascents*, Strecker remarks that he draws upon Matthew, Luke, and Acts. There is no comment on the question we are pursuing: Did the author also draw on John?

1:45; 6:14; 7:40), a far more prominent place, in fact, that it occupies in the Synoptics. One also observes, however, that in R 1, 41, 2, our author has drawn the motif of the Mosaic prophet not from John, but from Acts. In short, the prophet christology underlines both our author's dependence on Acts and his identity as a Jewish Christian.[113] It is not expressed in a way which shows him to have known and drawn on the Fourth Gospel.[114]

2. The *Ascents* and the Fourth Gospel share a polemic against followers of John the Baptist. In R 1, 60, 1 (cf. R 1, 54, 8) a disciple of the Baptist asserts that his master was the Christ, and not Jesus. It is however striking that while one could hardly imagine a point more appropriate for a quotation of John 1:20f., enriched perhaps by motifs from John 1:8 and 3:28ff., the author of the *Ascents* provides not so much as an allusion.

3. In R 1, 57, there is a reference to the issue whether worship of God takes place in Jerusalem or on Gerizim. It is a juncture at which the author could have supported his own concerns quite nicely by a quotation from—or at least an allusion to—the exchange between Jesus and the Samaritan woman in John 4: ". . . the hour is coming when neither on Gerizim nor in the Jerusalem temple will one worship the Father." Yet the author does not give even the slightest hint that Jesus ever uttered words similar to these. We thus conclude—again with Waitz and apparently with Strecker[115]—that the data we have treated thus far clearly weigh against the view which would see our second-century, Jewish-Christian author as dependent on the Fourth Gospel.

---

[113]Cf. the standard works on New Testament christology, and H.-J. Schoeps, *Theologie und Geschichte*, pp. 87ff.; R. N. Longenecker, *The Christology of Early Jewish Christianity* (Naperville, 1970), pp. 32ff.

[114]It is a striking and, I think, productively suggestive fact that references to the Fourth Gospel are relatively numerous in the massive book on the theology and history of Jewish Christianity by H.-J. Schoeps; yet the question we are investigating is not posed there.

[115]See notes 111 and 112 above.

C. The Scenes in R 1, 62-68
and the Gospel of John

We come then finally to the key passages which lie between R 1, 62 and R 1, 68 and which would seem to reflect motifs of persecution comparable to some in the Fourth Gospel. Here we have no guidance from previous interpreters. Even though a number of them have been particularly concerned with the question of possible dependence on John, none have sensed any marks of dependence in this material. It is relatively easy, therefore, to allow the analysis to proceed in an even-handed manner. Six passages demand our careful attention:

R 1, 62, 1

Interpreters who have analyzed the role of Scripture in the Pseudo-Clementines have regularly noted the presence of passages which show dependence upon conflated texts and/or allusions, a phenomenon common, in fact, in the New Testament itself, in rabbinic literature, and in the writings of the Church Fathers.[116] For our Jewish-Christian author, as for many rabbis and theologians, to think of one text is to have another called to mind, so that the two blend into a "combined text."

A clear example lies before us in R 1, 41. The author speaks of Jesus as the Mosaic prophet who,

... although he cured every sickness and infirmity among the people, worked innumerable miracles, and preached eter-

---

[116]The analysis of the role of Scripture made by Waitz in *Pseudo klementinen* remains the most comprehensive; the corresponding treatment in Strecker's *Judenchristentum* is far less extensive but generally more trustworthy. Waitz's conclusion that his investigation of the Scripture citations strongly confirmed his source analysis is largely denied by Strecker (p. 136). The conclusions of the present article lend some support to Waitz, though in a way which is rather differently nuanced.

nal life, was rushed to the cross by wicked men. This deed was, however, turned to good by his power.

Thus far the author is clearly drawing upon elements of the so-called "Jesus kerygma" in Acts (e.g., 2:22-24; 3:13-15; 4:10; 5:30; 13:29-32). He continues by turning to the Gospels of Luke and Matthew:

> In short, while he was suffering, all the world suffered with him; for the sun was darkened (Lk. 23:45), the mountains were torn apart, the graves were opened (Mt. 27:51b and c), the veil of the temple was rent (Mt. 27:51a and parallels). . . .

It belongs to the nature of a mixed text, of course, that it is created by addition. Hence, to say the obvious, if, in the present case, the elements drawn from Acts be subtracted, what remains is evidence of indebtedness to Luke and Matthew. Our question now becomes whether a similar phenomenon lies before us in R 1, 62, 1.

Here again we see the author employing a New Testament text, Acts 4. Allowing Caiaphas to stand in the place of the Sanhedrin (Acts 4:5f. mentions Caiaphas together with rulers, elders, scribes, Annas, John, Alexander, and all of the high-priestly family), he draws two motifs from the trial scene:

R 1, 62, 1	*Acts 4:6, 17, 18, 21, 29*
Then Caiaphas, again looking at me, sometimes in the way of *warning* and sometimes in that of accusation, said that *I ought for the future to cease preaching Christ Jesus*,	. . . Caiaphas . . . in order that it may spread no further among the people, let us *warn* them . . . so they called them and charged them *not to speak or teach at all in the name of Jesus* . . . and when they had further threatened them. . . .

John 16:2; 7:12, 47

lest I should cause *the de-struction of my life*, by being led astray after him (Christ) and by *leading others astray* [partly Syriac].[117]

. . . whoever *kills you* will think he is offering service to God. . . . He is *leading the people astray*.

The author's dependence on Acts is plain to see. From Acts 4:6, 17, 18, 21, 29 he has taken the picture of a Jewish authority, Caiaphas, warning a Jewish Christian, Peter, to cease preaching Christ Jesus. One notes also that when the Acts material is subtracted, three motifs remain: (1) For Peter to continue to preach Jesus Christ among his Jewish brethren would very likely lead to his death, not only because (2) he would show in this manner that he himself had been led astray, but also because (3) he would be leading others astray. Can we locate the origin of these additional motifs?

Perhaps the author himself conceived them, simply developing them out of the threatening atmosphere of the trial scene in Acts 4. One will want to note, however, another possibility. Rufinus rendered the (lost) Greek text by twice employing the expression *errore decipio*, which need mean nothing more specific than to deceive: " . . . being deceived myself, I should also deceive others." We are at a juncture at which it is profitable to compare Rufinus' Latin translation with the Syriac text, for after doing so we are led to conclude that this is one of those numerous instances in which Rufinus elected a somewhat general manner of expression where the original text was more specific. The key word in the Syriac is t‘ ’, which Frankenburg correctly rendered by the Greek verb *planan*.[118] Both of these terms *may* have the general force of "deceiving another person," but they also carry the specific denotation of "leading another person astray into

---

[117]The Latin and Syriac texts are discussed below.

[118]Frankenburg, *Die syrischen Clementinen mit griechischen Paralleltext* (Berlin, 1937), *ad loc.*

false belief." It is this specific denotation which best fits the context in R 1, 62, 1. Indeed Caiaphas' warning to Peter may very well stand on a well-defined point of Jewish law: those who lead others astray in a matter of idolatry are legally subject to execution as theological seducers (*Messithim*; *planoi*). The legal details are discussed in Mishna Sanhedrin 7, 10, the case of the seducer (*Messith*).[119]

Returning to the New Testament, one observes that the key term *planan* (to lead astray) emerges in John 7:12 and 47, and that at these two points the Peshitta renders by means of ţ' '. Beyond these verbal observations one notes also that the specific legal denotation of these terms—absent from Acts 4 and 5—seems to be clearly reflected in the New Testament nowhere except in the Fourth Gospel, where the prediction of the martyrdom of Jewish Christians at the hands of Jewish authorities (John 16:2) may be related to the charge that the former are deceived preachers who lead others astray into false worship (Jn. 7:12, 47; cf. 5:18).[120] Comparison of R 1, 62, 1b with these Johannine texts does not lead one to posit literary dependence. Some kind of relationship, however, would seem rather probable.

R 1, 62, 2

The passage continues immediately, via an adverbial expression.

R 1, 62, 2	Acts 4:13
Then, moreover, he charged me with *presumption*, because, although I was *unlearned*, a fisherman and a *rustic*,	. . . and perceiving that they were *uneducated and common men*, they were amazed. . . .

---

[119] See also Martyn, *History and Theology in the Fourth Gospel*, final pages of chapter 3, and Excursus C, not least the comments about the verb t'h.

[120] *Ibid.*

John 9:34

I dared to assume the office   You were *born in utter sin,*
of a teacher.   and *would you teach us?*

The author's dependence on Acts is clear, and again when the marks of his indebtedness to Acts are subtracted, a quite distinct motif remains, that of an authoritative Jewish questioner accusing a Jewish Christian of showing temerity, since, being himself unlearned, he has dared to assume the office of a teacher. Where did the author get this motif?

Not from Acts 4. In that text the learned are *amazed* (cf. Mk. 1:22 and Jn. 7:15) at the *boldness* of the unlearned, not *offended* at their *presumption* to be teachers. In another trial scene, however, the one in John 9, the climax is provided in part by precisely this motif, as the text above shows. There the authoritative examiners excoriate the formerly blind man for his temerity in presuming to teach them.

To be sure, one might also think of such texts as Mark 1:22, Luke 2:46f., and Matthew 13:54ff. (cf. John 7:15), but these contain only the motifs of a man teaching, even though he lacks formal training, and of others experiencing amazement at his activity. The added note provided in the charge of temerity and presumptuousness is, within the New Testament, peculiar to John 9:34.

Do we have, then, a mixed text, created by our author's drawing literarily on both Acts 4 and John 9? This is perhaps possible, but by no means does the evidence require it. One may in fact note literarily a contrast between R 1, 62, 2 and R 2, 48. The latter passage evidences a clear example of a mixed text, consisting of Matthew 11:27 plus John 1:1 and 5:23. As regards R 1, 62, 2, however, it will be wise, at least for the moment, to speak of a conflation which brings together elements drawn from Acts and a motif, which is, within the New Testament, peculiar to John.

R 1, 62, 5

In this passage one would not speak, I think, of a strong case for conflation, but in the context of the other passages it is sufficiently pertinent to be displayed.

R 1, 62, 5	*Acts 4:13*
[Peter remarks to the authoritative Caiaphas:] . . . if I, an *unlearned and uneducated man*, as you say, a fisherman and a rustic,	. . . and perceiving that they were *uneducated and common men* they were amazed. . . .

John 9:30-33

have more understanding than wise elders, this, I said, ought the more to strike terror into you.	[The formerly blind man remarks to the examining authorities:] The amazing thing is that *you do not know* where he (Jesus) comes from; *yet he opened my eyes*. . . .

Here again there is the element drawn from Acts 4:13, and one notes the possibility of a significant parallel with John 9:30-33.

R 1, 65, 1-3

R 1, 65-68 is not actually a literary sub-unit. The sub-unit begins at 1, 66 as a number of commentators have noted (Rehm places the paragraph at 1, 66, 2). But a consideration of the dramatis personae shows that 1, 66-71 is tied to the preceding in part by the introduction in 1, 65 of a new character who remains on stage, so to speak, into 1, 68. The character is Gamaliel, a figure our author has clearly drawn from Acts (he is mentioned only twice in the New Testament: Acts 5:34ff. and Acts 22:3). Note how he paints Gamaliel's picture: he has Gamaliel make two speeches, the last of the speeches made on day number one, and the first of those made on day number two. The former of these (1, 65) is occasioned by an uproar among the priests, which uproar had been caused, in turn, by Peter's prophecy that failure to terminate the sacrificial system would bring about the destruction of the temple. At the uproar, Gamaliel rises and restores order by a relatively brief speech.

R 1, 65, 1-3

When I (Peter) had thus spoken, the whole multitude of the priests were in a *rage*, because I had foretold the overthrow of the temple. When *Gamaliel, a chief of the people,* saw it—*who was secretly our brother in the faith,* but by our advice *remained among them*— . . . he *stood up and said,* "Be quiet for a little while, O *men of Israel,* for you do not perceive the trial which hangs over you. Wherefore, *refrain from these men. If what they are engaged in is of human counsel, it will soon come to an end; but if it is from God,* why will *you* sin without cause and gain nothing? For who can overpower the will of God? . . ."

Acts 5:33-35, 38, 39

When they heard this, they were

enraged and wanted to kill them. But a Pharisee *in the council* named Gamaliel, a teacher of the law *held in honor by all the people,*

stood up and said to them, "Men of Israel, take care what you do with these men. . . . *Keep away from these men and let them alone. For if this plan or this undertaking be of men, it will fail; but if it is of God, you will not be able to overthrow them, lest you be found opposing God."*

John 3:1; 7:50-52; 12:42; 19:38-40

Now there was a man of the Pharisees named Nicodemus, *a ruler of the Jews.* . . . Nicodemus, who had gone to him before, and who was one of them, said to them, "Does our Law judge a man without first giving him a hearing . . .?" They replied, "Are you from Galilee too?" . . . Many even of the *rulers believed in him* but for fear of the Pharisees they *did not confess it.* . . . After this Joseph of Arimathea came and took

> away his body. Nicodemus
> also . . . came. . . . They took
> the body of Jesus. . . .

Beyond what is set out in this exhibit, Gamaliel continues by promising himself to dispute with the Jewish Christians on the following day, and his speech partially calms the priests, who apparently anticipate that on the morrow Gamaliel will publicly convict the Christians of error (the reader of the *Ascents* knows, of course, that Gamaliel is a secret Christian who will do no such thing).

For the part of Gamaliel's first speech, exhibited above, approximately two-thirds of the whole, the author clearly drew upon Acts 5:33-35, 38-39. Indeed, the double conditional sentence so closely parallels the one in Acts 5:38-39, as to cause commentators to cite this passage as proof that our author is *literarily* dependent on Acts.

Preceding the speech, however, are two elements which call for separate comment, as possible "leftovers" vis-à-vis Acts 5. The *first*, *princeps populi* (a ruler of the people), may reflect Gamaliel's identification in Acts 5:34 as "a member of the Sanhedrin . . . a teacher of the Law, held in honor by all the people." One must ask more precisely, however, what Greek words our Jewish-Christian author is likely to have used here. To judge from Rufinus' text, we may doubt that he followed closely Acts 5:34, for in that case we should have expected Rufinus to render the Greek text by some such expression as *legisdoctor honorabilis universae plebi* (a teacher of the Law, held in honor by all the people). Moving the other way, that is, from Rufinus' translation to the Greek, one gets "a ruler of the people," an expression absent from the identification of Gamaliel in Acts 5 (cf. Acts 4:8). In a moment we shall inquire as to the possible origin of this expression.

The *second* leftover element is the pair of clauses enclosed by dashes: Gamaliel is secretly a Christian, but, on the advice of the apostles (or the whole Church), he remains among the non-Christian Jews. Where did our author find this motif?

A number of scholars speak of the present passage as the earliest indication of the legend that Gamaliel was a secret Christian.[121] That may be so, but—as in previous instances—one must still ask whether our author created a new motif, or whether he combined a New Testament text (Acts 5) with a motif reflected elsewhere in the New Testament.

Recalling the figure of Nicodemus in the Fourth Gospel may serve to suggest an affirmative answer, for both of the leftover elements find their best parallels in the Fourth Evangelist's portrait of Nicodemus. He is explicitly identified as a ruler of the Jews, and while the Fourth Evangelist's interpretative intentions as regards Nicodemus' full Christian allegiance may be debated, I believe it is at least clear that he intends to include Nicodemus among the secret believers to whom he refers in 12:42.[122]

It follows that the personage who emerges in R 1, 65 has probably been created by conflating the figure of Gamaliel (peculiar to Acts) with the figure of Nicodemus (peculiar to the Fourth Gospel), or with the equivalent of this latter figure. One may say that this particular conflation did not require an enormous amount of imagination, for in several respects the figures are remarkably similar: both Galamiel and Nicodemus are Pharisees; both are members of the Sanhedrin; and both function in ways advantageous to Jewish Christians who are confronted by hostile Jewish authorities. Indeed, the conflation of Gamaliel and Nicodemus is also attested in the *Acts of Pilate*. I shall return to that fact presently. For the moment the major point is the high degree of probability which attaches to the hypothesis of conflation in R 1, 65, 1-3.

---

[121] Schoeps, *Theologie und Geschichte*, p. 405; references to Schürer and Zahn are accurately given there.

[122] One recalls that the evangelist has Nicodemus accompany and assist the Synoptic Joseph of Arimathea in the sensitively executed task of burying Jesus (Jn. 19:38ff.); and one should note particularly the motif in 19:38—"but secretly for fear of the Jews"—a motif which would seem to suggest that neither Joseph nor Nicodemus is truly a Jew.

R 1, 67, 1 and R 1, 68, 1

The story of the first day of the disputation ends with R 1, 65. The apostles and their brethren prepare themselves for the second day by visiting "our James," and by praying through the night. In the morning, accompanied by James, they go up once more to the temple, where Gamaliel, the secret believer, resumes his clever and reasonable attempt to gain for the apostles a safe and effective hearing before both Caiaphas and the people as a whole.

R 1, 67, 1	*John 3:1ff.; 7:15, 50f. (cf. 9:34)*
If I, Gamaliel, deem it no reproach either to my learning or to my old age to learn something from young and unlearned men . . . ought not this to be the object of love and desire of all, to learn what they do not know, and to teach what they have learned?	(The texts are given in the discussion.)

(1) The motif of Gamaliel's willingness to be taught by those who are young and unlearned is a relatively easy extension from the portrait in Acts, but, in any case, it is precisely that, a new extension. And, again, it is a motif which in the Fourth Gospel is embodied by Nicodemus. It is this man who, although a ruler of the Jews and a teacher of Israel, comes by night (Jn. 3:1ff.) to receive instruction from a man who never studied (Jn. 7:15). (2) Moreover it is this same Nicodemus who later argues that the council itself should learn from this untutored man exactly what he has done (Jn. 7:50f.). In R 1, 67, 1 these are precisely the two motifs which our Jewish-Christian author has added to the portrait of Gamaliel drawn from Acts.

It should also be noted—as in R 1, 62, 1 above—that the

Caiaphas of the *Ascents* is presented in terms which cause him to look somewhat like the colleagues of Nicodemus in the Fourth Gospel. The latter refuse Nicodemus' plea to learn from the accused (7:52); and their equivalents in John 9, those who examine the blind man, make the same refusal: "You were born in utter sin, and will you teach us?"

R 1, 68, 1	*John 7:50-52*
These sayings of Gamaliel did not much please Caiaphas; and holding him in suspicion, as it seemed . . .	Nicodemus said to them. . . . They replied, "Are you from Galilee too?"

The speech of Gamaliel in Acts 5 is considered by his colleagues to be an eminently reasonable utterance. Far from holding him in suspicion, they accept his advice and act on it. The major motif of R 1, 68, 1 is clearly not drawn, then, from Acts. It finds its parallel, rather, in John 7:52. Here Nicodemus' speech to his colleagues-in-council does arouse their suspicions that he may have succumbed to the Christian message. Thus we see another datum which indicates that our Jewish-Christian author has conflated the Acts portrait of Gamaliel with motifs which in the New Testament attach only to the Johannine portrait of Nicodemus.

*   *   *

It is now time for us to gather up the loose ends in order to see what we may have before us as a whole.

1. Whereas there is clear evidence that our second-century, Jewish-Christian author drew direct quotations from Acts and from the Synoptic Gospels, there is not a single convincing case for a *quotation* from the Fourth Gospel.

2. The initial phase of our study of possible Johannine *allusions* produced results which are harmonious with the absence of quotations from John. Indeed, even where the subject matter would lead one to expect such allusions, they prove to be absent. Were one to judge on the basis of the data to this point—roughly

speaking, the data forthcoming from the research of previous scholars—he would be compelled to conclude either that the author was ignorant of the Fourth Gospel (as Waitz thought) or that he had a relationship to it so different from that which he had to the Synoptics as to cause him to give absolutely no indication of his knowledge of it.

3. Is this picture altered by the additional data we have studied in the passages from R 1, 62 to R 1, 68? For a moment one might consider the possibility, I suppose, that these data merely reflect the accidental emergence of similar motifs. For two major reasons, however, I should consider it quite probable that we are dealing with parallels which have arisen because of some kind of specific connection.

First, all six of them are found in a relatively short compass, rather than scattered here and there. They are primarily focused on only two figures: Peter—a Jewish Christian who dares to carry on a mission among his Jewish brethren—and Gamaliel—a member of the council who is secretly a Jewish Christian. They begin as soon as Peter takes up his direct speech, they emerge next in connection with Gamaliel, and they cease when Gamaliel steps off the stage. Thus the parallels do not constitute disparate snippets which might present accidental similarities.

Second, as I have already briefly noted, the conflation of the figures of Gamaliel and Nicodemus is evidenced elsehwere, and, in fact, is a work—the *Acts of Pilate*—which probably stems from the pen of a Jewish Christian of the same general period.[123] That fact encourages one to think that our author's portrait of Gamaliel does not possess features similar to those of Nicodemus simply by chance.

In short, then, the added data in R 1, 62, 65, 67, and 68 do indeed alter the picture. Taking them into account *requires* an explanation of the text of the *Ascents* which somehow involves the Fourth Gospel. Exactly how the Fourth Gospel is involved is a question which could lead to either of two hypotheses.

---

[123] See F. Scheidweiler, "The Gospel of Nicodemus, Acts of Pilate and Christ's descent into Hell," Hennecke-Schneemelcher, *New Testament Apocrypha* I, 444ff.

IV. Two Hypotheses

There are two major possibilities: A. Since the added data do not indicate a direct literary relationship, the most one may claim is that the author had at some time read the Fourth Gospel, and that he was therefore able to recall at least some of its motifs by memory:

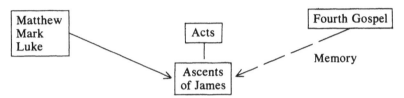

B. The data are also susceptible to explanation on the assumption that there was no link at all leading from the Fourth Gospel to the *Ascents*. In this case, one would be speaking of traditional elements which made their way along two independent routes both to the Fourth Gospel and to the *Ascents*:

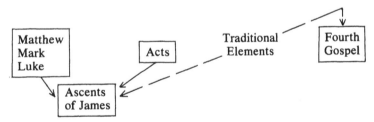

We may make our way forward by exploring the two hypotheses in the light of the Jewish-Christian identity of the author of the *Ascents*.

A. A memory link from the Fourth Gospel
to the *Ascents of James*

This is an attractive hypothesis on several counts:
1. We know that when R. E. Brown has called "a recasting and joining of canonical materials" is the key to the composition

of two second-century works: Tatian's *Diatessaron* (Rome ca. 175 A.D.?) and the Papyrus Egerton 2 (Egypt ca. 150 A.D.?); and the composition of each of these involved use of the Fourth Gospel.[124] Neither is the work of a Jewish Christian, and that fact must be borne in mind, but they do provide examples of a literary process *somewhat* similar to that posited by this first hypothesis.

2. The acceptance of this hypothesis would ease one of the difficulties we have observed earlier. At several junctures, we have had occasion to note that the *Ascents* seems to give conflicting signals: no use of the Fourth Gospel where such would be expected, several indications of its possible use in a context dominated by its indebtedness to Acts. These signals are perhaps not unduly puzzling on the hypothesis of a memory link, for memory is always selective. One could imagine that from the author's reading of the Fourth Gospel he recalled the figure of Nicodemus, but did not remember Jesus' conversation with the Samaritan woman, etc. Just why a Jewish Christian would remember and forget in the required pattern might be a question difficult or impossible to answer, but early Christian literature has bequeathed to us a host of such questions.

3. Returning to the specific phenomenon of the "doubling" of Gamaliel and Nicodemus, one may note that as a technique, doubling is quite common in early Christian literature, not least in the later layers of the Pseudo-Clementines themselves. To be sure, the specific parallel which is, as I mentioned above, so carefully developed in the *Acts of Pilate*, rests on a direct, *literary* borrowing from both Acts and the Fourth Gospel. A memory link as regards the figure of Nicodemus is, however, perfectly adequate to explain the pertinent data in the *Ascents*.

4. Moreover, a memory link as opposed to direct literary dependence could be seen as quite harmonious with the author's identity as a Jewish Christian. One recalls the presence in the Fourth Gospel of sharp polemic probably directed against Jewish Christians (e.g., John 8:31ff.).[125] On the assumption of such

---

[124] R. E. Brown, "The Relation of 'The Secret Gospel of Mark' to the Fourth Gospel," *CBQ* 36 (1974; Skehan Festschrift) 466-485 (477).

[125] See the section on John 8:31ff. in Chapter 3 of the present volume.

polemic, it is not overly difficult to imagine that this Gospel would constitute a special category in the mind of a Jewish-Christian author. If he allowed his memory to draw on it at all, he would surely do so in such a way as to pick the flowers from among the thorns.

In short, the data we have encountered in the disputation of R 1, 62ff. may open up to us a small part of a hitherto unattended chapter in the history of the interpretation of John, the chapter, namely, which deals with the Gospel's interpretation among Jewish Christians. As far as I can see, the possibility of such a chapter is hinted at neither by the scholars expert in the history of Johannine interpretation—from Loewenich to Pagels[126]—nor by those who specialize in the study of Jewish Christianity.[127]

To be sure, the pertinent data in the *Ascents* are neither numerous nor extensive. On the hypothesis of a memory link, one would say that they suffice only to indicate (a) that the (offensive?) Fourth Gospel had no honored place alongside the other Gospels in the literary treasury of the second-century church of Pella, but (b) that at least one member of that church—a writer of some talent—had read it and was willing to draw a few motifs from it by memory.

By the same token, however, mentioning a Jewish-Christian chapter in the history of the interpretation of John may lead one at least to ask whether an exploration of the recoverable attitudes of Jewish Christians toward the Fourth Gospel would, after all, provide support for the hypothesis of a memory link. There are good grounds for holding that our author lived in a Jewish-Christian community which had not been penetrated by Gnostic forms of thought.[128] A brief survey of the literature useful for the study of Jewish Christianity yields the hint that, while the Fourth Gospel was occasionally used among Gnosticizing Jewish Christians—e.g., those of the *Kerygmata Petrou*[129]—it may have

---

[126]See note 91 above.

[127]See the pertinent works of, among others, H.-J. Schoeps, J. Daniélou, M. Simon, G. Strecker, B. Bagatti, and E. Testa. Cf. also the Daniélou Festschrift mentioned in note 5 above.

[128]Strecker, *Judenchristentum*, p. 254 n.

[129]*Ibid.*, p. 218.

been mostly avoided in communities like that of our author.[130]
Even if this hint should prove correct, it would not exclude, of
course, a memory link on the part of one member of such a
community. Hence, I should be far from setting aside this first
hypothesis. I say only that a cursory survey hints that the presence in the Fourth Gospel of polemic against Jewish Christians
may in fact have caused that Gospel to be studiously avoided by
Jewish Christians who lacked the connecting bridge of Gnostic
thought-forms. In any case, one should at least consider seriously
the second alternative.

B. Traditional elements held in common
by the authors of the Fourth Gospel
and of the *Ascents of James*

There are several reasons to think that the parallels reflect
not a link with the Fourth Gospel itself—even by memory—but
rather the effects on the two documents of traditional elements
antedating both of them.

1. This hypothesis avoids altogether the difficulty of holding
that our Jewish-Christian author was willing to borrow from that
Gospel in which "the Jews who had believed in him" are characterized as having the devil as their father (Jn. 8:31, 44). Nor

---

[130]There is a fascinating and, as far as I can see, largely overlooked
passage in Epiphanius, *Panarion* (30, 3, 8) which *could* be cited, I suppose, to indicate use of the Fourth Gospel by Jewish Christians. It comes
in the discussion of the Ebionites. After saying that the latter accept and
use only the Gospel of Matthew, Epiphanius mentions that some Jewish
Christians have transmitted the following information: The Gospel of
John, translated from Greek into Hebrew, has been secretly stored in
some Jewish genizahs in Tiberias. This is the sort of datum which makes
one's head reel a bit, not only because it is so astonishing, but also
because the interpretative possibilities are so numerous. In the present
note there is sufficient space only to say that after pondering the text
itself in its context, and after consulting the corresponding texts (a) of the
pertinent anakephalaiosis (summary) in the *Panarion* (*GCS* 25, 236) and
(b) of *Anakephalaiosis* 30 (*PG* 42, 857), I see no grounds for drawing from
Panarion 30, 3, 8 the conclusion that the Fourth Gospel was read and
interpreted by non-Gnosticizing Jewish Christians.

should one think it truly strange that an author of the second half of the second century—especially a Jewish-Christian author—should be ignorant of the Fourth Gospel or should consciously avoid it. Nothing requires us to date the *Ascents* any appreciable distances at all from Justin, and while the apologist *may* have drawn on the Fourth Gospel, to a number of interpreters it seems far more likely that he did not do so.[131] It is now clear that well into the second century one or more of the written Gospels often circulated in the company of Gospel traditions in oral form.[132] Moreover, we may have evidence of such parallel circulation of written and oral Gospel materials in the *Ascents* itself. A comparison of R 1, 37 and R 1, 39 with Luke 21:20ff. may tell us that the Pella legend made its way along two independent routes, to Luke on the one hand, and to our author on the other. What we have called "Johannine motifs" in R 1, 62-68 could very well constitute an analogous case.

2. There is no instance of a verbal agreement extending beyond one or two words. This may be credited, of course, to a memory link, but it is perhaps a bit more readily explained as the result of a shared tradition. Repeatedly, when we subtracted the influence of Acts, what remained was made up, not of Johannine sentences, or even clauses, but rather of motifs which are paralleled in John.

3. Moreover—and this is, I believe, a weighty observation—these motifs all have a common *Sitz im Leben* (life situation). One notices that the pertinent data in the Fourth Gospel fall, without significant exception, in the first verses of Chapter 16 and in the latter parts of Chapters 7 and 9—that is to say, in texts which reflect the situation of a Jewish Christian being subjected to a hearing or trial before a Jewish court (a *Bet Din*; John 3:1; 7:12; 15 preserve supplementary notes).[133] From the Synoptic tradition we know that early Jewish Christians were re-

---

[131] See, e.g., the discussions in the commentaries by Barrett (pp. 93ff.) and Schnackenburg (ET 1, 199) and in Braun, *Jean le Théologien*, pp. 135ff., 290f.

[132] Cf. H. Köster, *Synoptische Überlieferung bei den Apostolischen Vätern* (Berlin, 1957); A. J. Bellinzoni, *The Sayings of Jesus*.

[133] See Martyn, *History and Theology*, Chapter 3.

peatedly brought before Jewish courts (Mk. 13:9a; Mt. 10:17; Lk. 12:11; 21:12a), so that it is technically proper to speak of that setting as a *Sitz im Leben*, and it is that single *Sitz im Leben* which lies behind all the Johannine data to which we have been led. To be sure, the scene in the *Ascents* is that of a public disputation to which the Jewish Christians have been invited, however urgently. For a talented author, however, such a scene is not far removed from the *Sitz im Leben* of a legal hearing.

In short, the hypothesis of shared elements of tradition does not require us to think of six disparate elements making their way along as many independent routes both to the fourth evangelist and to our Jewish-Christian author. One has only to imagine that both of these authors received what would be essentially a single piece of tradition, and this point proves, in fact, to be a distinct strength of our second hypothesis. If the author of the *Ascents* inherited a unified piece of tradition pertaining to the *Sitz im Leben* of a trial before a Jewish court—and this is all that is required by the data—it is not at all puzzling that he should compose the Samaritan debate and other pieces without reflecting in any way a knowledge of the Fourth Gospel. The hypothetical piece of tradition would amount to something like the following:

A Jewish Christian is on trial before a Bet Din on the capital charge of having led astray some of his fellow Jews;[a] in this setting, aware of the illumination of the Gospel, he offers instruction to his judges,[b] who, with one exception, refuse to be taught by an unlettered man, charging him with temerity;[c] the exception is a council member who secretly harbors pro-Christian sentiments;[d] he guardedly expresses these sentiments by suggesting that the court listen to the testimony of the accused,[e] and this move earns for him the suspicion of his colleagues.[f]

[a] John 16:2; 7:12, 47 (cf. Mark 13:9a); R 1, 62, 1
[b] John 9:30-33 (cf. Mark 13:9b); R 1, 62, 5
[c] John 7:52; 9:34; R 1, 62, 2; 1, 67, 1
[d] John 7:50ff.; 12:42; 3:1; R 1, 65, 1-3
[e] John 7:51; R 1, 67, 1
[f] John 7:52; R 1, 68, 1

In light of this hypothesis, we must alter in important ways the diagram used earlier to illustrate our second hypothesis:

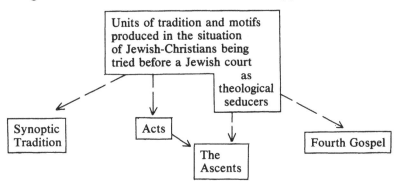

Ex hypothesi—let this expression be understood from this point forward, so as to avoid the cumbersome use of the English subjunctive—there is good reason to believe that this piece of tradition—*in the form involving the seducer charge*—was fixed in or quite near the setting in which the Fourth Gospel was written; and it would follow that the tradition probably reflected actual developments which had transpired in the life of John's own community.[134] The portrait of a secret believer among the synagogue rulers, for example, would probably not be *at this stage* (cf. Jn. 12:42) merely a "literary motif,"[135] although there can be little doubt that, along with other elements, it later became exactly that (*Acts of Pilate*). On the contrary, in its Johannine

----

[134]Martyn, *History and Theology*, Chapter 3.

[135]Contra Strecker, *Judenchristentum*, p. 253. The careful reader of Strecker's monograph senses that between the lines the author is carrying on a polemic against the historical credulity of H.-J. Schoeps. As regards this particular form of the historicity debate, I find myself in agreement, for the most part, with Strecker, as the following paragraph in the text above will show. If, in interpreting the *Ascents*, someone uses the adjective "historical" to claim that the document puts us in touch with specific events essentially like those which it purports to describe—largely the opinion of Schoeps—I should much prefer Strecker's repeated emphasis on "literary motifs." On the other hand, the adjective "historical" may also be justly used in a broader way to refer to a repeated *Sitz im Leben*, and this use is what seems called for by the Johannine parallels.

form the unit of tradition would have represented an historical specification of the Synoptic loging about Christians being brought before synagogue councils.

Its use by the author of the *Ascents*, on the other hand, shows that for him (and his community) it had become nothing other than a piece of tradition, available to this *littérateur* who wished to employ it for the sake of its literary potential. This can be seen already from the fact that the author employed it, not in the *Sitz im Leben* (repeated situation) of a trial before a Jewish court, but rather in an imaginary, "once-upon-a-time" disputation, in which the Jewish-Christian disputants of the Jerusalem church are presented as having been dramatically victorious over the chief priest himself. One notes also that the author rationalized a number of the tradition's motifs, virtually changing them into timeless aphorisms:

> . . . ought not this to be the . . . desire of all, to learn what they do not know? . . . For it is certain that neither friendship, nor kindred, nor lofty power, ought to be more precious to men than truth (R 1, 67, 1-2).

Finally, in reaching these conclusions, we must avoid two errors. From the hypothesis it follows clearly that we must not allow the author's literary gifts and his rationalistic tendencies to cause us to suppose that he created the disputation on the dual basis of the canonical Acts and his own imagination, thus fashioning nothing other than literary motifs. On the contrary, his fertile imagination seems clearly to have enjoyed the stimulus not only of Acts, but also of the piece of tradition we have hypothetically isolated. At the same time, we must not allow the author's dramatic gifts to cause us to think that he preserved accurate information about a disputation which actually transpired in the early days of the Jerusalem church. He is a talented *littérateur* who believes that his own Jewish-Christian church, far removed from the early days in Jerusalem and living even at considerable distance from persecution at the hands of Jewish courts, needs once again to learn of its identity in distinction both from the identity of its parent—non-Christian Judaism—and from that of its illegitimate sibling—Pauline Christianity. On the basis of our second hypothesis, one would say that for presenting the former of these two distinctions our author had at his disposal, among other materials, a piece of Jewish-Christian tradition which found its essential form at a time in the life of the community behind the Fourth Gospel when that community was a Jewish-Christian church.

CHAPTER 3

Glimpses into the History
of the Johannine Community

From Its Origin Through the Period of Its Life in Which
the Fourth Gospel Was Composed

INTRODUCTION

In composing the present chapter, I have taken for granted a
few presuppositions which ought to be made clear at the outset:

1. In three respects the Fourth Gospel is comparable to what
archaeologists call a "tell." (a) First, there are numerous literary
strata, and to some extent these strata may be differentiated from
one another.[136] (b) Second, much of the substance of the "materials" in the strata is of such a character as to reflect communal
interests, concerns, and experiences.[137] (c) Third, considered as
a whole, this literary "tell" exhibits a remarkable degree of stylis-

---

[136]See, e.g., the analysis proposed by R. E. Brown, John (I-XII), pp.
xxxiv-xl. The major criterion for strata differentiation is the aporia. See
note 138 below.

[137]This point has been grasped by many interpreters. See Martyn,
History and Theology, p. xviii and *passim*; David E. Aune, *The Cultic
Setting of Realized Eschatology in Early Christianity* (Leiden, 1972), pp.
73-84.

tic and conceptual homogeneity.[138] Now, taking into account all three of these observations, one sees that we are dealing with a stratified literary deposit from what archaeologists would call a single, continuous occupation. In other words, the literary history behind the Fourth Gospel reflects to a large degree the history of a single community which maintained over a period of some duration its particular and rather peculiar identity. It obviously follows that we may hope to draw from the *Gospel's literary history* certain conclusions about the *community's social and theological history*. In the present chapter there will not be sufficient space to demonstrate in every case the literary-critical grounds. I can only say that the fundamental attempt is to move from relatively secure points in the document's literary history to reasonable hypotheses as regards the community's social and theological history.

2. A second presupposition is that the Gospel was written for the Johannine community. That is to say, it was written for a community of people who had a shared history and who in the course of that history developed a highly symbolic language with numerous expressions which *they* would easily understand as referring to their shared history. In short, to a large extent the Gospel is written in the language of a community of initiates. It follows that those who would be historians of this community must not only engage in literary archaeology, but must also make at least a partial entry into this symbolic language. That is no small undertaking. On the contrary, it requires all of the scientific control and all of the informed, historical imagination we can corporately muster. The fact that these two gifts are somewhat unevenly distributed among us is one of the reasons we must help one another by mutual enrichment and by mutual correction (Rom. 1:11).

---

[138]E. Ruckstuhl, *Die literarische Einheit*; see also Professor Ruckstuhl's essay in M. de Jonge (ed.), *L'Évangile de Jean*. His critique of the work of R. T. Fortna is careful and weighty. Johannine source critics will have to reckon with Ruckstuhl's renewed challenge as regards the use of stylistic observations. The major criterion for strata differentiation, however, the criterion of the aporiae, remains intact. Cf. Robert Kysar, *The Fourth Evangelist*, Chapter 1.

3. In the course of this chapter it will become apparent that I believe studies in Jewish Christianity hold considerable promise for historians of the Johannine community and for Johannine interpreters in general. There are some new labors in this area, and I think they may be expected to bear some fruit in Johánnine studies.[139]

So much for presuppositions. I should also say a brief word about the indicative mood and the subjunctive mood. Considering the widespread use of the indicative mood in the work of historians, it has occurred to me that it would be a valuable practice for the historian to rise each morning saying to himself three times slowly and with emphasis, "I do not know." The direct pertinence of this suggestion to the present chapter will be at least partially grasped if the reader will bear in mind the necessity to interpret a good many of my indicative verbs as though they were in the subjunctive mood. The number of points in the history of the Johannine community about which we may be virtually certain is relatively small, and we need to be clear about that.

One of these relatively secure points is surely the highly probable correspondence to the *Birkath ha-Minim* (Benediction Against Heretics) of the expressions "to be put out of the synagogue" and "to put someone out of the synagogue" which emerge in John 9:22, 12:42 and 16:2. While concern for clarity has caused me to present the following "glimpses" in chronological order, the perception of them began not with observations and hypotheses pertinent to what I have termed the early period, but rather with this secure point of correspondence.[140] From this point I have tried to work both backward and forward literarily and historically.[141]

---

[139] In addition to the well-known works of Schoeps, Daniélou, Simon *et al.*, see Klijn and Reinink, *Patristic Evidence*. Cf. also Chapters 1 and 2 of the present volume.

[140] See Martyn, *History and Theology, passim.*

[141] See Meeks, *"Am I a Jew?"* In Meeks' generous and helpful appraisal of the essay I contributed to the Pittsburgh Festival of the Gospels (*Jesus and Man's Hope* I, pp. 247-273), he remarks that while my "fascinating proposals" constitute a "prolific working hypothesis . . . the weakest point . . . is just the starting point: the attempt to reconstruct a

I. THE EARLY PERIOD

The Conception of a Messianic Group Within
the Community of the Synagogue

The statement of Martin Dibelius, "In the beginning was the sermon," is not only famous;[142] it has also been enormously influential in New Testament studies. Perhaps, indeed, it is this very statement which lies ultimately behind the wide agreement today that "the Fourth Gospel began life as separate homilies."[143] The question is whether we can determine which of the recoverable homilies are likely to be the earliest.

A strong case may be made, I believe, for holding that a recoverable literary stratum behind 1:35-49 constitutes part of a very early sermon, perhaps indeed one of those evangelistic sermons, which by definition must have lain at the origin of the Johannine community.[144] There are several reasons for holding this opinion:

   1. Verse 43 contains clear indications of editorial activity on

---

single, unitary *narrative* source independently of form- and redaction-critical study of the *discourse* material" (p. 184). This is a critique of the source-critical labors of Robert Fortna and of my taking those labors as my first hypothesis (Pittsburgh essay, p. 248). At the present juncture three things must be said: (1) I believe Fortna's analysis to be the best and most helpful source criticism of the Fourth Gospel we have to date. (2) Meeks is surely right that Fortna's work must be reviewed on the basis of form- and redaction-critical study of the discourses. This constitutes a *desideratum* in Johannine studies. (3) Actually both in the Pittsburgh essay and in the present one the "starting point" of my analysis, as distinguished from the point at which the presentation of results begins, is John 9:22.

[142]Martin Dibelius, *Die alttestamentlichen Motive in der Leidensgeschichte des Petrus- und des Johannes-Evangeliums*, p. 242 of the reprint in *Botschaft und Geschichte* I (Tübingen, 1953).

[143]Lindars, *Behind the Fourth Gospel* (London, 1971), p. 47.

[144]Verse 49 is fixed as the end of the pericope by the observation that John 1:50 is probably the evangelist's composition, placed as it is to function as a bridge leading from the tradition behind 1:35-49 to the logion of verse 51. As regards beginning the pericope with verse 35 cf. M. de Jonge, "Jesus as Prophet and King in the Fourth Gospel," in *ETL* 49

the part of *someone*. We recall some vexing syntactical problems, discussed at some length in Chapter 1 above.[145] There is moreover a structural problem which is created by verse 43.[146] Elsewhere in this tightly-knit pericope the present tense of the verb "to find" serves as the means by which the witness-chain is continuously extended from John the Baptist outward (vv. 41 and 45; cf. 35ff.). As it stands, verse 43 breaks this chain by allowing Jesus to be the subject of "he found." Several explanations are possible, of course.[147] In my opinion the most probable explanation is to identify the syntactical and structural problems as *aporias* introduced into the text by someone who edited an earlier tradition or source. In its earlier form verse 43 probably mentioned Andrew (or Simon) as the subject of "he found."[148] Thus

---

(1973), p. 163f, where 1:19-34 is correctly identified as a pericope. In the present essay I am using the terms "sermon" and "homily" to refer to messages actually preached in the Johannine group/community. I do not intend to imply that the very words of the recoverable literary stratum behind John 1:35-49 constituted such a message, but rather that they *encapsulate part* of an early sermon. At a later point I shall make a similar suggestion about John 8:31ff. These suggestions are also to be distinguished from the claim that we have before us an example representative of a form-critical category which can be identified as a "homily." See the trenchant observations made on this subject by K. P. Donfried, *The Setting of Second Clement in Early Christianity* (Leiden, 1974), pp. 25-34.

[145] The syntactical problems are also discussed in R. E. Brown, *John, ad loc.*; it is one of the disappointing features of the generally helpful commentary by Barnabas Lindars that *problems* posed by the text are not infrequently smoothed over, rather than wrestled with. Lindars' comment on 1:43 is typical of such treatment: "But awkward as it is the text can stand . . . the verse is only aimed at bringing Philip on to the stage, because of his part in what follows."

[146] The structural imbalance was seen and clearly stated by M.-E. Boismard, "Les traditions johanniques concernant le Baptiste", in *RB* 70 (1963) 5-42 (especially p. 40).

[147] F. Spitta, W. Wilkens, and M.-E. Boismard allotted verse 43 to the hand of a post-Johannine redactor. The references to Spitta and Wilkens are given by Boismard on p. 42 of the article cited above in note 146.

[148] See R. E. Brown, *John, ad loc.*, and Chapter 1 of the present volume.

the pericope originally portrayed Jesus in a remarkably passive role. He does not take the major initiative to call disciples. On the contrary, it is the others who *find* him.

2. With this observation it is harmonious that alongside the striking use of "to find" the verb "to come" emerges in pregnant expressions:

come and see (v. 39),
come and see (v. 46),
to come to Jesus (equivalent expressions in vv. 39, 46, and 47).

Aside from the Baptist, all of the characters in the underlying tradition *come to Jesus* and thereby become his disciples.

3. The roles given to "to find" and "to come" and the concomitant passivity of Jesus constitute an *aporia* when compared with key passages in the Fourth Gospel in which the initiative of Jesus (or of God) is polemically affirmed. Two are particularly striking:[149]

6:44 (cf. also 6:65)
No one can come to me
unless the Father . . . draws him. . . .
15:16 (cf. also 15:19)
You did not choose me,
but I chose you.

The "someone" who edited the earlier tradition or source behind 1:35-49 was very probably the fourth evangelist himself. Part of his motivation for altering verse 43 presumably lay in the desire to show Jesus taking the initiative in this instance (cf. also v. 48c).

4. The roles given to "to find" and "to come" also differentiate the underlying tradition rather sharply from the Synoptic pericopes commonly referred to as "The *Call* of the Disciples."[150]

---

[149] Cf. also Jn. 5:14 and 9:35.
[150] For a discussion of Hahn's analysis of this pericope see note 65.

In the latter, as the name correctly implies, Jesus consistently takes the entire initiative to call disciples. In the tradition underlying John 1:35-49, to the contrary, we have already noted that Jesus is dominantly presented as a passive figure who is successively *found* by men who *come to him.*

From these four observations it follows with some degree of probability that we may view the earlier stratum below John 1:35-49 as a tradition antedating the literary efforts of the evangelist and as a non-Synoptic form of the pericope about the coming of Jesus' first disciples. Moreover, because of the dual accent on "finding" and "coming," it is quite easy to imagine that the earlier form of John 1:35-49 was in fact a sermon which lay, along with others, at the origin of the Johannine community. One can readily envisage that the preacher who painted the dynamic picture of men who come to Jesus and find him to be the Messiah did so in the hope that his hearers would behave in like manner, that they also would *come* to Jesus, and that, *finding* him to be the Messiah, they also would become Christians.

If some of the hearers did so, if the underlying sermon did in part play a role in the origin of the Johannine community, then from where did the converts come? Not from the general world of Greco-Roman culture. There is, of course, a conceptual movement which corresponds to the spatial movement of the verb "to come," and that conceptual movement does not include a step from messianic ignorance to the awakening of messianic expectations. It is not they who have never been told of him who come to see, and it is not they who have never heard of him who come to understand (cf. Is. 52:15; Rom. 15:21). On the contrary, the preacher takes for granted that his hearers already hold certain well-formed messianic expectations, and these expectations constitute in his view a sort of launching pad for a *heilsgeschichtlich* christological trajectory which has its fulfillment in Jesus of Nazareth. *He* is the Mosaic prophet, the eschatological Elijah, the expected Messiah. The preacher of the sermon, therefore, like John the Baptist, points to Jesus, so that those who have been brought up on the traditional Jewish expectations may now *find* the one so long expected.

From these observations it would seem obvious that the preacher was addressing Jews and thus that the homily underlying John 1:35-49 is one of the rare examples within the largely Gentile-Christian New Testament of what Paul referred to as the Gospel of the circumcision (Gal. 2:7). This tells us, in turn, that the evangelization which brought the Johannine community into existence was very probably carried out wholly within the bosom of the synagogue. As regards the Johannine community, "In the beginning was the sermon of the Gospel of the circumcision."

Of course this Gospel of the circumcision will have included considerably more than the account of messianic discovery portrayed in the sermon underlying 1:35-49. There will also have been numerous pieces of Jesus-tradition which were used to support and to make concrete for the hearers the confessions paradigmatically made by Andrew, Peter, Philip, and Nathanael. We cannot know the precise contours of this additional material, but there is good reason to assume that it *included* elements of the passion-resurrection narrative and the early strata of a number of the Johannine miracle stories, several of which may have been collected and shaped under the influence of similar collections which lie behind the Synoptic Gospels, and also under the influence of the Elijah/Elisha cycles in 1 and 2 Kings.[151] In any case, already in this early evangelistic preaching Jesus' miracles were probably called "signs," and it was expected that most Jews who heard and therefore saw these signs would come rather uncritically to believe that Jesus was the promised Messiah.

We may surmise that before a great many years had passed, it occurred to one of the preachers of this inner-synagogue messianic group to collect some of the traditions and homilies into what Ernst Haenchen thought of as a rudimentary, written Gospel.[152] What motivated him to do this? Had he got at least a glimpse of the Gospel of Mark (cf. Lindars' suggestion regarding

---

[151]See R. E. Brown, "Jesus and Elisha", in *Perspective* 12 (1971) 85-104, especially p. 97.

[152]Haenchen's actual words are "What Bultmann called the "Signs Source" can very well have been the gospel of this community: a sort of rudimentary Gospel of Mark. . . ."; p. 303 of *Aus der Literatur zum Johannesevangelium 1929-1956*, in *TR* 23 (1955) 295-335. It may also be pertinent to recall that Haenchen identified as Jewish-Christian the miracle story underlying the first part of John 5; p. 48 of *Johanneische Probleme*, in *ZTK* 56 (1959) 19-54.

what he terms the first edition of John's Gospel)?[153] Or are we to consider the possibility that the Gospel form emerged independently at two junctures in early Christian history? Here we are, I think, in the shadows. In any case, already within the early period, one of the Christian Jews of the inner-synagogue group seems to have penned a document similar, I believe, to the signs source or signs Gospel, which in our time has been spoken of and investigated, to some degree independently of one another, by Rudolph Bultmann, Ernst Haenchen, Robert Fortna, Jürgen Becker, Nikolaus Walter, Willem Nicol, Günther Reim, and Moody Smith.[154] This signs source or signs Gospel was precisely "an essay in christology," which, far from terminating the further formation of oral homilies, clearly now served the author and his preaching colleagues in the task of proclamation.

For our present concerns the importance of the signs source/Gospel lies, of course, in the fact that it affords the historian a glimpse of the messianic group as it lived in the community of the synagogue during the early period. Several notes of importance demand attention:

1. During this period the group's evangelistic preaching seems to have met with considerable success. We may allow for some exaggeration, to be sure. Yet there seem to be genuine reflections of remarkable evangelization in 2:11, 4:53 (note particularly the expression "and he himself believed, and his whole house"), 6:14, etc.; and, by the same token, such dark and pes-

---

[153]B. Lindars, *Behind the Fourth Gospel*, pp. 12f.: "It is likely that John had at least *seen* Mark."

[154]R. Bultmann, *Das Evangelium des Johannes*, and D. Moody Smith, *The Composition and Order of the Fourth Gospel: Bultmann's Literary Theory* (New Haven, 1965); E. Haenchen, the article cited above in note 152, and his unpublished commentary; R. T. Fortna, *The Gospel of Signs*, and a series of redaction-critical essays, the latest being "Christology in the Fourth Gospel: Redaction-Critical Perspectives", in *NTS* 21 (1974-75) 489-504; Jürgen Becker, "Wunder und Christologie", in *NTS* 16 (1969-70) 130-148; N. Walter, "Die Auslegung überlieferter Wundererzählungen im Johannes-Evangelium", in *Theologische Versuche* II (1970) 93-107; W. Nicol, *The Sēmeia in the Fourth Gospel*; G. Reim, *Studien zum alttestamentlichen Hintergrund des Johannesevangeliums*; D. Moody Smith, "The Milieu of the Johannine Miracle Source", in *Jews, Greeks, and Christians* (see note 139 above).

simistic logia as the one in 12:37 are to be assigned literarily to a later stage of the group's history. In the early period the group saw that the Messiah who had come to his own was in fact being widely received among them.

2. It was remembered, to be sure, that in Jerusalem not all of the Messiah's own had received him. Indeed the Johannine evangelists must surely have told the story of Jesus' crucifixion in a way which included inculpating roles played by the authorities of the Jewish people. In recognizing this fact, we are reminded that the preaching of the Christian Gospel was always and everywhere scandalous and offensive. We may also assume, however, that the scandal was focused and accurately defined by midrashic demonstration that in the Messiah's betrayal and death Scripture had been fulfilled.[155]

3. While we can scarcely be certain, it seems that this very early group had for the most part a relatively simple understanding of faith. The signs and the paradoxically scandalous and redemptive proclamation of the passion-resurrection led rather simply to faith, and there was only one level of faith.[156]

4. I have already said that the group was made up altogether of Jews, probably bilingual, but clearly living within the theological, social, and cultural security of the synagogue. In this early period—a period which probably began before the Jewish war, as Moody Smith has recently argued[157]—the group experienced no social dislocation and felt relatively little alienation from their heritage.[158] Here three points in particular demand attention:

---

[155]Cf. John 19:24 etc. and Fortna, *The Gospel of Signs*, pp. 229f.

[156]That the author of the signs source had an understanding of the relationship between signs and faith which was rather different from that of the evangelist is suggested by most of the scholars listed above in note 154. See also an unpublished essay by Paul W. Meyer of Princeton Theological Seminary entitled *Seeing, Signs, and Sources in the Fourth Gospel*.

[157]D. Moody Smith, "Johannine Christianity: Some Reflections on Its Character and Delineation", in *NTS* 21 (1974-75) 222-248, especially p. 246.

[158]Those readers who were in attendance at the (1975) *Journées Bibliques* will recall that this statement elicited some rather spirited disagreement. In what now follows I am responding to the questions raised.

(a) If the group was "at home" within the synagogue, what was its stance toward Torah? The question is difficult to answer with both precision and certainty, but there are several factors which converge to suggest quite strongly that the group was Torah-observant. The traditions of this early period give not the slightest indication that this inner-synagogue group engaged in debates about the validity of Torah; form-critical analysis clearly shows that the references to breach of Sabbath in 5:9. 10. 16. 18 and in 9:14. 16 belong to the later strata, and the same is to be said of the discussion of circumcision and of breach of Sabbath in 7:22ff. Moreover, as we shall shortly see, the group's later exit from the synagogue provides pertinent evidence which points to the conclusion that its members were Torah-observant Jews. It is clear that they desired to remain within the synagogue; their exit was in fact a traumatic expulsion carried out against their will (contrast, e.g., Acts 18:6f.). One does not have the impression of a group which even dreamed of being free from Torah observance. And on what grounds did the authorities expel them? Not on the grounds that the group was lax with regard to Torah observance per se, but rather only on the grounds of their messianic confession of Jesus (9:22, etc.). One is reminded that the *Birkath ha-Minim* seems to have been directed against the confession of Jesus as Messiah, not against discrete breach of Torah.[159] One thinks furthermore of the witness given by the Jewish-Christian author of the "Ascents of James" who says that his community differs from the unbelieving Jews in one regard only: the confession of Jesus as the Christ.[160] And finally one is put in mind of numerous references to law-observant Jewish Christians in the Acts of the Apostles. Note in particular the words which Luke allows the elders of the Jerusalem church to speak to Paul:

> You see, brother, how many thousands there are among the Jews of those who have believed; they are all zealous for the law. . . . (Acts 21:20).

---

[159] Martyn, *History and Theology*, Chapter 2.

[160] Clementine Recognitions 1, 43. 2; B. Rehm, *Die Pseudoklementinen II, Rekognitionen in Rufins Übersetzung* (GCS, 51) (Berlin, 1965). For the source analysis of the *Ascent of James* see G. Strecker, *Das Judenchristentum in den Pseudoklementinen*, pp. 221ff, and above chapter two.

Whatever the precise stance toward Torah may have been in the case of Jesus,[161] we have every reason to believe that numerous Jewish-Christian groups were quite observant of Torah. And the pertinent data in the Fourth Gospel indicate that in its early period the Johannine group was probably a case in point.

(b) If the group was "at home" in the synagogue, what stance did it take toward the Gentile mission? Regarding this question the early strata in the Gospel are utterly silent. I see, in fact, no indication that in the early period the Johannine group even had any knowledge of the mission to the Gentiles. To be sure, one must bear in mind that this period stretched from a relatively early date to some point in the eighties. That fact alone may be judged as sufficient grounds for concluding that the group knew of the Gentile mission. Could Christians in any locale and of any sort have lived into the eighties ignorant of that momentous and vigorously debated development? Nevertheless, it is the marks of the vigorous debate which are most notably absent. As is always the case, one must exercise great caution in the interpretation of silence. I shall only suggest that whatever the Johannine group knew of the mission among the Gentiles, it would seem that they somehow managed to avoid being drawn into debates about it. And that suggestion brings us back to the major point: In the early period the group experienced no social dislocation and felt little alienation from their Jewish heritage.

(c) One is not surprised, therefore, to observe that in the strata pertinent to the early period there are no notes of dualism[162] and no indications of world-foreignness. I have already pointed out that Jesus' crucifixion, with its midrashic explication, served to focus the offensive character of the good news. It must have been recognized that the Gospel—even this Gospel

---

[161] It is of course a non sequitur to argue that the Johannine group's attitude toward Torah must have been such and such because Jesus' attitude was such and such. We must proceed on the basis of data in the Fourth Gospel.

[162] Cf. J. Becker, "Beobachtungen zum Dualismus im Johannesevangelium", in ZNW 65 (1974) 71-87, an attempt to show that the Johannine dualism had a history of development within the Johannine community: "The thinking characteristic of the earliest phase is pre-dualistic" (85).

of the circumcision—was not an announcement of the continuation of "life as usual." On the contrary, God's long-awaited, eschatological prophet-Messiah had come to grant genuinely new deliverance to his people. We must also note, however, that the Johannine evangelists seem clearly to have proclaimed the "new" without introducing such radical categories of discontinuity as are associated with dualism and world-foreignness. In the early strata Jesus himself, far from being a stranger, is quite plainly the expected Jewish Messiah. Correspondingly, the early homily and the signs Gospel itself indicate no feelings of suspicion, fear, or hostility toward the messianic group on the part of the Jewish authorities. In short, however theologically revolutionary their message must have been, the group was able to view the synagogue as the primary expression of the properly ordered kosmos.

5. I have referred above to the signs Gospel as an essay in christology. In fact, its massive concentration on the christology of the miracle worker produced a picture of the Messiah so numinous that that picture was destined in time to assume the proportions of "God striding across the face of the earth."[163] In the early period, however, there seems to have been no fear that such a christology could pose a threat to monotheism. On the contrary, we see in this period only *a group of Christian Jews*[164] who stand in a relatively untroubled stream of social and theological continuity precisely within the synagogue.

II. THE MIDDLE PERIOD

Part of the Group Is Born as a Separate Community by
Experiencing Two Major Traumas:
Excommunication from the Synagogue and Martyrdom

---

[163]The expression is derived, of course, from ones coined by F. C. Baur; E. Käsemann has suggestively revived the expression in our time. See, e.g., *The Testament of Jesus*, pp. 8f (German ed., p. 22).

[164]Here and later the reader will see that I have tried to grasp certain aspects of the history of the Johannine community by two means: a

In the course of the middle period there were momentous developments and alterations, both in the group's setting and within the group itself. The history of the Johannine tradition is particularly revealing here, for in contrast to the relatively tranquil waters which lie behind the earliest homily and the signs Gospel, one sees reflected in the next stages of tradition rather complex and stormy seas. The middle period is marked off, indeed, by the fact that the authorities now began to be quite suspicious of the rapidly growing messianic group, and both they and some rank-and-file synagogue members demanded that the group prove the validity of its messianic proclamation on the basis of exegesis. There ensued a number of midrashic debates, and in the course of the debates there emerged a widening spectrum of opinion about the group's message, ranging from absolute commitment (6:68) to partial faith (2:23ff., etc.) to outright unbelief (7:12. 47, etc.).[165]

And beyond such sobering developments lay two major traumas suffered by the messianic group and rather clearly reflected in dramatic expansions of two of the earlier miracle stories.

The First Trauma

In the dramatic expansion of the story of the man born blind (Jn. 9)—a dramatic expansion which may originally have been composed orally—we can see a clear reflection of the first trauma. Not far into the middle period the rapid growth of the messianic group caused the authorities not only to be suspicious, but also to take a radical step designed to terminate the flow of converts into the group. They introduced the reworded *Birkath ha-Minim* into the synagogue service in order to be able to iden-

---

distinction between "group" and "community," and a distinction between "Christian Jews" and "Jewish Christians." The possibility that the Beloved Disciple was an historical person who played a role in the early period cannot be pursued in the present book.

[165] It is not my intention to suggest that differences of opinion arose overnight in the middle period or that there was absolute unanimity in the early period.

tify and excommunicate those who confessed Jesus as Messiah (9:22. 34).[166]

From the logion of 12:42 and indeed from the role played by the blind man's parents in Chapter 9, it is clear that to a degree this step had the desired effect. Some of the members of the messianic group, and perhaps even more of those who were merely inclined toward the messianic faith, turned away from the confession in order to remain safely within the community of the synagogue. We shall return to these persons at a later point. Many members of the messianic group, however, paid the price of their convictions and suffered excommunication. From this point forward we may refer to these people, I think, as *the Johannine community*, for it is obvious that the outworking of the *Birkath ha-Minim* in the city in question changed the Johannine circle— against their will—from a messianic *group* within the synagogue into a separate *community* outside that social and theological setting. In this trauma the members suffered not only social dislocation but also great alienation, for the synagogue/world which had been their social and theological womb, affording nurture and security, was not only removed, but even became the enemy who persecutes. We may surmise that the roots of the dualistic patterns of thought and of the world-foreignness which came to full fruition only later are to be traced, in fact, to the sufferings of this middle period.

The Second Trauma

As I have said above, the use of the reworded *Birkath ha-Minim* narrowed the flow of converts, but it clearly did not terminate the flow altogether. The authorities therefore concluded that further restrictive measures were necessary, and in light of the Johannine community's increasing tendency to view Jesus as a numinous and somewhat other-worldly figure, the authorities were apparently able to argue that confession of such a figure constituted not only unacceptable messianism, but also a violation of monotheism (5:18). In short, they were able not only to

---

[166]Martyn, *History and Theology*, Chapter 2.

excommunicate those who confessed Jesus as Messiah, but also to arrest some of the evangelists from the separated community and to subject them to trial and, indeed to execution as *Messithim/Planoi* (seducers), as ditheists who led other Jews into the worship of a second god alongside Adonai.[167]

It is not difficult to see that this second trauma deepened the community's fear and distrust. Johannine evangelists were now not only socially dislocated and alienated. They were also subjected to the possibility of being "snatched away" out of life (cf. 10:28f.; 15:18). It is here that we may see what Wayne Meeks has suggestively termed a harmonic reinforcement between social experience and christology.[168] Expelled from the synagogue, the Johannine community was bound to search for a mature interpretation of the expulsion, and that search led it to new christological formulations. The logos hymn, for example, is probably to be assigned to this middle period, and its wording may very well reflect the rude awakening of the twin traumas:

The Messiah came to his own world,
and his own people did *not* receive him.[169]

---

[167]*Ibid.*, chp. 3. Note furthermore the use of the verb t' ' in the Syriac text of Clementine Recognitions i, 62.1; W. Frankenberg, *Die syrischen Clementinen mit griechischen Paralleltext*. The passage is discussed in some detail in Chapter 2 of the present volume.

[168]Wayne A. Meeks, *The Man From Heaven in Johannine Sectarianism*, in *JBL* 91 (1972) 44-72, especially p. 71. A similar point is made by David E. Aune, *The Cultic Setting of Realized Eschatology in Early Christianity* (note 137 above). Aune unfortunately takes the additional step, however, of repeatedly using expressions which suggest that the flow was unidirectional: *from* social experience *to* christology. For example, "The Johannine Jesus was relevant for the faith and life of the community primarily because he was the personification and embodiment of the religious needs, values and aspirations of the community projected onto and superimposed over the historical Jesus" (p. 101). Later on the same page: ". . . the Johannine Jesus is in reality a reflection of the salvific needs and ideals of the community. . . ." One can easily imagine the fourth evangelist shuddering at such statements. Recall John 1:18, 3:13, 3:31-36, 6:44, etc.

[169]The interpretation of John 1:11 is one of those points at which a hermeneutical rule attributed orally by E. Käsemann to W. Bauer is of

The *heilsgeschichtlich* pattern of thought presupposed in the earlier christological trajectory from traditional expectations to their fulfillment in Jesus is now being significantly altered by the dualistic, above/below pattern.

To be sure, the Messiah is none other than the eternal sophia-logos through whom God created all that is; yet after the two major traumas, the community began to perceive that he came to his own world/synagogue as the stranger from above.[170] This perception *may* be reflected, moreover, in certain aspects of the Gospel's theological geography. If Judea is the Messiah's "native land," the locus of those who were originally "his own," and the place where his teaching had to be given, then there may be considerable significance in the indications that it was impossible for Jesus to "remain" there. That is to say, the Johannine community, having found it impossible to remain in the synagogue, may have perceived a prefiguring of that development in the geography of the Messiah's story.[171] In any case, in the middle period the community began to take *onto itself* with increasing intensity the characteristics of the stranger from above.[172] Socially, having been excommunicated and having subsequently experienced persecution to the death, they no longer find their

---

crucial importance: Before one inquires into the author's intention, he must ask how the first readers are likely to have understood the text. In light of the history of the Johannine community (not to mention the history of other communities as reflected in Mark 12:1-12 and Romans 9:1ff.), one may be virtually certain that the first readers and hearers understood John 1:11 as a reference to contemporary Jewish unbelief. The author of that verse took no steps to exclude this obvious interpretation. It follows that he probably intended it. (We may also note that he did not balance his reference to Jewish unbelief with a reference to the Gentile mission, as was done by the traditioners behind Mark 12:1-12, Luke 14:15-24, etc.)

[170] Again I have borrowed a note from the uncommonly perceptive article by Wayne A. Meeks, "The Man from Heaven". Cf. also E. Käsemann, *The Testament of Jesus*, p. 22: ". . . the stranger from the world above. . . ."

[171] The interpretation of John 4:44 is notoriously difficult. See R. E. Brown, *John, ad loc,* and contrast R. T. Fortna, "Theological Use of Locale in the Fourth Gospel," in *Anglican Theological Review* Suppl. Series 3 (1974) 95-112.

[172] Again cf. both Meeks and Aune as cited above in note 168.

origin and their intelligible point of departure in the synagogue and in its traditions. On the contrary, they, like their Christ, become people who are not "of the world" and who are for that reason hated by the world. In this process they cease, in fact, to be *Christian Jews* and become instead *Jewish Christians*. To express it theologically, they cease even to be "Jews" and become instead—like Nathanael—"truly Israelites" who now constitute the *new* "his own" because the stranger has come from above and has chosen them out of the world/synagogue.

III. THE LATE PERIOD

Movement Toward Firm Social and Theological Configurations

The history of the traditions and of the literary activity proper to the late period brings us not only to further homilies, but also to the climactic writing of the fully Johannine Gospel in its first and second editions.[173] The period also finds the Johannine community forming its own theology and its own identity not only vis-à-vis the parent synagogue, but also in relation to other Christian groups in its setting.[174] The period is, thus, extraordinarily rich and complex, and could easily form in its own right the subject for several essays. Because of the present need for brevity, I shall concentrate attention in the remaining space on three expressions, the first of which reaches back into the middle period, and the other two of which appear to be significantly revealing of developments during this late period. The three expressions are:

1. the disciples of Moses (9:28);
2. the Jews who had believed in him (8:31);
3. the other sheep (10:16).

---

[173] Cf. the five-stage analysis made by R. E. Brown as cited above in note 136. Contrary to Lindars' own opinion I find his analysis of two major editions to be quite harmonious with the hypothesis of a signs source/Gospel: B. Lindars, *The Gospel of John*, pp. 46ff.

[174] Cf. R. E. Brown, "Other Sheep Not of This Fold: The Johannine Perspective on Christian Diversity in the Late First Century," *JBL* 97 (1978) 5-22.

1. The Disciples of Moses

One scarcely needs to emphasize the importance of the term "disciples" for our attempts to discern the community behind the Gospel. In fact, not only significant aspects of the community's life in general, but also glimpses of the *history* of the community are revealed in the ways in which this term is employed in the various strata.

In the earliest evangelistic sermons and in the signs Gospel, where the term seems to have been employed a number of times, the word "disciples" was apparently used in only two formulations: "disciples of John" and "disciples of Jesus." Moreover, the role of the disciples of John was quite clear. They were on stage, so to speak, in order to become disciples of Jesus in order to exemplify the movement which persons experience by *becoming* disciples of Jesus. That movement was characterized, as we have already seen, by simple and largely unquestioned continuity. Jesus was the prophet-Messiah foretold by Moses (1:45). Hence, while one who became a disciple of Jesus would cease actively to be a disciple of the Baptist, he would nevertheless move along a line which stands in unquestioned continuity with the witness and writings of Moses. Far from abandoning Moses, he would simply have attached himself to the one of whom Moses wrote.

In the middle period, as we have noted, that simple and unquestioned *heilsgeschichtlich* continuity was decisively shattered. In the face of numerous conversions within the synagogue, the Jewish authorities felt that they had to take drastic steps. Quite naturally, these repressive steps had ultimately to be based on Moses, and that fact led the authorities to combine their use of the *Birkath ha-Minim* with a midrashic attack. This combination, in turn, led to a startlingly new "either . . . or." In the excommunication drama of John 9, when the Jews are asked by the formerly blind man whether they wish to become disciples of Jesus, they answer angrily,

You are his disciple; but we are disciples of Moses (9:28).

In the middle period in which this drama was formulated, the authorities obviously laid down a new dictum. *Either* one is a loyal disciple of Moses, remaining true to the ancient Jewish community, *or* one has become a disciple of Jesus, thereby ceasing to be a disciple of Moses.

To the original, inner-synagogue group of Christian Jews, who knew Jesus to be the one of whom Moses wrote, this formulation must have come as a great shock. It is clear, however, that before long the shock would have not only to be endured, but also to be interpreted. What is the true meaning of this newly formulated "either . . . or"?

It is quite clear that the members of the original group of Christian Jews did not all perceive the new "either . . . or" in the same way, and correspondingly their experiences of it and the stances they developed toward it were rather varied. It hardly needs to be said once again that the Johannine community experienced it in the form of excommunication. It is equally clear, as I have also said earlier, that the same was not true of all members of the original messianic group. Some managed to remain within the bosom of the synagogue by presenting themselves in public as disciples of Moses and children of Abraham, while considering themselves in private to be *also* disciples of Jesus. A Johannine logion probably to be assigned to the middle period refers to these people as persons who have believed in Jesus, but who, in order to avoid excommunication, refused to make a public confession of that belief (12:42). And in another logion (6:66) one hears similarly that many of the original messianic group "turned back" and did not keep the kind of social company which would make their confession public. Perhaps we may refer to these people as believing Jews who wish to remain Christian Jews, but who are determined to do so in secret. Such a suggestion leads us to take up the next expression.

2. The Jews Who Had Believed in Him

With this expression we return to the late period, for it occurs in a homily (8:31ff.) which was probably composed in that period. The modern critical judgment to delete the words "the Jews who had believed in him" as a gloss[175] has no manuscript support, and may be in fact one of the numerous judgments which reflect our generally inadequate knowledge of the varieties of Christian Jews and Jewish Christians in the period after 70 A.D.

Bearing in mind a pregnant suggestion made in 1932 by Schwartz to the effect that the Johannine polemic often becomes understandable as a reaction against some form of Jewish Christianity, we may proceed not by deleting the troublesome phrase, but by inquiring for the precise identity of these Jews who have for some time believed in Jesus.[176]

It is a distinct service of C. H. Dodd to have made a strong case for the thesis that the evangelist refers here to Jewish Christians of his own time,[177] but Dodd's thesis needs also to be strengthened and in various regards corrected.[178]

From the description of Jesus' interlocutors, and from the mouths of the interlocutors themselves, there are numerous indications that they represent, in fact, not Jewish Christians, but rather Christian Jews who wish proudly to hold some sort of dual allegiance. Let me mention five observations:

1. One must reiterate the straightforward identification in verse 31 which finds, as Dodd showed, significant parallels in instances in Acts where the perfect participle of "to believe"

---

[175] After incorrectly crediting Dodd and Brown with this view, Lindars states it as his own: *The Gospel of John, ad loc.*, and *Behind the Fourth Gospel*, p. 80. Dodd's argument was constructed by accepting the text as it stands (see note 177 below); Brown suggested that verse 31 and the troublesome phrase in verse 32 be allotted to the final redactor: *John, ad loc.*

[176] E. Schwartz, "Unzeitgemässe Beobachtungen zu den Clementinen", in *ZNW* 31 (1932) 191.

[177] C. H. Dodd, "A l'arrière-plan d'un dialogue johannique", in *Revue d'histoire et de philosophie religieuses*, 37 (1957) 5-17; *Behind a Johannine Dialogue*, in *More New Testament Studies* (Manchester, 1968), pp. 41-57.

[178] See particularly Rudolf Schnackenburg, *Das Johannesevangelium*, II. Teil, Freiburg, 1971, pp. 258ff; Bruce Schein, *Our Father Abraham*, Yale Dissertation, Ann Arbor, Michigan (microfilm), 1972; Gilbert Bartholomew, *An Early Christian Sermon-Drama: John 8:31-59*, Columbia University-Union Theological Seminary Dissertation, Ann Arbor, Michigan (microfilm), 1974.

emerges. One of these has already commanded our attention: "those among the Jews who had believed" (21:20). Note, moreover, the syntax of the expression in John 8:31; *here* the participle "those who had believed" is adjectival, merely modifying the noun "the Jews."

2. These people characterize themselves as "descendants of Abraham" (vv. 33 and 39). While this designation could be claimed by any Jew, the group's identification in verse 31 as "the Jews who had believed in him" should remind us of the evidence in Paul's letters suggesting that the expression "descendants of Abraham" was used as a self-designation among early Christian Jews (2 Cor. 11:22; cf. Gal. 3:6-29).[179]

3. It follows easily that in John 8 this self-designation may have had at least two points of reference. The interlocutors could have linked their existence as Christians with being "descendants of Abraham," but *antecedently* they are descendants of Abraham precisely because they are Jews. Perhaps they would be happy to call themselves "descendants of Abraham" particularly because it could be a phrase with ambiguity. To the ears of the Jewish authorities it would mean only that those who use it are loyal Jews, while to the users themselves it could also be a secret expression of their Christian inclinations. In any case, when the issue of freedom arises, they proudly call on their blood descendance from Abraham to show that they have never been enslaved. Impressed as they are with Jesus' word (v. 30), they do not need *it* to make them free.

4. One notes also their proud and indeed polemical claim to the inheritance of monotheism. *Others* may move in the direction of a christology which approaches ditheism, a form of apostasy from Adonai, symbolized as being born of fornication or adultery.[180] *They* emphatically remain monotheists, as the syntax of verse 41b makes clear: "We have *one* father: God."

5. But we may note that, at least initially, it appears to be only the high christology, and only the absolute claims for Christ,

---

[179] See the pertinent discussion in the work of B. Schein as cited in the preceding note.

[180] Note the comments to John 8:41 made by R. E. Brown, *John, ad loc.*

which are offensive to these Christian Jews. For them Jesus may be allowed to stand *within Heilsgeschichte*, within the prophetic line, and while that means that he is not greater than Abraham and the prophets (v. 53), it nevertheless means that he is to be affirmed *along with them*. At some point these Christian Jews have desired to take their stand both on their Jewish descent and on Jesus' word.

This intention to hold a dual allegiance seems, moreover, to be clearly reflected in the polemic formulated by the Johannine preacher responsible for this homily. Formal analysis of his sermon shows that both of the first two major sections begin with a highly emphatic reference to Jesus' word (vv. 31 and 37).

Verse 31

The expression "in my word" not only employs the emphatic pronoun, but also stands syntactically in the emphatic position. Given the context, one might paraphrase the protasis:

If you take a constant stand absolutely in *my* word. . . .

And the apodosis significantly employs the adverb "truly" which is nowhere else linked with the construction "to be disciples." Thus, a further paraphrase:

You Jews who have believed in me! If you take a constant stand absolutely in *my* word, you are *truly* my disciples. . . .

What would seem to be the alternative? Either to take one's stand in the word of someone else—an interpretation which would conflict with verse 30—or to attempt, as I have just suggested, to stand simultaneously and more or less equally in the words of Jesus and in the words of another teacher. In that case, implies the preacher, one is not *truly* a disciple of Jesus.

It is here, indeed, that we catch a clear glimpse of the community's considered interpretation—in the late period—of the "either . . . or" formulated some time earlier by the Jewish authorities. Shocked as the Johannine community must initially have been to hear it said that one must be either a disciple of Moses or a disciple of Jesus, they necessarily had eventually to interpret that formulation not only in the light of their own heritage from ancient Israel, but also in the light of the behavior of their former colleagues who, in view of the threat of excommunication, tried secretly to maintain a dual allegiance. Given this latter development, the Johannine community perceived that *Jesus' word* had to be granted absolute priority, and that only on the basis of his word could one understand the witness borne to him by the Fathers. Thus it was that the Johannine preacher heard Jesus declare with divine solemnity:

Before Abraham was I am (8:58).

In place of the *heilsgeschichtlich* christology "from behind,"[181] we now find the full emergence of the dualistic christology "from above." Indeed, the initially shocking "either . . . or," formulated so polemically by the Jewish authorities, is now turned back on them and on the so-called Christian Jews by being interpreted quite radically in dualistic terms.

From the point of view of the Johannine community it is quite insufficient to say that one is either a disciple of Moses or a disciple of Jesus. Rather one is *either* from above—from God—*or* one is from below—from the devil.

Verse 37

Here the believing Jews, the "descendants of Abraham," are said to have taken the wrong path as a result of the fact that "my word finds no room among you." It is in this second section that "the Jews who had believed in him" prove to be fundamentally undistinguishable from "the Jews" in general, in preparation for verse 48 where they are, in fact, so identified. But *ex hypothesi*

---

[181] For this suggestive expression I am indebted to Dr. Adriaan Krijger, a pastor-theologian in The Hague and one of my stimulating colleagues during an unforgettable period at the Ecumenical Institute for Advanced Theological Studies in Jerusalem, 1974-75.

this means only that, from the point of view of the separated Johannine community, the attempt on the part of these secret believers, these so-called Christian Jews, to straddle the fence is wholly unsuccessful; their attempt constitutes, in fact, what Wayne Meeks has correctly characterized as a diabolic lie.[182] Because they do not take their stand absolutely in the word of Jesus, they only prove that his word does not have any place at all among them, and that in the final analysis they are not "the Jews who had believed in him," but merely "the Jews."

Theologically it is therefore no cause for surprise to the Johannine community when these former colleagues of theirs turn out to be horribly instrumental in the martyrdom of some of the Johannine evangelists, presumably by functioning as informers intent on preserving monotheism (vv. 37, 40, 44, 59).

In the present context I cannot offer further analysis. I can only summarize by suggesting that together with 2:23ff., 11:46 and 12:42, the homily of 8:31ff. forms one of several references to a group whose distinct identity emerged in the late period, and whom, following the syntax of 8:31, we ought carefully to characterize not as Jewish Christians, but rather as Christian Jews. Indeed, in light of the foregoing analysis, one might suggest a final paraphrase of 8:31 as follows:

> Jesus then said to those who understood themselves to be Christian Jews: If you take a constant stand absolutely in my word, you will be genuinely liberated as Jewish Christians.

The point is that with the emergence in the late period of this group of Christian Jews, the social configuration in which the Johannine community finds itself is not completely grasped when one speaks of the polarity vis-à-vis the parent synagogue. The social configuration is more complex; it is at least trilateral, involving first the parent synagogue, second the group of secretly Christian Jews who have been able to remain within the synagogue, and third the separated Johannine community, a

---

[182]Wayne A. Meeks, "The Man From Heaven" (note 168), p. 69.

community made up almost wholly of Jewish Christians (also a few Samaritan Christians[183]).

Our last question is whether even this trilateral configuration is adequate as a representation of the social complexity of the late period. And the posing of this question leads us finally to the expression in 10:16.

3. *The Other Sheep*

Aside from Chapter 10 the word "sheep" occurs in the Fourth Gospel only four times—twice in the pericope of the temple cleansing and twice in Chapter 21. In Chapter 10 it occurs no less than fifteen times, and it is obviously used in ways which are quite revealing as regards the history of the Johannine community.

Notice first that the word is distributed throughout most of Chapter 10. In the parables at the opening of the chapter (vv. 1-5) the word "sheep" appears five times, and in the explanations which follow these parables the word appears another seven times. Finally, leaving aside verse 16 for the moment, the word emerges twice more in verses 26 and 27. In all fourteen instances the primary reference is quite clear. The sheep stand in the first instance for the Johannine community.

a. It is they who hear the voice of the Good Shepherd and who follow him; and it is they whom he calls by name.

b. It is they who flee from alternative shepherds and who refuse to listen to them because they do not recognize the voices of those shepherds.

c. It is they whose lives are threatened by the wolf when he comes to snatch them away and to scatter them; and it is they who, when they are thus endangered, are abandoned by the hired hand, who chooses to avoid the possibility of his own death by leaving the community behind.

d. And, finally, it is they who receive the absolute assurance

---

[183] On the whole I find convincing the interpretation of John 4:10-15 offered by H. Leroy, *Rätsel und Missverständnis*, pp. 88-99. See the review by R. E. Brown, in *Biblica* 51 (1970) 152-154.

from the Good Shepherd that, however threatened they may be, no one will ever be able actually to snatch them out of his hand or out of the hand of his Father.

I should not want to claim that it is the only viable interpretation, but in light of the history of the Johannine community which has emerged in the foregoing analyses, I am led at least to suggest that the parables and their interpretations must be taken together as an allegory, in the reading of which those who were initiates by virtue of having shared a common history—that is to say, the members of the Johannine community—would easily recognize the following representations:

1. the sheep   stand for the Johannine community.

2. strangers   stand for the Jewish authorities ("the
   thieves   Pharisees" of Chapter 9) who in fact kill, de-
   robbers   stroy, snatch away, and scatter the Johan-
   the wolf   nine community.

3. hireling   may stand for the secretly believing "rulers"
               who avoid the possibility of their own execu-
               tion by abandoning the Johannine commu-
               nity when it is endangered.

4. the Good   stands for Jesus, as he is active through
   Shepherd   Johannine evangelists who are prepared to
               face martyrdom for the community and who
               both receive and transmit this absolute as-
               surance that, however threatening the Jewish
               authorities may become, they shall never be
               able to snatch any member of the community
               out of the hands of Jesus and of the Father.

We come now to verse 16. If we accept the wording of papyrus 66, the text reads:

And I have other sheep, that are not of this fold.
I must gather them also,

and they will heed my voice,
and there will be one flock, one shepherd.

The problems are numerous. In the present setting we can consider only one: Who are the "other sheep"?

The dominant answer, given by Bultmann, Barrett, Schnackenburg, Brown, and Lindars, is to identify the "other sheep" as Gentiles who will believe as a result of the Gentile mission.[184] In light of the common opinion of these five exegetes the least one can say is that this interpretation may be correct.

There are, however, certain factors which indicate a different interpretation, as Hans Joachim Schoeps suggested a number of years ago, and as H. B. Kossen has more recently suggested, apparently without being influenced by the views of Schoeps.[185] Could it be that the other sheep are Jewish Christians belonging to conventicles known to but separate from the Johannine community? Let us return to the text, taking it one clause at a time. Several points seem either quite clear or at least probable:

1.   "I have other sheep"

These other sheep already exist. The reader or hearer is simply informed of their existence.

2.   "that are not of this fold"

How will the Johannine community have understood "this fold"? Up to this point in Chapter 10 every reference to sheep has been a reference to them. It is their community, therefore, which is "this fold."

3.   "I must gather (or lead) them also"

We cannot be sure of the text, of course, but I think the motif of unification which is so strong in the last clause of the

---

[184]See the commentaries of these scholars, *ad loc.*

[185]H. J. Schoeps, *Jewish Christianity*, p. 131; H. B. Kossen, "Who Were the Greeks of John XII 20?", in *Studies in John* (J. N. Sevenster Festschrift, Leiden, 1970), pp. 97-110, especially pp. 107f. Cf. also M. L. Appold, *The Oneness Motif in the Fourth Gospel* (Tübingen, 1976), pp. 11, 262ff.

verse provides weighty support for the reading of P66.[186]
One may also note that P66 preserved, almost alone, the
correct reading in John 7:52. I shall return to the interpretation of this clause.

4.   "and they will heed my voice,
       and there will be one flock, one shepherd."

The prophecies with which the verse closes strongly
emphasize unification. The gathering of the "other sheep"
will lead to there being one flock under one shepherd.

We may take our bearings, I think, from this emphatic
prophecy of unification, which is obviously the goal of the entire
logion. And that leads us, as regards the identity of the other
sheep, to return to the clause, "I must gather them also."

Why, we may ask, should there be such an emphasis on
unification, and why for the sake of the unification must the other
sheep be *gathered*?

The obvious answer is that they have been scattered. Are
there indications that such is, in fact, the case?

The posing of this question takes us first to John 11:52, for
that verse—the ironic prophecy of Caiaphas—is very closely
bound to 10:16 by these same two motifs: unification, and the
gathering which leads to unification. The important point to
notice is that 11:52 also contains the word "scatter abroad" in the
expression "the children of God who are scattered abroad." If one
takes seriously *all* of the elements of 11:52 and their deep roots in
both the traumas and the hopes of exilic and post-exilic Judaism,
he may be led to the following interpretation: The high priest of all
Jews is made to prophesy that Jesus will die in behalf of the
Jewish nation both in its homeland and in its scattering, its dispersion.[187]

Now, returning to John 10, we note, interestingly enough,

---

[186] For the contrary judgment see R. Schnackenburg, *Das Johannesevangelium*, *ad loc.*; by implication W. A. Meeks accepted the reading of P66: *The Prophet-King*, p. 318n: ". . . the reference in 10:16 about
'other sheep' which must be 'gathered'. . . ."

[187] Interpretative opinion on John 11:52 is sharply divided. W. C.
van Unnik, J. A. T. Robinson, A. F. J. Klijn, and L. van Hartingsveld

the presence of the verb "scatter" in verse 12. In the picture of the wolf the Johannine community is reminded that the Jewish authorities scatter those who are the sheep of the Good Shepherd. To what, precisely, does this refer? In all probability it is a Johannine *reinterpretation* of the widespread and classic motif of Jewish dispersion. *In the experience of the Johannine community* the scattering of the sheep occurred when the *Birkath ha-Minim* was imposed in their city.

It seems probable, however, that under Jamnian authority the *Birkath ha-Minim* was in fact introduced over a wide geographical area.[188] It follows, I think, that the portrait of the "other sheep" is drawn in such a way as to refer *primarily* to other Jewish Christians who, like those of the Johannine community, have been *scattered* from their parent synagogues by experiencing excommunication. It is, then, a vision of the Johannine community that the day will come when all of the conventicles of scattered Jewish Christians will be gathered into one flock under the one Good Shepherd.

If these interpretative suggestions have some merit, we may

----

read the verse very much as I have suggested (bibliographical data given on p. 106 of the article by H. B. Kossen cited above in note 185). C. K Barrett, R. Schnackenburg, and R. E. Brown, on the other hand, represent commentators who argue for a reference to the Gentile mission. It seems to me that Schnackenburg and Brown do not read the verse in its own right, but rather interpret it against its grain because they have already judged 10:16 to contain a reference to the Gentile mission.

[188]The *Birkath ha-Minim* was one of the "ordinances" issued from Jamnia. On the ordinances in general see J. Neusner, *A Life of Rabban Yohanan Ben Zakkai* (Leiden, 1962), pp. 155ff.; Neusner, *Development of a Legend* (Leiden, 1970), pp. 206ff.; J. Goldin, "The Period of the Talmud" in Vol. 1 of L. Finkelstein, ed., *The Jews: Their History, Culture, and Religion* (New York, 1949). To make decisions regarding the synagogue liturgy was one of the major prerogatives claimed by the Jamnia academy in its attempt to supply stability and cohesiveness in the post-war period, and Berakoth 28b (cf. j Berakoth 8a) explicitly identifies the *Birkath ha-Minim* as one of the stabilizing ordinances. It is true that the claims to authority made by the Jamnia academy were resented in some quarters, but the specific ordinances known to us seem generally to have been recognized. See also the discussion in Martyn, *History and Theology*, pp. 32-41, and Justin, *Dialogue*, 16 and 17, cf. Eusebius, *H. E.* iv, 18, 7.

conclude this rather brief and fragmentary historical *sketch* by suggesting that by the time the Fourth Gospel itself was written, the social and theological configuration in which the Johannine community found itself was in fact not trilateral but rather at least quadrilateral:

1. We see first, of course, the Johannine community.

2. We see, second, that the Johannine community is sharply differentiated from the parent synagogue, to the point, in fact, of being polarized with a breakdown in communication—John 3:11 and 15:18ff. The synagogue and its "Jews" form the clearest representation of the alien "world."

3. We see, third, that the community is, if anything, even more sharply differentiated and alienated from a group of so-called Christian Jews who remain within the synagogue—John 8:31ff. and 12:42—and who are therefore "of this world."

4. But we see also, fourth, that the Johannine community is aware of the existence of other communities of Jewish Christians who have also suffered excommunication and with whom there is the hope of unification.[189]

One final word. To most interpreters, John 7:35 and 12:20 are clear references to Greeks who will come to believe via the Gentile mission;[190] similarly the title accorded to Jesus by the Samaritans—Savior of the world—is thought to indicate a vision of universality; and in any case there can be no doubt that the picture of Peter in Chapter 21 as shepherd and (Roman?) martyr—to say nothing of data in the Johannine epistles pertinent to the development of "early Catholicism"—indicates a relationship with the emerging "great Church" which lives on the frontier of the Gentile mission. It remains to be said, however, that if the quadrilateral picture of social and theological relationships which I have just sketched is accurate, and if the earlier glimpses I have offered are generally valid, then the history of the Johannine

---

[189]Concerning the number of groups in the Johannine purview see also R. E. Brown, "Other Sheep" (note 174 above).

[190]See, as examples, R. Schnackenburg, *Das Johannesevangelium*, II. Teil, *ad loc.*; R. E. Brown, *John*, pp. lxxvii f. and *ad loc.*

community from its origin through the period of its life in which the Fourth Gospel was composed forms to no small extent a chapter in the history of *Jewish* Christianity.[191]

---

[191] Unfortunately the learned book by O. Cullmann, *Der johanneische Kreis* (Tübingen, 1975), came into my hands too late to be used in the writing of this chapter. As always, I find numerous aspects of Cullmann's work to be helpfully instructive. Were there time and space here, I should like especially to pursue the questions which arise from a comparison of the Johannine community with the Jewish-Christian communities reflected in discrete strata of the Pseudo-Clementines. Cf. Cullmann, *op. cit.*, pp. 62-66 and Chapter 2 of the present volume.

APPENDIX

The Pseudo-Clementine Recognitions
Book One, Chapters 33-71

The Pseudo-Clementines were originally written in Greek, and for the *Homilies* we have good Greek manuscripts and a critically edited text: B. Rehm, *Die Pseudoklementinen I* (Homilien), *GCS* 42 (Berlin, 1953). In the case of the *Recognitions* we are dependent on (a) a Latin translation made in the early fifth century by Rufinus, who surely thought he was translating a Greek text originally written by Clement of Rome, and (b) a Syriac translation of Books 1-4 also made from a Greek text and stemming from the same general period. To facilitate the reader's grasp of the arguments presented in Chapter 2 of the present volume I provide here the standard English translation of *Recognitions* 1, 33-71. It was made for the *Ante-Nicene Fathers* by Thomas Smith from the Latin text available to him in the 1880's, and for a general comprehension of the text it is quite adequate.

The scholar who wishes to pursue some points in detail will be able to work with the critical edition of the Latin text by B. Rehm, *Die Pseudoklementinen II* (Rekognitionen in Rufins Übersetzung), *GCS* 51 (Berlin, 1956) and to consult the Syriac given in W. Frankenburg, *Die syrischen Clementinen mit griechischen Paralleltext* (Berlin, 1937). Frankenburg's rendering of the Syriac into Greek, while a genuine aid, is unreliable at points. See also the text-critical and interpretative comments presented in G. Strecker, *Judenchristentum*, 221-254.

CHAP. 33 — ABRAHAM: HIS POSTERITY.

"Therefore Abraham, when he was desirous to learn the 1
causes of things, and was intently pondering upon what had been
told him, the true Prophet appeared to him, who alone knows the
hearts and purpose of men, and disclosed to him all things which 2
he desired. He taught him the knowledge of the Divinity; intimated the origin of the world, and likewise its end; showed him
the immortality of the soul, and the manner of life which was
pleasing to God; declared also the resurrection of the dead, the
future judgment, the reward of the good, the punishment of the
evil, — all to be regulated by righteous judgment; and having
given him all this information plainly and sufficiently, He departed again to the invisible abodes. But while Abraham was still 3
in ignorance, as we said to you before, two sons were born to
him, of whom the one was called Ismael, and the other Helies-
dros. From the one are descended the barbarous nations, from
the other the people of the Persians, some of whom have adopted 4
the manner of living and the institutions of their neighbours, the
Brachmans. Others settled in Arabia, of whose posterity some
also have spread into Egypt. From them some of the Indians and 5
of the Egyptians have learned to be circumcised, and to be of
purer observance than others, although in process of time most of
them have turned to impiety what was the proof and sign of
purity.

CHAP. 34 — THE ISRAELITES IN EGYPT.

"Nevertheless, as he had got these two sons during the time 1
while he still lived in ignorance of things, having received the
knowledge of God, he asked of the Righteous One that he might
merit to have offspring by Sarah, who was his lawful wife, though
she was barren. She obtained a son, whom he named Isaac, from 2
whom came Jacob, and from him the twelve patriarchs, and from
these twelve seventy-two. These, when famine befell, came into 3
Egypt with all their family; and in the course of four hundred

years, being multiplied by the blessing and promise of God, they
4   were afflicted by the Egyptians. And when they were afflicted the
true Prophet appeared to Moses, and struck the Egyptians with
ten plagues, when they refused to let the Hebrew people depart
from them, and return to their native land; and he brought the
5   people of God out of Egypt. But those of the Egyptians who
survived the plagues, being infected with the animosity of their
6   king, pursued after the Hebrews. And when they had overtaken
them at the sea-shore, and thought to destroy and exterminate
them all, Moses, pouring out prayer to God, divided the sea into
two parts, so that the water was held on the right hand and on the
left as if it had been frozen, and the people of God passed as over
a dry road; but the Egyptians who were pursuing them, rashly
7   entering, were drowned. For when the last of the Hebrews came
out, the last of the Egyptians went down into the sea; and
straightway the waters of the sea, which by his command were
held bound as with frost, were loosed by his command who had
bound them, and recovering their natural freedom, inflicted
punishment on the wicked nation.

CHAP. 35—THE EXODUS.

1   "After this, Moses, by the command of God, whose providence is over all, led out the people of the Hebrews into the
wilderness; and, leaving the shortest road which leads from
Egypt to Judaea, he led the people through long windings of the
wilderness, that, by the discipline of forty years, the novelty of a
changed manner of life might root out the evils which had clung to
them by a long-continued familiarity with the customs of the
2   Egyptians. Meantime they came to Mount Sinai, and thence the
law was given to them with voices and sights from heaven, written in ten precepts, of which the first and greatest was that they
should worship God Himself alone, and not make to themselves
3   any appearance or form to worship. But when Moses had gone up
to the mount, and was staying there forty days, the people, although they had seen Egypt struck with the ten plagues, and the

sea parted and passed over by them on foot, manna also given to them from heaven for bread, and drink supplied to them out of the rock that followed them, which kind of food was turned into whatever taste any one desired; and although, being placed under 4 the torrid region of heaven, they were shaded by a cloud in the day-time, that they might not be scorched by the heat, and by night were enlightened by a pillar of fire, lest the horror of dark-ness should be added to the wasteness of the wilderness;—those 5 very people, I say, when Moses stayed in the mount, made and worshipped a golden calf's head, after the fashion of Apis, whom they had seen worshipped in Egypt; and after so many and so great marvels which they had seen, were unable to cleanse and wash out from themselves the defilements of old habit. On this 6 account, leaving the short road which leads from Egypt to Judaea, Moses conducted them by an immense circuit of the des-ert, if haply he might be able, as we mentioned before, to shake off the evils of old habit by the change of a new education.

CHAP. 36—ALLOWANCE OF SACRIFICE FOR A TIME.

"When meantime Moses, that faithful and wise steward, per- 1 ceived that the vice of sacrificing to idols had been deeply in-grained into the people from their association with the Egyptians, and that the root of this evil could not be extracted from them, he allowed them indeed to sacrifice, but permitted it to be done only to God, that by any means he might cut off one half of the deeply ingrained evil, leaving the other half to be corrected by another, and at a future time; by Him, namely, concerning whom he said himself, 'A prophet shall the Lord your God raise unto you, 2 whom ye shall hear even as myself, according to all things which He shall say to you. Whosoever shall not hear that prophet, his soul shall be cut off from his people.'

CHAP. 37 — THE HOLY PLACE.

1   "In addition to these things, he also appointed a place in
2   which alone it should be lawful to them to sacrifice to God. And
all this was arranged with this view, that when the fitting time
should come, and they should learn by means of the Prophet that
God desires mercy and not sacrifice, they might see Him who
should teach them that the place chosen of God, in which it was
suitable that victims should be offered to God, is his Wisdom; and
that on the other hand they might hear that this place, which
seemed chosen for a time, often harassed as it had been by hostile
invasions and plunderings, was at last to be wholly destroyed.
3   And in order to impress this upon them, even before the coming
of the true Prophet, who was to reject at once the sacrifices and
the place, it was often plundered by enemies and burnt with fire,
4   and the people carried into captivity among foreign nations, and
then brought back when they betook themselves to the mercy of
God; that by these things they might be taught that a people who
offer sacrifices are driven away and delivered up into the hands of
the enemy, but they who do mercy and righteousness are without
sacrifices freed from captivity, and restored to their native land.
5   But it fell out that very few understood this; for the greater
number, though they could perceive and observe these things, yet
were held by the irrational opinion of the vulgar: for right opinion
with liberty is the prerogative of a few.

CHAP. 38 — SINS OF THE ISRAELITES.

1   "Moses, then, having arranged these things, and having set
over the people one Auses to bring them to the land of their
fathers, himself by the command of the living God went up to a
2   certain mountain, and there died. Yet such was the manner of his
3   death, that till this day no one has found his burial-place. When,
therefore, the people reached their fathers' land, by the providence of God, at their first onset the inhabitants of wicked races
are routed, and they enter upon their paternal inheritance, which
4   was distributed among them by lot. For some time thereafter they
were ruled not by kings, but judges, and remained in a somewhat

peaceful condition. But when they sought for themselves tyrants 5 rather than kings, then also with regal ambition they erected a temple in the place which had been appointed to them for prayer; and thus, through a succession of wicked kings, the people fell away to greater and still greater impiety.

CHAP. 39—BAPTISM INSTITUTED IN PLACE OF SACRIFICES.

"But when the time began to draw near that what was want- 1 ing in the Mosaic institutions should be supplied, as we have said, and that the Prophet should appear, of whom he had foretold that He should warn them by the mercy of God to cease from sacrific- ing; lest haply they might suppose that on the cessation of sac- 2 rifice there was no remission of sins for them, He instituted bap- tism by water amongst them, in which they might be absolved from all their sins on the invocation of His name, and for the future, following a perfect life, might abide in immorality, being purified not by the blood of beasts, but by the purification of the Wisdom of God. Subsequently also an evident proof of this great 3 mystery is supplied *in the fact*, that every one who, believing in this Prophet who had been foretold by Moses, is baptized in His name, shall be kept unhurt from the destruction of war which impends over the unbelieving nation, and the place itself; but that those who do not believe shall be made exiles from their place and kingdom, that even against their will they may understand and obey the will of God.

CHAP. 40—ADVENT OF THE TRUE PROPHET.

"These things therefore having been forearranged, He who 1 was expected comes, bringing signs and miracles as His creden- tials by which He should be made manifest. But not even so did 2 the people believe, though they had been trained during so many ages to the belief of these things. And not only did they not believe, but they added blasphemy to unbelief, saying that He was a gluttonous man and a belly-slave, and that He was actuated by a demon, even He who had come for their salvation. To such 3 an extent does wickedness prevail by the agency of evil ones; so

that, but for the Wisdom of God assisting those who love the truth, almost all would have been involved in impious delusion.
4 Therefore He chose us twelve, the first who believed in Him, whom He named apostles; and afterwards other seventy-two most approved disciples, that, at least in this way recognising the pattern of Moses, the multitude might believe that this is He of whom Moses foretold, the Prophet that was to come.

CHAP. 41—REJECTION OF THE TRUE PROPHET.

1   "But some one perhaps may say that it is possible for any one to imitate a number; but what shall we say of the signs and miracles which He wrought? For Moses had wrought miracles and
2 cures in Egypt. He also of whom he foretold that He should rise up a prophet like unto himself, though He cured every sickness and infirmity among the people, wrought innumerable miracles, and preached eternal life, was hurried by wicked men to the
3 cross; which deed was, however, by His power turned to good. In short, while He was suffering, all the world suffered with Him; for the sun was darkened, the mountains were torn asunder, the graves were opened, the veil of the temple was rent, as in lamen-
4 tation for the destruction impending over the place. And yet, though all the world was moved, they themselves are not even now moved to the consideration of these so great things.

CHAP. 42—CALL OF THE GENTILES.

1   "But inasmuch as it was necessary that the Gentiles should be called into the room of those who remained unbelieving, so that the number might be filled up which had been shown to Abraham, the preaching of the blessed kingdom of God is sent
2 into all the world. On this account worldly spirits are disturbed, who always oppose those who are in quest of liberty, and who make use of the engines of error to destroy God's building; while those who press on to the glory of safety and liberty, being rendered braver by their resistance to these spirits, and by the toil of

great struggles against them, attain the crown of safety not
without the palm of victory. Meantime, when He had suffered, 3
and darkness had overwhelmed the world from the sixth even to
the ninth hour, as soon as the sun shone out again, and things
were returned to their usual course, even wicked men returned to
themselves and their former practices, their fear having abated.
For some of them, watching the place with all care, when they 4
could not prevent His rising again, said that He was a magician;
others pretended that He was stolen away.

CHAP. 43 — SUCCESS OF THE GOSPEL.

"Nevertheless, the truth everywhere prevailed; for, in proof 1
that these things were done by divine power, we who had been
very few became in the course of a few days, by the help of God,
far more than they. So that the priests at one time were afraid, lest
haply, by the providence of God, to their confusion, the whole of
the people should come over to our faith. Therefore they often
sent to us, and asked us to discourse to them concerning Jesus,
whether He were the Prophet whom Moses foretold, who is the
eternal Christ. For on this point only does there seem to be any 2
difference between us who believe in Jesus, and the unbelieving
Jews. But while they often made such requests to us, and we 3
sought for a fitting opportunity, a week of years was completed
from the passion of the Lord, the Church of the Lord which was
constituted in Jerusalem was most plentifully multiplied and
grew, being governed with most righteous ordinances by James,
who was ordained bishop in it by the Lord.

CHAP. 44 — CHALLENGE BY CAIAPHAS.

"But when we twelve apostles, on the day of the passover, 1
had come together with an immense multitude, and entered into
the church of the brethren, each one of us, at the request of
James, stated briefly, in the hearing of the people, what we had
done in every place. While this was going on, Caiaphas, the high 2

priest, sent priests to us, and asked us to come to him, that either we should prove to him that Jesus is the eternal Christ, or he to us that He is not, and that so all the people should agree upon the one faith or the other; and this he frequently entreated us to do.

3   But we often put it off, always seeking for a more convenient time."

4   Then I, Clement, answered to this: "I think that this very question, whether He is the Christ, is of great importance for the establishment of the faith; otherwise the high priest would not so frequently ask that he might either learn or teach concerning the Christ."

5   Then Peter: "You have answered rightly, O Clement; for as no one can see without eyes, nor hear without ears, nor smell without nostrils, nor taste without a tongue, nor handle anything without hands, so it is impossible, without the true Prophet, to know what is pleasing to God."

6   And I answered: "I have already learned from your instruction that this true prophet is the Christ; but I should wish to learn what *the Christ* means, or why He is so called, that a matter of so great importance may not be vague and uncertain to me."

CHAP. 45—THE TRUE PROPHET: WHY CALLED THE CHRIST.

1   Then Peter began to instruct me in this manner: "When God had made the world, as Lord of the universe, He appointed chiefs over the several creatures, over the trees even, and the mountains, and the fountains, and the rivers, and all things which He had made, as we have told you; for it were too long to mention

2   them one by one. He set, therefore, an angel as chief over the angels, a spirit over the spirits, a star over the stars, a demon over the demons, a bird over the birds, a beast over the beasts, a serpent over the serpents, a fish over the fishes, a man over men,

3   who is Christ Jesus. But He is called *Christ* by a certain excellent rite of religion; for as there are certain names common to kings, as Arsaces among the Persians, Caesar among the Romans, Pharaoh among the Egyptians, so among the Jews a king is called *Christ*.

And the reason of this appellation is this: Although indeed He was   4
the Son of God, and the beginning of all things, He became man;
Him first God anointed with oil which was taken from the wood of
the tree of life: from that anointing therefore He is called *Christ*.   5
Thence, moreover, He Himself also, according to the appoint-
ment of His Father, anoints with similar oil every one of the pious
when they come to His kingdom, for their refreshment after their
labours, as having got over the difficulties of the way; so that their
light may shine, and being filled with the Holy Spirit, they may be
endowed with immortality. But it occurs to me that I have suffi-   6
ciently explained to you the whole nature of that branch from
which that ointment is taken.

CHAP. 46 — ANOINTING.

"But now also I shall, by a very short representation, recall   1
you to the recollection of all these things. In the present life,   2
Aaron, the first high priest, was anointed with a composition of
chrism, which was made after the pattern of that spiritual ointment of which we have spoken before. He was prince of the
people, and as a king received first-fruits and tribute from the
people, man by man; and having undertaken the office of judging
the people, he judged of things clean and things unclean. But if   3
any one else was anointed with the same ointment, as deriving
virtue from it, he became either king, or prophet, or priest. If,   4
then, this temporal grace, compounded by men, had such efficacy, consider now how potent was that ointment extracted by
God from a branch of the tree of life, when that which was made
by men could confer so excellent dignities among men. For what   5
in the present age is more glorious than a prophet, more illustrious than a priest, more exalted than a king?"

CHAP. 47 — ADAM ANOINTED A PROPHET

To this I replied: "I remember, Peter, that you told me of the   1
first man that he was a prophet; but you did not say that he was   2

anointed. If then there be no prophet without anointing, how could the first man be a prophet, since he was not anointed?"

3 Then Peter, smiling, said: "If the first man prophesied, it is certain that he was also anointed. For although he who has recorded the law in his pages is silent as to his anointing, yet he has evi-

4 dently left us to understand these things. For as, if he had said that he was anointed, it would not be doubted that he was also a prophet, although it were not written in the law; so, since it is certain that he was a prophet, it is in like manner certain that he was also anointed, because without anointing he could not be a

5 prophet. But you should rather have said, If the chrism was compounded by Aaron, by the perfumer's art, how could the first man be anointed before Aaron's time, the arts of composition not yet

6 having been discovered?" Then I answered: "Do not misunderstand me, Peter; for I do not speak of that compounded ointment and temporal oil, but of that simple and eternal *ointment*, which you told me was made by God, after whose likeness you say that that other was compounded by men."

CHAP. 48 — THE TRUE PROPHET, A PRIEST.

1   Then Peter answered, with an appearance of indignation: "What! do you suppose, Clement, that all of us can know all

2 things before the time? But not to be drawn aside now from our proposed discourse, we shall at another time, when your progress is more manifest, explain these things more distinctly.

3   "Then, however, a priest or a prophet, being anointed with the compounded ointment, putting fire to the altar of God, was

4 held illustrious in all the world. But after Aaron, who was a priest, another is taken out of the waters. I do not speak of Moses, but of Him who, in the waters of baptism, was called by God His Son.

5 For it is Jesus who has put out, by the grace of baptism, that fire

6 which the priest kindled for sins; for, from the time when He appeared, the chrism has ceased, by which the priesthood or the prophetic or the kingly office was conferred.

CHAP. 49—TWO COMINGS OF CHRIST.

"His coming, therefore, was predicted by Moses, who deliv- 1
ered the law of God to men; but by another also before him, as I
have already informed you. He therefore intimated that He 2
should come, humble indeed in His first coming, but glorious in
His second. And the first, indeed, has been already accom- 3
plished; since He has come and taught, and He, the Judge of all,
has been judged and slain. But at His second coming He shall 4
come to judge, and shall indeed condemn the wicked, but shall
take the pious into a share and association with Himself in His
kingdom. Now the faith of His second coming depends upon His 5
first. For the prophets—especially Jacob and Moses—spoke of
the first, but some also of the second. But the excellency of 6
prophecy is chiefly shown in this, that the prophets spoke not of
things to come, according to the sequence of things; otherwise
they might seem merely as wise men to have conjectured what the
sequence of things pointed out.

CHAP. 50—HIS REJECTION BY THE JEWS.

"But what I say is this: It was to be expected that Christ 1
should be received by the Jews, to whom He came, and that they
should believe on Him who was expected for the salvation of the
people, according to the traditions of the fathers; but that the
Gentiles should be averse to Him, since neither promise nor announcement concerning Him had been made to them, and indeed
He had never been made known to them even by name. Yet the 2
prophets, contrary to the order and sequence of things, said that
He should be the expectation of the Gentiles, and not of the Jews.
And so it happened. For when He came, He was not at all ac- 3
knowledged by those who seemed to expect Him, in consequence
of the tradition of their ancestors; whereas those who had heard
nothing at all of Him, both believe that He has come, and hope
that He is to come. And thus in all things prophecy appears faith- 4
ful, which said that He was the expectation of the Gentiles. The 5

Jews, therefore, have erred concerning the first coming of the
6   Lord; and on this point only there is disagreement betwixt us and
them. For they themselves know and expect that Christ shall
come; but that He has come already in humility—even He who is
7   called Jesus—they do not know. And this is a great confirmation
of His coming, that all do not believe on Him.

CHAP. 51 —THE ONLY SAVIOUR.

1   "Him, therefore, has God appointed in the end of the world;
because it was impossible that the evils of men could be removed
by any other, provided that the nature of the human race were to
2   remain entire, i.e., the liberty of the will being preserved. This
condition, therefore, being preserved inviolate, He came to invite
to His kingdom all righteous ones, and those who have been
desirous to please Him. For these He has prepared unspeakable
good things, and the heavenly city Jerusalem, which shall shine
above the brightness of the sun, for the habitation of the saints.
3   But the unrighteous, and the wicked, and those who have de-
spised God, and have devoted the life given them to diverse wick-
ednesses, and have given to the practice of evil the time which
was given them for the work of righteousness, He shall hand over
4   to fitting and condign vengeance. But the rest of the things which
shall then be done, it is neither in the power of angels nor of men
to tell or to describe. This only it is enough for us to know, that
God shall confer upon the good an eternal possession of good
things."

CHAP. 52—THE SAINTS BEFORE CHRIST'S COMING.

1   When he had thus spoken, I answered: "If those shall enjoy
the kingdom of Christ, whom His coming shall find righteous,
shall then those be wholly deprived of the kingdom who have died
2   before His coming?" Then Peter says: "You compel me, O Clement, to touch upon things that are unspeakable. But so far as it is
3   allowed to declare them, I shall not shrink from doing so. Know

then that Christ, who was from the beginning, and always, was ever present with the pious, though secretly, through all their generations; expecially with those who waited for Him, to whom He frequently appeared. But the time was not yet that there 4 should be a resurrection of the bodies that were dissolved; but this seemed rather to be their reward from God, that whoever should be found righteous, should remain longer in the body; or, at least, as is clearly related in the writings of the law concerning 5 a certain righteous man, that God translated him. In like manner others were dealt with, who pleased His will, that, being translated to Paradise, they should be kept for the kingdom. But as to those who have not been able completely to fulfil the rule of righteousness, but have had some remnants of evil in their flesh, their bodies are indeed dissolved, but their souls are kept in good and blessed abodes, that at the resurrection of the dead, when they shall recover their own bodies, purified even by the dissolution, they may obtain an eternal inheritance in proportion to their good deeds. And therefore blessed are all those who shall attain 6 to the kingdom of Christ; for not only shall they escape the pains of hell, but shall also remain incorruptible, and shall be the first to see God the Father, and shall obtain the rank of honour among the first in the presence of God.

CHAP. 53 — ANIMOSITY OF THE JEWS.

"Wherefore there is not the least doubt concerning Christ; 1 and all the unbelieving Jews are stirred up with boundless rage against us, fearing lest haply He against whom they have sinned should be He. And their fear grows all the greater, because they 2 know that, as soon as they fixed Him on the cross, the whole world showed sympathy with Him; and that His body, although they guarded it with strict care, could nowhere be found; and that innumerable multitudes are attaching themselves to His faith. Whence they, together with the high priest Caiaphas, were com- 3 pelled to send to us again and again, that an inquiry might be instituted concerning the truth of His name. And when they were 4 constantly entreating that they might either learn or teach con-

cerning Jesus, whether He were the Christ, it seemed good to us
to go up into the temple, and in the presence of all the people to
bear witness concerning Him, and at the same time to charge the
5 Jews with many foolish things which they were doing. For the
people was now divided into many parties, ever since the days of
John the Baptist.

CHAP. 54—JEWISH SECTS.

1   "For when the rising of Christ was at hand for the abolition of
sacrifices, and for the bestowal of the grace of baptism, the
enemy, understanding from the predictions that the time was at
hand, wrought various schisms among the people, that, if haply it
might be possible to abolish the former sin, the latter fault might
2 be incorrigible. The first schism, therefore, was that of those who
were called Sadducees, which took their rise almost in the time of
John. These, as more righteous than others, began to separate
themselves from the assembly of the people, and to deny the
resurrection of the dead, and to assert that by an argument of
infidelity, saying that it was unworthy that God should be wor-
3 shipped, as it were, under the promise of a reward. The first
author of this opinion was Dositheus; the second was Simon.
4 Another schism is that of the Samaritans; for they deny the resurrection of the dead, and assert that God is not to be worshipped in
5 Jerusalem, but on Mount Gerizim. They indeed rightly, from the
predictions of Moses, expect the one true Prophet; but by the
wickedness of Dositheus they were hindered from believing that
6 Jesus is He whom they were expecting. The scribes also, and
7 Pharisees, are led away into another schism; but these, being
baptized by John, and holding the word of truth received from the
tradition of Moses as the key of the kingdom of heaven, have hid
8 it from the hearing of the people. Yea, some even of the disciples
of John, who seemed to be great ones, have separated themselves
from the people, and proclaimed their own master as the Christ.
9 But all these schisms have been prepared, that by means of them
the faith of Christ and baptism might be hindered.

CHAP. 55 — PUBLIC DISCUSSION.

"However, as we were proceeding to say, when the high 1
priest had often sent priests to ask us that we might discourse
with one another concerning Jesus; when it seemed a fit opportunity, and it pleased all the Church, we went up to the temple,
and, standing on the steps together with our faithful brethren, the 2
people kept perfect silence; and first the high priest began to
exhort the people that they should hear patiently and quietly, and
at the same time witness and judge of those things that were to be
spoken. Then, in the next place, exalting with many praises the 3
rite of sacrifice which had been bestowed by God upon the human
race for the remission of sins, he found fault with the baptism of
our Jesus, as having been recently brought in in opposition to the
sacrifices. But Matthew, meeting his propositions, showed 4
clearly, that whosoever shall not obtain the baptism of Jesus shall
not only be deprived of the kingdom of heaven, but shall not be
without peril at the resurrection of the dead, even though he be
fortified by the prerogative of a good life and an upright disposi-
tion. Having made these and such like statements, Matthew
stopped.

CHAP. 56 — SADDUCEES REFUTED.

"But the party of the Sadducees, who deny the resurrection 1
of the dead, were in a rage, so that one of them cried out from
amongst the people, saying that those greatly err who think that
the dead ever arise. In opposition to him, Andrew, my brother, 2
answering, declared that it is not an error, but the surest matter of
faith, that the dead rise, in accordance with the teaching of Him of
whom Moses foretold that He should come the true Prophet. 'Or 3
if,' says he, 'you do not think that this is He whom Moses
foretold, let this first be inquired into, so that when this is clearly
proved to be He, there may be no further doubt concerning the
things which He taught.' These, and many such like things, Andrew proclaimed, and then stopped.

CHAP. 57—SAMARITAN REFUTED.

1   "But a certain Samaritan, speaking against the people and against God, and asserting that neither are the dead to rise, nor is that worship of God to be maintained which is in Jerusalem, but that Mount Gerizim is to be reverenced, added also this in opposition to us, that our Jesus was not He whom Moses foretold as a
2   Prophet to come into the world. Against him, and another who supported him in what he said, James and John, the sons of
3   Zebedee, strove vigorously; and although they had a command not to enter into their cities, nor to bring the word of preaching to them, yet, lest their discourse, unless it were confuted, should hurt the faith of others, they replied so prudently and so power-
4   fully, that they put them to perpetual silence. For James made an oration concerning the resurrection of the dead, with the approbation of all the people; while John showed that if they would abandon the error of Mount Gerizim, they should consequently acknowledge that Jesus was indeed He who, according to the
5   prophecy of Moses, was expected to come; since, indeed, as Moses wrought signs and miracles, so also did Jesus. And there is no doubt but that the likeness of the signs proves Him to be that prophet of whom he said that He should come, 'like himself.' Having declared these things, and more to the same effect, they ceased.

CHAP. 58—SCRIBES REFUTED.

1   "And, behold, one of the scribes, shouting out from the midst of the people, says: 'The signs and miracles which your Jesus
2   wrought, he wrought not as a prophet, but as a magician.' Him Philip eagerly encounters, showing that by this argument he ac-
3   cused Moses also. For when Moses wrought signs and miracles in Egypt, in like manner as Jesus also did in Judaea. it cannot be doubted that what was said of Jesus might as well be said of Moses. Having made these and such like protestations, Philip was silent.

CHAP. 59—PHARISEES REFUTED.

"Then a certain Pharisee, hearing this, chid Philip because he   1
put Jesus on a level with Moses. To whom Bartholomew, answer-   2
ing, boldly declared that we do not only say that Jesus was equal
to Moses, but that He was greater than he, because Moses was   3
indeed a prophet, as Jesus was also, but that Moses was not the
Christ, as Jesus was, and therefore He is doubtless greater who is
both a prophet and the Christ, than he who is only a prophet.
After following out this train of argument, he stopped. After him   4
James the son of Alphaeus gave an address to the people, with the
view of showing that we are not to believe in Jesus on the ground
that the prophets foretold concerning Him, but rather that we are
to believe the prophets, that they were really prophets, because
the Christ bears testimony to them; for it is the presence and   5
coming of Christ that show that they are truly prophets: for tes-   6
timony must be borne by the superior to his inferiors, not by the
inferiors to their superior. After these and many similar statements, James also was silent. After him Lebbaeus began vehe-   7
mently to charge it upon the people that they did not believe in
Jesus, who had done them so much good by teaching them the
things that are of God, by comforting the afflicted, healing the
sick, relieving the poor; yet for all these benefits their return had
been hatred and death. When he had declared these and many
more such things to the people, he ceased.

CHAP. 60—DISCIPLES OF JOHN REFUTED.

"And, behold, one of the disciples of John asserted that John   1
was the Christ, and not Jesus, inasmuch as Jesus Himself declared that John was greater than all men and all prophets. 'If,   2
then,' said he, 'he be greater than all, he must be held to be greater
than Moses, and than Jesus himself. But if he be the greatest of   3
all, then must he be the Christ.' To this Simon the Canaanite,
answering, asserted that John was indeed greater than all the

prophets, and all who are born of women, yet that he is not
4 greater than the Son of man. Accordingly Jesus is also the Christ,
whereas John is only a prophet: and there is as much difference
between him and Jesus, as between the forerunner and Him
whose forerunner he is; or as between Him who gives the law,
and him who keeps the law. Having made these and similar
5 statements, the Canaanite also was silent. After him Barnabas,
who also is called Matthias, who was substituted as an apostle in
the place of Judas, began to exhort the people that they should
6 not regard Jesus with hatred, nor speak evil of Him. For it were
far more proper, even for one who might be in ignorance or in
doubt concerning Jesus, to love than to hate Him. For God has
7 affixed a reward to love, a penalty to hatred. 'For the very fact,'
said he, 'that He assumed a Jewish body, and was born among the
Jews, how has not this incited us all to love Him?' When he had
spoken this, and more to the same effect, he stopped.

CHAP. 61—CAIAPHAS ANSWERED.

1   "Then Caiaphas attempted to impugn the doctrine of Jesus,
2 saying that He spoke vain things, for He said that the poor are
blessed; and promised earthly rewards; and placed the chief gift
in an earthly inheritance; and promised that those who maintain
righteousness shall be satisfied with meat and drink; and many
3 things of this sort He is charged with teaching. Thomas, in reply,
proves that his accusation is frivolous; showing that the prophets,
in whom Caiaphas believes, taught these things much more, and
did not show in what manner these things are to be, or how they
are to be understood; whereas Jesus pointed out how they are to
be taken. And when he had spoken these things, and others of like
kind, Thomas also held his peace.

CHAP. 62—FOOLISHNESS OF PREACHING.

1   "Therefore Caiaphas, again looking at me, and sometimes in
the way of warning and sometimes in that of accusation, said that

I ought for the future to refrain from preaching Christ Jesus, lest I should do it to my own destruction, and lest, being deceived myself, I should also deceive others. Then, moreover, he charged 2 me with presumption, because, though I was unlearned, a fisherman, and a rustic, I dared to assume the office of a teacher. As he 3 spoke these things, and many more of like kind, I said in reply, that I incurred less danger, if, as he said, this Jesus were not the Christ, because I received Him as a teacher of the law; but that he was in terrible danger if this be the very Christ, as assuredly He is: for I believe in Him who has appeared; but for whom else, who 4 has never appeared, does he reserve his faith? But if I, an un- 5 learned and uneducated man, as you say, a fisherman and a rustic, have more understanding than wise elders, this, said I, ought the more to strike terror into you. For if I disputed with any 6 learning, and won over you wise and learned men, it would appear that I had acquired this power by long learning, and not by the grace of divine power; but now, when, as I have said, we 7 unskilled men convince and overcome you wise men, who that has any sense does not perceive that this is not a work of human subtlety, but of divine will and gift?

CHAP. 63 — APPEAL TO THE JEWS.

"Thus we argued and bore witness; and we who were un- 1 learned men and fishermen, taught the priests concerning the one only God of heaven; the Sadducees, concerning the resurrection of the dead; the Samaritans, concerning the sacredness of Jerusalem (not that we entered into their cities, but disputed with them in public); the scribes and Pharisees, concerning the kingdom of heaven; the disciples of John, that they should not suffer John to be a stumbling-block to them; and all the people, that Jesus is the eternal Christ. At last, however, I warned them, that 2 before we should go forth to the Gentiles, to preach to them the knowledge of God the Father, they should themselves be reconciled to God, receiving His Son; for I showed them that in no way 3 else could they be saved, unless through the grace of the Holy Spirit they hasted to be washed with the baptism of threefold

4 invocation, and received the Eucharist of Christ the Lord, whom alone they ought to believe concerning those things which He taught, that so they might merit to attain eternal salvation; but that otherwise it was utterly impossible for them to be reconciled to God, even if they should kindle a thousand altars and a thousand high altars to Him.

CHAP. 64—TEMPLE TO BE DESTROYED.

1 " 'For we,' said I, 'have ascertained beyond doubt that God is much rather displeased with the sacrifices which you offer, the 2 time of sacrifices having now passed away; and because ye will not acknowledge that the time for offering victims is now past, therefore the temple shall be destroyed, and the abomination of desolation shall stand in the holy place; and then the Gospel shall be preached to the Gentiles for a testimony against you, that your 3 unbelief may be judged by their faith. For the whole world at different times suffers under divers maladies, either spreading generally over all, or affecting specially. Therefore it needs a 4 physician to visit it for its salvation. We therefore bear witness to you, and declare to you what has been hidden from every one of you. It is for you to consider what is for your advantage.'

CHAP. 65—TUMULT STILLED BY GAMALIEL.

1 "When I had thus spoken, the whole multitude of the priests were in a rage, because I had foretold to them the overthrow of 2 the temple. Which when Gamaliel, a chief of the people, saw— who was secretly our brother in the faith, but by our advice remained among them—because they were greatly enraged and 3 moved with intense fury against us, he stood up, and said, 'Be quiet for a little, O men of Israel, for ye do not perceive the trial which hangs over you. Wherefore refrain from these men; and if what they are engaged in be of human counsel, it will soon come to an end; but if it be from God, why will you sin without cause, and prevail nothing? For who can overpower the will of God?

Now therefore, since the day is declining towards evening, I shall 4
myself dispute with these men to-morrow, in this same place, in
your hearing, so that I may openly oppose and clearly confute
every error.' By this speech of his their fury was to some extent 5
checked, especially in the hope that next day we should be publicly convicted of error; and so he dismissed the people peace-
fully.

CHAP. 66 — DISCUSSION RESUMED.

"Now when we had come to our James, while we detailed to 1
him all that had been said and done, we supped, and remained
with him, spending the whole night in supplication to Almighty
God, that the discourse of the approaching disputation might
show the unquestionable truth of our faith. Therefore, on the 2
following day, James the bishop went up to the temple with us,
and with the whole church. There we found a great multitude,
who had been waiting for us from the middle of the night. There- 3
fore we took our stand in the same place as before, in order that,
standing on an elevation, we might be seen by all the people.
Then, when profound silence was obtained, Gamaliel, who, as we 4
have said, was of our faith, but who by a dispensation remained
amongst them, that if at any time they should attempt anything
unjust or wicked against us, he might either check them by skil-
fully adopted counsel, or might warn us, that we might either be
on our guard or might turn it aside; — he therefore, as if acting 5
against us, first of all looking to James the bishop, addressed him
in this manner: —

CHAP. 67 — SPEECH OF GAMALIEL.

"If I, Gamaliel, deem it no reproach either to my learning or 1
to my old age to learn something from babes and unlearned ones,
if haply there be anything which it is for profit or for safety to
acquire (for he who lives reasonably knows that nothing is more

precious than the soul), ought not this to be the object of love and desire to all, to learn what they do not know, and to teach what

2 they have learned? For it is most certain that neither friendship, nor kindred, nor lofty power, ought to be more precious to men

3 than truth. Therefore you, O brethren, if ye know anything more, shrink not from laying it before the people of God who are present, and also before your brethren; while the whole people shall

4 willingly and in perfect quietness hear what you say. For why should not the people do this, when they see even me equally with themselves willing to learn from you, if haply God has revealed

5 something further to you? But if you in anything are deficient, be not yet ashamed in like manner to be taught by us, that God may

6 fill up whatever is wanting on either side. But if any fear now agitates you on account of some of our people whose minds are prejudiced against you, and if through fear of their violence you dare not openly speak your sentiments, in order that I may deliver you from this fear, I openly swear to you by Almighty God who liveth for ever, that I will suffer no one to lay hands upon you.

7 Since, then, you have all this people witnesses of this, my oath, and you hold the covenant of our sacrament as a fitting pledge, let each one of you, without any hesitation, declare what he has learned; and let us, brethren, listen eagerly and in silence.'

CHAP. 68—THE RULE OF FAITH.

1   "These sayings of Gamaliel did not much please Caiaphas; and holding him in suspicion, as it seemed, he began to insinuate

2 himself cunningly into the discussions: for, smiling at what Gamaliel had said, the chief of the priests asked of James, the chief of the bishops, that the discourse concerning Christ should not be drawn but from the Scriptures; 'that we may know,' said

3 he, 'whether Jesus be the very Christ or no.' Then said James, 'We must first inquire from what Scriptures we are especially to

4 derive our discussion.' Then he, with difficulty, at length overcome by reason, answered, that it must be derived from the law; and afterwards he made mention also of the prophets.

CHAP. 69—TWO COMINGS OF CHRIST.

"To him our James began to show, that whatsoever things 1
the prophets say they have taken from the law, and what they
have spoken is in accordance with the law. He also made some 2
statements respecting the books of the Kings, in what way, and
when, and by whom they were written, and how they ought to be
used. And when he had discussed most fully concerning the law, 3
and had, by a most clear exposition, brought into light whatever
things are in it concerning Christ, he showed by most abundant
proofs that Jesus is the Christ, and that in Him are fulfilled all the
prophecies which related to His humble advent. For he showed 4
that two advents of Him are foretold: one in humiliation, which
He has accomplished; the other in glory, which is hoped for to be
accomplished, when He shall come to give the kingdom to those
who believe in Him, and who observe all things which He has
commanded. And when he had plainly taught the people concern- 5
ing these things, he added this also: That unless a man be baptized
in water, in the name of the threefold blessedness, as the true
Prophet taught, he can neither receive remission of sins nor enter
into the kingdom of heaven; and he declared that this is the pre-
scription of the unbegotten God. To which he added this also: 'Do 6
not think that we speak of two unbegotten Gods, or that one is
divided into two, or that the same is made male and female. But 7
we speak of the only-begotten Son of God, not sprung from another source, but ineffably self-originated; and in like manner we
speak of the Paraclete.' But when he had spoken some things also 8
concerning baptism, through seven successive days he persuaded
all the people and the high priest that they should hasten straightway to receive baptism.

CHAP. 70—TUMULT RAISED BY SAUL.

"And when matters were at that point that they should come 1
and be baptized, some one of our enemies, entering the temple
with a few men, began to cry out, and to say, 'What mean ye, O 2

men of Israel? Why are you so easily hurried on? Why are ye led
headlong by most miserable men, who are deceived by Simon, a
3   magician?' While he was thus speaking, and adding more to the
same effect, and while James the bishop was refuting him, he
began to excite the people and to raise a tumult, so that the people
4   might not be able to hear what was said. Therefore he began to
drive all into confusion with shouting, and to undo what had been
arranged with much labour, and at the same time to reproach the
priests, and to enrage them with revilings and abuse, and, like a
5   madman, to excite every one to murder, saying, 'What do ye?
Why do ye hesitate? Oh, sluggish and inert, why do we not lay
6   hands upon them, and pull all these fellows to pieces?' When he
had said this, he first, seizing a strong brand from the altar, set the
7   example of smiting. Then others also, seeing him, were carried
8   away with like madness. Then ensued a tumult on either side, of
the beating and the beaten. Much blood is shed; there is a confused flight, in the midst of which that enemy attacked James, and
threw him headlong from the top of the steps; and supposing him
to be dead, he cared not to inflict further violence upon him.

CHAP. 71 — FLIGHT TO JERICHO.

1   "But our friends lifted him up, for they were both more
numerous and more powerful than the others; but, from their fear
of God, they rather suffered themselves to be killed by an inferior
2   force, than they would kill others. But when the evening came the
priests shut up the temple, and we returned to the house of
James, and spent the night there in prayer. Then before daylight
3   we went down to Jericho, to the number of 5,000 men. Then after
three days one of the brethren came to us from Gamaliel, whom
we mentioned before, bringing to us secret tidings that that
enemy had received a commission from Caiaphas, the chief
4   priest, that he should arrest all who believed in Jesus, and should
go to Damascus with his letters, and that there also, employing
the help of the unbelievers, he should make havoc among the
faithful; and that he was hastening to Damascus chiefly on this
5   account, because he believed that Peter had fled thither. And

about thirty days thereafter he stopped on his way while passing through Jericho going to Damascus. At that time we were absent, having gone out to the sepulchres of two brethren which were whitened of themselves every year, by which miracle the fury of 6 many against us was restrained, because they saw that our brethren were had in remembrance before God."

CHAPTER 4

Source Criticism and *Religionsgeschichte* in the Fourth Gospel

THE TIME AVAILABLE FOR this working paper made necessary the familiar choice: either to work with some care on perhaps two or three passages, or to try a bird's-eye view of a part of the Johannine landscape. Had I chosen the former route, the passages would probably have been drawn from the passion narrative, where (1) the discipline of source criticism, (2) the comparative study of religious ideas, and (3) the informed quest for John's place in the history of early Christian thought seem to me to intersect in unusually productive ways. I suspect that current divergent opinions regarding John's attitude toward Jesus' death might be at least set in better order by such labor.[1]

1. First published in *Jesus and Man's Hope*, I, edited by G. Buttrick (Pittsburg: Pittsburg Theological Seminary, 1970), 147–73. Among the numerous works which might be mentioned are W. Thüsing, *Die Erhöhung* und *Verherrlichung Jesu im Johannesevangelium*, Neutestamentliche Abhandlungen 21.1–2 (Münster: Aschendorff, 1960); E. Haenchen, "Historie und Geschichte in den johanneischen Passionsberichten," *Zur Bedeutung des Todes Jesu*, edited by H. Conzelmann et al (Gütersloh: Exegetische Beiträge, 1968), 55–78; E. Käsemann, *The Testament of Jesus*, translated by G. Krodel, Johannine Monograph Series 6 (1968; Eugene, OR: Wipf & Stock, 2017). See also the reviews of this last work by G. Bornkamm, "Zur Interpretation des Johannesevangeliums: Eine Auseinandersetzung mit Ernst Käsemanns Schrift 'Jesu letzter Wille nach Johannes 17'"; *Evangelische Theologie* 28:1 (1968) 8–25, translated by John Ashton as "Towards the Interpretation of John's Gospel;" in his *The Interpretation of John* (1986, London: T. & T. Clark, 1997), 97–120; and W. A. Meeks, *Union Seminary Quarterly Review* 24:4 (1969) 414–20

As it is, I have chosen the more general alternative that necessarily leads to the more sketchy result. But it suits my present purpose well enough simply to suggest some of the gains that may be had if one will be reckless enough to try to ride uphill and downhill on three horses at once, and, much of the time, by night.

I. Hypotheses and Probes

I can indicate the area under conscious purview and the general approach by stating two working hypotheses and two critical probes.

Hypothesis #1: Fortna's Signs Gospel is reasonably similar to the Fourth Evangelist's narrative source.[2]

I do not find Fortna's analysis equally compelling in all of its parts, and toward the end of this paper I will cite one or two instances of disagreement. There are others, but it is not to be expected that a source analysis of John will be uniformly convincing to anyone, save its author, and probably not even to him. In the main, I find Fortna's work to be a solid working hypothesis. One of the questions posed in this paper—stated below—is whether the placing of Fortna's work as one hypothesis alongside others will lead to increased or lessened confidence in it and/or modifications of it.

---

2. Still in its dissertation stage at the time of the writing of this essay, this work was soon published as *The Gospel of Signs: A Reconstruction of the Narrative Source Underlying the Fourth Gospel*, SNTSMS 11 (Cambridge: Cambridge University Press, 1970). The page numbers listed in parentheses reference the dissertation.

Hypothesis #2: Between the production of Signs Gospel and the writing of the Fourth Gospel lie dynamic developments of various sorts, which played important roles in causing the Fourth Evangelist to handle Signs Gospel as he did.

One might think that so obvious a hypothesis is superfluous, but a survey of recent literature indicates the contrary. To cite a single example, I must say that *in regard to this hypothesis*, Bornkamm's generally telling review of Käsemann's *Jesu Letzter Wille* is a step backward.[3] For it is one of the numerous and distinct services of Ernst Käsemann, curiously overlooked in Bornkamm's review, to renew and make potent in our time the voice of F. C. Baur.[4]

> Nothing is gained when someone conjures up an inaccurately pictured ghost of the terrible "Tübingen School," only to pose as a modern St. George when he has laid it again in its grave. Much will be gained if we can re-learn how to analyze "the concrete, the individual, the peculiar" in the history of early Christian thought, and only after having done that to attempt a synthetic picture which is therefore drawn on the basis of the stubborn details rather than drafted according to modern desires for a balanced harmony.[5]

3. Günther Bornkamm's review (see note 1) was reprinted in *Gesammelte Aufsätze* Band III (1968) 104–21; pages cited below are from this reprint.

4. See particularly Käsemann's "Einfuhrung" for Volume 1 of F. C. Baur's *Ausgewählte Werke in Einzelausgaben*, edited by K. Scholder (Stuttgart: Bad-Cannstatt, 1963), 1–146. The pervasive influence of F. C. Baur is apparent in most of Käsemann's works; only to a lesser degree, perhaps, that of W. Bauer.

5. In much of his work, Käsemann's overt emphasis is on the first of these two demands, but the second is surely present. In the American context—as distinct from the Continental and the British—I suspect both must be emphasized. As one surveys the labors of SBL, for example, one is reminded of A. Schweitzer 's eulogistic remark about F. C. Baur, with emphasis on the first words: "He was the last who dared to conceive, and to deal with, the history of dogma in the large and general sense," *Paul and His Interpreters: A Critical History*, translated by W. Montgomery (London: A. & C. Black, 1911), vi.

A careful reading of Käsemann's Johannine studies will cause one at the very least to reexamine an assumption, conscious or unconscious, that John wrote in response almost exclusively to forces internal to himself, caring very little whether his work would be read or not.[6] The Fourth Gospel does belong somewhere in the history of early Christian thought, even if we are not able to fix that "somewhere" as easily as in the case, let us say, of Galatians (which is problematic enough, itself). And, the chances of our finding its historical locus are vastly increased if we will listen for clues to the dynamism of the setting. John is not fighting mad as he writes—contrast Paul in several instances—but neither is he pronouncing the benediction at the graduation exercises of Ephesus University, even if, as a modern parallel, a commencement speaker might be tempted to enlighten some graduating seniors regarding their true parentage (John 8:44a).

In short, there are numerous data in the Gospel which indicate that John is a theologian with opponents perhaps every bit as active and aggravating as those Paul knew in Corinth. In part, and in some

6. In his excellent introduction to *The Gospel According to St. John* (London: SPCK, 1955), C. K. Barrett discusses the Gospel's purpose by drawing a picture which is stretched against the background of "two urgent problems" faced by the church at the turn of the first century: eschatology and gnosticism. But the tenor of his discussion is thoroughly set by the following statements:

> it may be doubted whether he [John] was very interested in its publication. It is easy, when we read the gospel, to believe that John, though doubtless aware of the necessity of strengthening Christians and converting the heathen, wrote primarily to satisfy himself. His gospel must be written: it is no concern of his whether it was also read. . . . It [the traditional material] cried aloud for rehandling; its true meaning had crystallized in his mind, and he simply conveyed this meaning to paper . . . ; no book ever was less a party tract than John. (115)

I do not suppose Barrett had Käsemann's lecture, "Ketzer und Zeuge," in mind as he wrote this last sentence. The lecture was given in Göttingen on June 30, 1951 (published in *ZTK* 48 (1951) 292–311), and the manuscript of the commentary was completed in Durham on December 31 of the same year, with no mention of Käsemann in the index. However that may be, the influence of Baur and of Bauer is dominant on the one side and very nearly absent on the other.

sense of the term, John apparently writes in order to *win*. Käsemann has helped us to see this.

Probe #1: Do the two working hypotheses intersect in ways that are illuminating to one or both of them?

Again, we are dealing with the more-or-less obvious. The surveyor knows that a point fixed by measuring along a single line is more reliable if it is confirmed by the intersection of two reasonably drawn lines. To be specific, if it is reasonably clear that John is a theologian with opponents, it is equally clear that the scholar who searches for clues to the identity and beliefs of those opponents will need as many scientific controls as he or she can get. One recalls how the pendulum has swung almost off its mooring in the various attempts to identify Paul's opponents at certain points in his work. The relative success—so it seems to me, at any rate—in the case of the Corinthian correspondence is due in no small part to the fact that *literary criticism* has provided us with *several documents* representing successive *stages* in the volatile give-and-take, perhaps even including snippets of the opponents' work.[7] Will Fortna's source-critical labors provide a similar helpful control for a renewed attempt to distinguish *stages* in the Johannine tradition?[8]

---

7. John Hurd, *The Origin of I Corinthians* (London: SPCK, 1965); S. Schulz, "Die Decke des Moses: Untersuchungen zu einer vorpaulinischen Uberlieferung in II Cor 37–18," *ZNW* 49 (1958) 1–30 (an important thesis regarding the presence in II Corinthians 3 of a midrash composed by Paul's opponents and edited by him); Günther Bornkamm, "Die Vorgeschichte des sogenannten Zweiten Korintherbriefes," *Sitzungsberichte der Heidelberger Akademie der Wissenschaften, Philosophisch-historische Klasse*, 1961, 2; Dieter Georgi, *Die Gegner des Paulus im 2. Korintherbrief: Studien zur religiösen Propaganda in der Spätantike, Wissenschaftliche Monographien zum alten und neuen Testament* 11 (Vluyn-Neukirchen: Neukirchener, 1964). Note again the roles played here by Baur and Käsemann (e.g., Georgi, 7–16).

8. For the Corinthian correspondence compare Hurd's bold chart (290–93) and Georgi's attempt to sketch the sequence of developments (25–29).

But, to return for a moment to Hypothesis #2, it is putting Fortna and Käsemann together that has caused me to formulate it as I have: the dynamic relations between John's source and its use. I can scarcely believe that John expended the massive effort necessary to rethink and reshape—perhaps one should say recreate—the Signs Gospel (and other available traditions), and to do so as he did, merely because some inadequacies in the Signs Gospel offended his theological sensitivities.[9] In other words, we are dealing here not with two stages (the Signs Gospel and the Fourth Gospel), but rather with at least three: the writing of the Signs Gospel; subsequent and thus chronologically intervening developments, including activities on the part of "opponents;" and the writing of the Fourth Gospel. This being so, an adequate understanding of the third stage will require careful consideration of *both* its predecessors.[10]

Probe #2: Do the two hypotheses intersect in ways which are illuminating with regard to both the general history of religious ideas (*Religionsgeschichte*) and the history of early Christian theology (*Theologiegeschichte*)? Conversely, are they supported by what we already know of *Religionsgeschichte* and *Theologiegeschichte*?

In an age which seems thoroughly entranced with redaction criticism, for the sake of quickly acquired theological pay dirt, one needs, perhaps, to recall that patient labors in the general history of religious ideas and

9. One must also bear in mind that according to the hypothesis the Signs Gospel was the Gospel of John's church, used and no doubt in some sense venerated in its worship.

10. It is a helpful and illuminating exercise to relate Schnackenburg's comments on Tradition and Redaction, *The Gospel According to St. John, Volume One* (1968, New York: Seabury, 1980), 59–74 (6–70 in the German edition) to his discussion of Theological and Topical Interests, 153–72 (146–53). Likewise, the corresponding sections in Raymond E. Brown, *The Anchor Bible*, 29 (New York: Doubleday, 1966), xxxiv–xxxix and lxvii–lxxix, offers an equally illuminating treatment.

in the history of specifically Christian thought are themselves carried out by *Neutestamentler* for the sake of theological precision, gained by observations similar to those proper to *Redaktionskritik*.[11] That is to say, each of the three disciplines under consideration here—source criticism, *Religionsgeschichte*, and *Theologiegeschichte*—forms a basis for possible redaction criticism or something similar to it. Therefore, mutual criticism among the three is imperative. But to limit ourselves to the two working hypotheses, it will be sufficient, perhaps, to say that these will acquire added probability to the extent that a) the Signs Gospel proves to be readily identifiable *religionsgeschichtlich*, and *theologiegeschichtlickh*; b) the intervening stage or stages posited between the Signs Gospel and the Fourth Gospel; and c) John's own contribution are similarly identifiable, or at least comprehensible.

It may be further clarifying for me to add that the impulse to attempt the present paper came to me when I began to ask myself how three recent monographs might fit together, or not fit together,

---

11. Scarcely needed in the circle of Festival participants, but probably helpful in a wider context, is S. Schulz's reminder:

> Der Sinn aller religionsgeschichtlich-kritischen Arbeit—nicht nur am Joh-Ev—ist zuletzt nicht der, den für uns in Frage kommenden johanneischen Reden ihre Besonderheit zu nehmen, sondern diese vielmehr herauszustellen (note to G. Kittel, *Spätjudentum*, p. 19). Denn jeder religionsgeschichtlich-kritische Vergleich zeigte zur Genüge, daß mit der Übernahme einer religionsgeschichtlichen Vorstellung immer auch ihre Verarbeitung verbunden war; d.h. sie wurde kritisiert, modifiziert und neu zentriert. Und in diesem Prozeß der verarbeitenden Neuauslegung liegt das Theologisch-Entscheidende und Bedeutsame. (English translation: The meaning of all religious historical-critical work—not only in the Johannine Gospel—finally, is not to take up the Johannine speeches that we consider to be peculiar, but rather to highlight them [note to G. Kittel, *Spätjudentum*, p. 19]. For every historical and critical comparison of religions was sufficient to show that the assumption of a religious history was always related to its processing; i.e. it was criticized, modified and re-centered. And, in this process of reworking realignment lies that which is theologically decisive and important.)

Siegfried Schultz, *Komposition und Herkunft der Johanneischen Reden* (Stuttgart: W. Kohlhammer, 1960), 140.

on the Johannine shelf: Käsemann's *The Testament of Jesus*, Meeks's *The Prophet-King*, and Fortna's *The Gospel of Signs*. Käsemann seeks to fix the historical place of John's theology—mainly Christology—by means of carefully and boldly constructed *theologiegeschichtlich* comparisons. Meeks explores an aspect of John's Christology partly by following a similar approach (*Prophet-King*, 60ff.), but mainly by placing great weight on *religionsgeschichtliche* comparisons, an avenue Käsemann explicitly leaves aside (*Testament*, 66). The results reached in these two monographs are not entirely harmonious, to say the least.[12] Now Fortna has propounded a far-reaching source analysis, relying very little on either of these kinds of conceptual comparisons, but making some concluding observations which do indeed speak to the questions of *Religionsgeschichte* and *Theologiegeschichte*, and which are now being expanded in papers and in a forthcoming *redaktionsgeschichtlichen* monograph.[13]

However, the major point here is not the need for ecumenical, scholarly interchange, but rather the methodological imperative to allow mutual critique among the three disciplines. Points that are fixed by the supportive intersection, so to speak, of two or of all three are surely worth very serious consideration.

↶

It should be obvious that in a relatively brief working paper one can make only a modest beginning in the very large task to which the two

12. See Meeks's review of *Testament* (note 1). On the whole, Meeks's own monograph has apparently not received the thorough treatment in written reviews that it deserves: W. A. Meeks, *The Prophet-King: Moses Traditions in the Johannine Christology*, Johannine Monograph Series 5 (1967, Eugene, OR: 2017). An exception is the review by R. Schnackenburg in *BZ* 13 (1969) 136–38, where the book is given a serious and responsible critique.

13. Note particularly his paper read at the meeting of SBL in Berkeley; December 20, 1968: "Source and Redaction in the Fourth Gospel's Portrayal of Jesus' Signs," published in the *Journal of Biblical Literature* 89.2 (1970) 151–66.

hypotheses and the two probes point. Three factors lighten the load somewhat and enable me at least to make an attempt.

I do not take it as my task, at the present juncture, explicitly to test Hypothesis #1. An initial testing was provided by the oral examination of Fortna's work in dissertation form. Further evaluation will doubtless be provided by reviewers and others.[14]

With regard to Hypothesis #2, I will consciously impose a limitation. In stating that hypothesis I have spoken of *various* developments taking place between the production of the Signs Gospel and the writing of the Fourth Gospel. The range of these developments may be rather large. Were one proceeding on the basis of the present state of Johannine research, rather than following a more inductive path, several possibilities would demand attention. *Perhaps* between the Signs Gospel and the Fourth Gospel arose:

A. a struggle with followers of John the Baptist

B. a hardening of battle lines between synagogue and church

C. inner-church problems, such as:

    1. overemphasis on the anticipated glories of Jesus future coming;

    2. loss of a sense of contact with and memory of the earthly Jesus, with concomitant danger that Christianity might devolve into a mystery religion;

---

14. Raymond Brown has given a critique of certain aspects for the Gospels Seminar of SBL at the Toronto meeting, November 17, 1969. It is a helpful probe, purposely emphasizing points of disagreement. On the whole, I find myself measurably less skeptical than Brown. See also the paper prepared by D. Moody Smith for the same occasion. Smith is mainly concerned to provide a critique of the source-critical aspects of E. Haenchen's emerging commentary, but he also offers some evaluative comments about Fortna's monograph. (Editor's note: see also the extensive treatments of Bultmann's and Fortna's source theories in Paul N. Anderson, *The Christology of the Fourth Gospel: Its Unity and Disunity in the Light of John 6* (1996, Eugene, OR: Cascade, 2010), and especially the engagement with Robert Kysar in the *Review of Biblical Literature* 1 (1999) 38–72.)

3. Docetism;

4. growth of a hardening and institutionally oriented orthodoxy which pits itself with increasing fervor against the
   growth of Hellenistic enthusiasm in the church;

5. theological developments which are not truly christo-
   centric.[15]

It can be seen that a range of possible developments is large indeed. I
do not intend to attempt even a survey of the whole picture, but rather
to look for *some of the intervening developments which seem fairly directly and simply reflected in the Evangelist's handling of the Signs Gospel.*
If the results of my sketch are taken as an overall view, they will be
misinterpreted.

Finally, I shall not be mechanical in relating the two probes to
the two hypotheses. For the time being, I am content to pose a series
of questions and to allow the probes and hypotheses to form a general
methodological context.

II. Questions and Developing Answers

A. Who is Jesus?

We may begin at a point many interpreters identify as the very center
of Johannine theology: the remarkable and massive concentration on
Christology. When we raise the question which is surely a key to the
Gospel—Who is Jesus?—do we hear answers along the line which affect the degree of probability attaching to our hypotheses?

---

15. I have sketched these possibilities on the basis of suggestions offered in such
works as the commentaries by Schnackenburg and Brown and the monographs by
Käsemann and Meeks. They are not intended to comprise an exhaustive list.

The Signs Gospel

Fortna finds in the Signs Gospel a single-minded focusing on Christology that appears to be even more exclusive than that often attributed to the Fourth Gospel. The reader of the Signs Gospel is *not* told
that a new age has dawned or is about to dawn. He is not taught that
suffering and sin are now destroyed (Jesus does not perform miracles in order to alleviate suffering or to attack sin and evil), that the
Spirit is bestowed on believers, that in Jesus Christ God has begun
to build an *ecclesia*, that in the *ecclesia* the sacraments are centrally
important. He is told again and again who Jesus is: the Christ, the
Messiah of Israel.

On the face of it, source criticism is not strongly supported
here by *Religionsgeschichte* and *Theologiegeschichte*. Fortna speaks of
the Signs Gospel's uniqueness in this regard, vis-à-vis not only first-
century Christian literature (p. 234), but also Jewish apocalyptic (p.
228). It is a kind of Christological oddity, and its being such does
not especially increase one's confidence in the source analysis. On
the other hand, the Fourth Gospel is itself nearly as single-mindedly
oriented to Christology. Käsemann is fully justified in thinking of
John when he quotes Zinzendorf: "I have but one passion. That is He
and only He." Furthermore, when one ponders the question "What
percentage of the religious literature of the Hellenistic age has come
down to us?," he will be very slow to label any document a *religionsgeschichtlich* "bastard."

More important are observations that may be made regarding the Signs Gospel's optimistic assumption that a simple recount-
ing of Jesus' signs will lead the reader to confess him as Messiah.
Fortna points here to Old Testament traditions about Elijah, Elisha,
and Moses, and he refers his reader to Dieter Georgi's pages on
θεῖοι ἄνδρες in Jewish tradition. There are, then, several possible
recognizable conceptual milieu for the Signs Gospel's sign-working
Messiah, a figure who apparently raised not only Lazarus, but also
himself, from the dead. The milieus are all OT-Jewish in character.

Post-Signs Gospel Developments

With only a pinch of imagination one can pursue the question of Jesus' identity into the intervening period between the Signs Gospel and the Fourth Gospel. For the moment I will limit myself to three suggestions, each of which is given some strength, I think, by the intersection of source criticism and *Religionsgeschichte*:

1. "To the Bet ha-Midrash!"

Some of the persons exposed to the Signs Gospel, specifically some of the potential Jewish converts for whom, at least in part, it was written (Fortna, p. 234), reacted quite reasonably by saying, in effect: "Very well, if your claim that Jesus was the Messiah [note the tense] is to be sustained, it must stand up under careful and extensive midrashic examination, carried out by those whose training equips them for such work" (Consider John 5:39; 6:30ff; 7:17, all non-Signs-Gospel passages.)

We see a similar reaction in the case of Trypho; and there are numerous data in Christian documents that indicate that many early Christian preachers not only encountered such Jewish reactions, but also accepted the demanding challenge, as did Justin in the second century.

The challenge has epistemological implications, notably those evident in the assumption that one can "book a through train" from rational midrashic discussion to dependable conclusions. God gave the Torah. He stands, therefore, at the beginning of the line extending from Moses.[16] If He acts today, He will do so in forms that are consistent with, and perhaps even pre-given in, the Torah. When He gave the Torah, He did not keep anything back. Hence, one can pronounce judgment on the basis of authoritative midrash.

16. The theological implications of such patterns of thought have been several times voiced by Käsemann. See, e.g., "The Structure and Purpose of the Prologue to John's Gospel," in his *New Testament Questions of Today* (Philadelphia: Fortress, 1969), 138–67.

2. "Moses is the one who ascended and received the heavenly secrets."

A bit more exotic, on the face of it, is a second possible intervening development, corresponding, I suppose, to the Signs Gospel's portrait of Jesus as the Elijah-like, Elisha-like, Moses-like, prophetic θεῖος ἀνήρ. The opponents evidently countered such a portrait by identifying themselves as followers of Moses himself, who on Sinai ascended to heaven where the heavenly secrets were imparted to him.

The Jewish data that support such a possible development, as well as the relevant Johannine data, have been carefully collected and sifted by Wayne Meeks.[17] What calls for emphasis here is the fact that the Johannine data suggesting such a reaction on the part of the Signs Gospel readers fall outside the Signs Gospel. In this important matter, then, Fortna's source criticism and Meeks's work in the history of religious ideas are mutually supportive. And again we see an intervening development, which involves extra-church opponents.

3. "You are Ditheists!"

We are not to assume, of course, that Jewish opponents did all of the talking in the interval between the Signs Gospel and the Fourth Gospel, or that the Johannine theologians limited their counter-response to a simple repetition of the Signs Gospel's materials. There are data in the Fourth Gospel which suggest that at some point(s) the Johannine church so elevated Jesus as the θεῖος ἀνήρ, the God striding across the face of the earth,[18] as to evoke from Jewish opponents the charge of ditheism. That is to say, the Johannine community apparently used the Signs Gospel and embroidered on it in ways that caused the Jewish opponents to see perhaps in it, and certainly in the use being made of it, an abrogation of monotheism.

17. *The Prophet-King.*

18. Käsemann, *Testament*, and passim, citing Baur, Wetter, and Hirsch. I doubt that the reader of Käsemann's *Testament* will fully understand it until he or she makes some careful comparisons with F. C. Baur's work on the Fourth Gospel, a task to which Käsemann's footnotes invite him. See also note 33 below.

In *Religionsgeschichtlichen* terms, we *may* see a move here which corresponds in some rough way to a move from the materials (proper to the Signs Gospel?) by which van der Woude and Hahn investigate the Prophet to those (added in the interval between the Signs Gospel and the Fourth Gospel?) cited by Wetter as he made a similar attempt.[19] But I am not at all sure about that. Perhaps it merits further investigation. I want only to suggests that such passages as 5:18ff; 8:53; and 10:33 reflect a charge which Jewish opponents hurled at the Johannine community with considerable reason, between the writing of the Signs Gospel and that of the Fourth Gospel. It may also be relevant to note that the "Logos Hymn" could have played a part in such developments. For it moves implicitly in the direction of ditheism, as Conzelmann has recently pointed out.[20]

With regard to the opponents, there are numerous possible parallels. Perhaps one should consider some of the Rabbinic references which show polemic against those who hold the doctrine of "Two Powers in Heaven," though it would not be necessary to limit the field at this point to Rabbinic data.[21]

The Fourth Gospel

1. Confronted by opponents who enthusiastically exclaim, "To the Bet ha-Midrash" and knowing quite well the simple implications

---

19. A. S. van der Woude, *Die messianischen Vorstellungen der Gemeinde von Qumran* (Assen: Van Gorcum, 1957); F. Hahn, *Christologische Hoheitstitel*, FRLANT 83 (Göttingen: Vandenhoeck & Ruprecht, 1963); G. P. Wetter; *Der Sohn Gottes* (Göttingen: Vandenhoeck & Ruprecht, 1916). See also Meeks, *The Prophet-King*, 22ff.

20. H. Conzelmann, *An Outline of the Theology of the New Testament*, translated by John Bowden (New York: Harper & Row, 1969), 335.

21. See, e.g., R. Travers Herford, *Christianity in Talmud and Midrash* (1903), 255ff., 291 ff.; G. F. Moore, *Judaism* (1927), I. 364ff.

in the Signs Gospel regarding the relationship between signs and faith,[22] John appears to react in several ways:

a. He makes the frequent failure of the signs an important theme in his Gospel.[23] John 12:37ff shows the Evangelist pondering the development of dominant Jewish opposition which has characterized the interim since the writing of the Signs Gospel. The signs are now seen as the dividing *krisis*, rather than as simple occasions for faith.

b. He corrects the Signs Gospel in such a way as to deny that the question of Jesus' identity can be settled by midrash.[24]

c. He makes clear that this all-important question is not "Was he Messiah?," but rather, "Who is he?" I have pointed out that Bornkamm, in his review of Käsemann's *Jesu Letzter Wille*, steps back from the heritage of F. C. Baur in that he does not ask about the dynamic setting of the Fourth Gospel. However, he does provide some very helpful comments, including an accurate listing of four aspects of John's critical stance toward his tradition. The first two are relevant here:

> Nicht zufällig ist darum mindestens implizit und potentiell, oft aber auch explizit den Wunderberichten eines der grossen Ich-bin-Worte zugeordnet (6,35; 9,5, vgl. 5, 12; 11, 25). Nicht zufällig darum der häufige Umschlag aus dem Vergangenheitstempus der Erzählung in das Gegenwartstempus der Reden (p. 116).

22. Cf. E. Haenchen "Johanneische Probleme," *ZThK* 56 (1959) 19–54; "Der Vater, der mich gesandt hat," *NTS* 9 (1962–63) 208–16; Fortna, "Source and Redaction"; Paul Meyer, "Seeing Signs and Sources in the Fourth Gospel," a paper read at AAR in Dallas, November, 1968. I do not cite all of these studies as support for the statement in the text, but rather as relevant to the question whether or not John and the Signs Gospel had distinguishable attitudes toward the signs. Haenchen, Fortna, and Meyer are not of a common mind on this question.

23. Fortna, "Source and Redaction."

24. J. Louis Martyn, *History and Theology in the Fourth Gospel* (New York: Harper & Row, 1968), 112ff.

d. John senses the epistemological naïveté present both in the Signs Gospel and in the arguments of the opponents; hence he emphasizes:

1. What Bornkamm (ibid.) lists as a fourth aspect of John's critical stance toward his tradition: *Verwerfungen* (geological faults) which make clear that there are no "through trains" from this side.

2. The role of the Paraclete in perception. Note that John points forward to the five paraclete sayings by three times appending to a Signs Gospel passage an emphatic note about the transition from ignorance to true understanding (2:17; 2:22; 12:16). In each of these cases the transition involves perceiving the true relationship between ἡ γραφή and Jesus' deeds/words. The verb μνησθῆναι, absent from the Signs Gospel, is very important to John as an epistemological-hermeneutical key.

3. The dualism of *present* election. There are numerous facets to this emphasis. John accomplishes it in part by employing what Bornkamm calls the language and perspective of gnosis (p. 118): the exclusive character of the claim to revelation, the enmity to the world, the esoterica. But he employs such language and perspectives in order to sharpen the epistemological issue. Unlike the author of the Signs Gospel, John is interested in exploring various patterns which can arise when the verbs "to see" and "to believe" are related to one another.[25] (Note, e.g., 6:36f.) Perhaps Peder Borgen's ingenious exegesis of v. 36 is correct;[26] either way the point here is the same: *seeing* and *believing* cannot be properly related to one another apart from the motif of *present election*. God does not stand only at the beginning of either creation or Torah-revelation (Sinai).[27]

e. I am inclined to think that John's introduction and shaping of Son of Man tradition, wholly absent from the Signs

25. Fortna, "Source and Redaction."

26. P. Borgen, *Bread from Heaven: An Exegetical Study of Manna in the Gospel of John and the Writings of Philo*, the Johannine Monograph Series, 4 (1965, Eugene, OR: 2017), 74.

27. See note 16.

Gospel, and his—so I think—creation of two-level dramas are also to be listed here, i.e., as adjustments of the Signs Gospel in the face of inadequacies in it which have been revealed in the course of Jewish opposition to it.[28]

2. Confronted by opponents who not only are disciples of Moses (9:28; cf. 5:39, 45), but also claim that Moses received the heavenlies on the occasion of his Sinai ascent, John counters quite dogmatically:

> No one has ever seen God (1:18), except, of course, the Son, and him who has truly seen the Son (14:8f.). No one has ascended to heaven, except the Son of Man, not even Moses (3:13).[29]

John's exegesis of the "Logos Hymn" (i.e., 1:14–18) cannot be fully grasped, I think, unless one a) gives due weight to *both* of the emphatic elements, v. 14 *and* vv. 17–18, and b) notes that the literary seam preceding v. 14 coincides with a disjuncture in *religionsgeschichtlich* background.[30] For our present purposes it is, perhaps, enough to say that John is considerably more interested in Moses than was the author of the Signs Gospel, and that the reason for this increased interest apparently lies with the intervening volatile developments vis-à-vis the synagogue. Unlike the author of the Signs Gospel, John finds it necessary to deny claims made for Moses.

3. To the charge of ditheism, a charge nowhere reflected in the Signs Gospel, John constructs a careful response.[31] Here it is important to

---

28. *History and Theology*, passim.

29. I paraphrase 3:13 according to the results of Meeks's exegesis, *The Prophet-King*, 297–301.

30. Points to be developed in a forthcoming study in which Käsemann's structural analysis is accepted as correct.

31. "If the formulae of his commission through the Father and his unity with the Father are isolated from each other, the result will be subordinationism or ditheism. Both formulae are correlative and complementary, because only together do they describe the truth that Jesus is nothing but the revealer and, on the other hand, that Jesus

see that John does not place the lengthy sermon of 5:19–47 immediately after the healing (raising—v. 8) sign of 5:1–9a. Nor is it the
Sabbath conflict as such which introduces this long speech of Jesus
on the relation of the Son to the Father. The transition is accomplished, rather, by 5:18b. One is not surprised, therefore, to find that
the sermon in 5:19–47 is preached at least in part to those who do
not honor the Son at all, while claiming nevertheless to honor God (v.
23). Verse 21 (cf. 26) may very well be an indirect challenge to those
who regularly recite the *Shemoneh Esreh*, the second benediction of
which reads in part:

> Thou art strong . . . Thou livest forever, bringing the dead back to
> life . . . Thou supportest the living and revivest the dead . . . Blessed
> be thou, O God, who bringeth the dead back to life.

Why do the addresses not honor the Son? From their point of view they
refuse to do so in order to remain true monotheists (v. 18). John is also
a monotheist. Therefore he is at pains to show his opponents—among
other things—"wi er den Monotheismus (den die Juden auf ihre Weise
vertreten) mit der Zweiheit van Vater und sohn vereint: Der Sohn kann
nichts von Selbst tun; er tut nur, was er den Vater tun sieht."[32]

Here we may receive a valuable clue to John's place in the history
of Christian thought. There is a theological "both . . . and" in the Fourth
Gospel, and there is a theological "both . . . and" in 1 John. The two
are related, yet significantly different. The Evangelist's "both . . . and"
is directed to opponents (Jews) who want the Father without the

---

is the only revealer of God and therefore belongs totally on the side of God while he is
on earth" (Käsemann, *Testament*, 11).

32. E. Haenchen, "Johanneische Probleme," *ZThK* 56 (1959) 50. Doesn't John thereby
diminish the initiative of Jesus (contra Fortna, "Source and Redaction")? I think so. I
quite agree with Käsemann, that Jesus' obedience "is the form and concretion of Jesus'
glory during the period of his incarnation" (*Testament*, 10f). Nevertheless, compared
with the Signs Gospel's portrait, that of John emphasizes at points Jesus' subordination to
the Father, and, I think, for the reasons suggested above.

wondrous Son, and who hurl at John the charge "Ditheist!" The Epistle
writer directs his "both . . . and" to inner-church opponents who want
Christ without Jesus, and against whom he hurls the charge "Docetist!"
Apparent ditheism and unreflecting docetism (Käsemann's term) are
coupled in the Johannine community until first one development and
then another cause them to be separated and individually handled vis-
à-vis disparate opponents. Or, to put it another way, the unreflecting
docetism of the Signs Gospel and of the "Logos Hymn"—Käsemann's
term may be somewhat more satisfactory for the Signs Gospel than
for the Fourth Gospel, though I suspect it is suggestive for both[33]—
has come home to roost by the time of the First Epistle. Paradoxically,
docetic opponents must now be faced by a member of a community
which at an earlier date had to find a way simultaneously to honor the
θεῖος ἀνήρ and, being largely Jewish, to remain monotheistic.

Results thus far:

Posing the question of Jesus' identity in these ways leads, I think, to a)
increased confidence in the hypothesis of the Signs Gospel, to b) the
view that dynamic and influential developments do lie chronologically
between the Signs Gospel and the Fourth Gospel, to c) the conclusion
that some of these developments constitute a sharp debate between
John's church and a mostly hostile Jewish community, and to d) the
conviction that John's own theological stance is in part formed by this
post-Signs-Gospel debate.

33. Essentially, therefore, I find myself standing with Käsemann as regards "un-
reflektierter Doketismus" (contra Bornkamm, 1968 review). To believe that John *intended* 1:14 to guard against docetism one would have to hold, it seems to me, that
he was asleep when he wrote the words καὶ ἐσκήνωσεν ἐν ἡμῖν. But even that would
be scarcely possible, since these words carefully point forward to "the paradoxical 'a
little while' of the farewell discourses in 14:19; 16:16ff.; as already in 7:33; 12:35; 13:33"
(*Testament*, 10 n. 10).

B. Can one follow Moses and Jesus?

The Signs Gospel

The question does not come up in the mind of the author; thus it is neither posed nor answered as such. Assumed, however, is a clear continuity between Moses and Jesus. Indeed, there is good reason to believe that when the Signs Gospel was produced, the community of messianic believers was, in John's city, a group within the synagogue fellowship. John 1:45 is typical of a simple and unsophisticated strain in the Signs Gospel: "We have found the one of whom Moses and the prophets wrote."

Intervening Developments

I have already suggested that John was far more interested in the Moses-Jesus question than was the author of the Signs Gospel, and that the reason for his being so lies in certain intervening developments. Of these developments, 9:28 is typical. To the question "Can one follow Moses and Jesus?," the answer is now a resounding "no!"[34] With this come two further moves on the part of the opponents: excommunication of those

---

34. That this resounding "No" should come from the "orthodox" Jewish authorities in John's setting, rather than from thinkers in his own messianic community, tells us something of the distance between John's world and that of Paul. It has frequently been pointed out that Torah as the way of salvation is not the problem for John that it is for Paul (e.g., Bultmann, *Theology of the New Testament*, 2.8). But to make this observation in the correct context, to make it with precision, and only then to explicate it theologically are tasks not yet fully accomplished.

confessing Jesus as Messiah,[35] and trial and execution of Jewish-Christian evangelists who continue the mission among Jews.[36]

The Fourth Gospel

Here again, in light of what has already been said, no lengthy comment is needed. It is John, not the author of the Signs Gospel, I think, who knows and ponders the two awesome moves just mentioned, and who

---

35. Here a good bit turns, of course, on the literary analysis of John 9. Bultmann allotted the drama of that chapter to the Semeia-Quelle: see D. Moody Smith, *The Composition and Order of the Fourth Gospel: Bultmann's Literary Theory*, Johannine Monograph Series 3 (1965, Eugene, OR: Wipf & Stock, 2015), 42f. But he regarded 9:22 as a remark which the Evangelist inserted in the Signs Source: Rudolf Bultmann, *Das Evangelium des Johannes* (Göttingen: Vandenhoeck & Ruprecht, 1957), 254 n. 10; "Der Stil des Evglisten ist deutlich." For Bultmann, the three ἀποσυνάγωγος references point to a period that stretches approximately from Paul to Justin (428). Ray Brown gives 9:22 to stage 5, the final redaction by someone other than the Evangelist, because—if I read him correctly—(a) it is inconceivable in stage I, and (b) it is literarily parenthetical. I feel the force of both reasons, but in light of 12:42 and especially 16:2, and noting the harmony between 9:22 and 9:34, I am afraid I do not see ample justification for bringing in the final redactor at this point. Haenchen allots most of John 9 to the source, much as did Bultmann, and he does not find himself convinced by such exegetes as Hirsch and Windisch who refer to the Evangelist as a gifted dramatist on the basis of that chapter. Whether it is truly consistent to give the post-miracle scenes in chapter 5 to the Evangelist and to deny him what appear to be corresponding scenes in chapter 9 is a question I must ponder.

There seem to me to be at least three good grounds for crediting the Evangelist with the drama of chapter 9: (1) the apparent relationship of 9:4a to 14:12; (2) the structural similarity as regards scene presentation of the trial before Pilate (Paul Meyer in Meeks, *The Prophet-King*, 293). I quite agree with Haenchen (*Einleitung*, §6, 3, a privately circulated section of Haenchen's forthcoming commentary) that for the Evangelist, "der eigentliche Sinn der Geschichte nicht in dem legitimierenden Wunder lag, sondern in dem Hinweis von V. 9,5: 'Ich bin das Licht der Welt.'" (English translation: the real meaning of the story was not the legitimating miracle, but in the reference in v. 9:5: "I am the Light of the world.") But that does not tell me that John cannot be responsible for the drama. Quite the opposite. It supports such an interpretation if one perceives that John is interested not only in the class of this *Hinweis*, but also in the *wie*, namely the two-level drama.

36. *History and Theology*, 45–77

hears "the resounding 'No!'" In light of these developments he works out a profoundly dialectic stance toward the Moses-Jesus issue.[37]

C. What Significance Has Jesus' Death?

I have remarked above (in the initial paragraph of the paper) that the disciplines of source criticism, *Religionsgeschichte*, and *Theologiegeschichte* seem to intersect in unusually productive ways as one pursues them through the Johannine passion narrative. In the space and time remaining, let me offer a few suggestions.

The Signs Gospel

The reader of the Signs Gospel makes his way through what Fortna calls the Exordium, the Baptist's testimony, the conversion of the first disciples, and all seven of the signs without encountering a single note which is preparatory for Jesus' death. There are no *Streitgespräche*, no hostile murmurings, not even any opposition to the faith awakened by Jesus' signs. We certainly have no guarantee that Fortna's reconstruction presents the whole of this hypothetical document; indeed he explicitly avoids such a claim.[38] Nevertheless, one who works with the Signs Gospel as a hypothesis is clearly justified in pointing out the absence of a correspondent to Mark 3:6. The signs produce faith, not a death plot.

Thus, the weight of showing motivation on the part of Jesus' enemies in the passion story is placed squarely, and virtually exclusively, on the confrontation provoked by Jesus' cleansing of the Temple. Even here, however—that is, within the limits of the Temple-cleansing pericope itself—the accent may fall not so much on Jesus' death as on his resurrection. To the authorities' demand for a legitimizing sign, Jesus responds, Λύσατε τὸν ναὸν τοῦτον καὶ ἐν τρισὶν ἡμέραις ἐγερῶ αὐτόν

---

37. See Martyn, *History and Theology*, 112f.

38. *Gospel of Signs*, 242.

(John 2:10). To the author of the Signs Gospel, this old piece of tradition (Bultmann argues well) is a clear reference to Jesus' death and resurrection, perhaps implying that he will raise himself from the dead.[39] In any case, the saying refers primarily to Jesus' chief σημεῖων, the one that shows his messiahship more clearly than any other: his resurrection.[40]

It would seem reasonable to conclude that the author of the Signs Gospel was not greatly interested in Jesus' death, and did not see great significance in it. To paraphrase Käsemann's statement about the Fourth Gospel and apply it to the Signs Gospel, the passion comes into view only at the very end, is provided with virtually no preparation, and is overshadowed by Jesus' signs, which find their proper climax in his resurrection.[41]

Intervening Developments

These are somewhat more difficult to identify in this case than in the earlier instances. As before, one tries, of course, to look forward from the Signs Gospel and backward from the Fourth Gospel. Doing so here suggests that some factors caused the death of Jesus to be far more important to John than it was to his predecessor. Let me suggest that two intervening developments already mentioned played roles here also.

1. It is clear that John's church knows the experience of Christian martyrdom. The prophecy of 16:2, spoken virtually from heaven (17:11f.) by the departing Lord, points to just such a development, and redaction-criticism will indicate it to lie chronologically between the Signs Gospel and the Fourth Gospel. Jewish Christians have somehow been brought to their deaths by Jews. A priori, it is not likely that such experience would fail to leave some kind of marks on the tradition of

39. Fortna, "Source and Redaction."

40. Ibid.

41. *Testament*, 7: "Apart from a few remarks that point ahead to it, the passion comes to view in John only at the very end."

the passion narrative. We shall see in a moment whether that may be the case, but let me mention 11:16 and 12:10, which lie outside the passion story and are non-Signs Gospel.

2. In a rather different way, another development already discussed may belong here: the polemical claim that Moses is the one who ascended into heaven. It is difficult to say with certainty which is claim and which counter-claim, but that there is polemic seems clear enough.

The Fourth Gospel

1. We begin with the cleansing of the Temple, because with respect to the passion, John's handling of this pericope is his most obvious alteration of the Signs Gospel, and because some interpreters have taken the relocation—it is a relocation on virtually any theory of tradition-history—to indicate John's interest in Jesus' death. In handling this pericope, John did at least four things: (1) He moved it to a position very early in the Gospel, separating it rather completely from the passion narrative. (2) He introduced the motif of literalistic misunderstanding on the part of "the Jews." (3) He portrayed the opposite to such literalistic misunderstanding: the perspective which is provided in a memory informed by Jesus' resurrection. I have spoken above about the epistemological weight John attached to the verb μνησθῆναι pointing ahead to the coming of the Paraclete. By introducing this motif so early in his Gospel, John signals that the whole of the story is to be understood from Jesus' glorification backwards (so also Bornkamm, p. 114). (4) It is not entirely surprising, then, that John ignores the verb Λύσατε, whereas he twice repeats and thus highlights the verb ἐγερῶ (vv. 20 and 22). In this way he accents the hermeneutical importance of the resurrection, looking forward again to 14:26.

These alterations show two things: first, that John places the so-called "Book of Signs" not in the shadow of Jesus' death—the cleansing pericope no longer has about it even the small odor of death it possessed in the Signs Gospel—but rather in the light of Easter and of the coming of the Paraclete. Second, that having removed the Signs Gospel's sole passion-motivation pericope from its passion setting, John will have to show the adversaries' motivation in some other way.

2. The second of these points calls for exploration. How does John portray the motivation for Jesus' passion-adversaries?

a. While the Signs Gospel lacks a note corresponding to Mark 3:6, the Fourth Gospel does indeed have one, namely 5:18. We have already noted that this verse is the major link by means of which John makes his way from the drama of the paralytic to the lengthy speech about the Son's relation to the Father. Now we note that it is also the first of a weighty series of references to Jesus' death, by means of which John points forward to 11:53, a verse he took from the Signs Gospel: 5:18; 7:1, 19–20, 25; 8:22, 37, 40, 44; 11:50–51.[42] Furthermore, John extends the same line beyond the verse taken from the Signs Gospel: 12:10 ("also"), 24, 33; 18:14, 31–32; 19:7.

John takes the verb ἀποκτεῖναι from the Signs Gospel only once (11:53). Elsewhere, about eleven times, he either draws it from other traditional materials or introduces it himself, alternatives which may amount to very nearly the same thing if, as the hypothesis has it, the Signs Gospel is John's narrative source. Add to this that the seven references employing ἀποθνήσκειν are all non-Signs Gospel, and it would seem reasonable to conclude that John is far more concerned with Jesus' death than was the author of the Signs Gospel. But is it equally obvious that by constructing the long lines leading up to and away from the Signs Gospel verse (11:53), he is providing a picture of the Jewish motivation for killing Jesus, a picture to replace the one portrayed in the Signs Gospel by the cleansing of the Temple pericope.

b. Several factors suggest that John's portrait of this motivation is drawn in light of the first of the intervening developments mentioned

---

42. Bornkamm is fully justified, of course, in taking exception to the statement of Käsemann quoted in my preceding note (1968 review, 114).

above, the appearance of ditheism, the charging of Jewish-Christian evangelists as Beguilers, and their execution. This development seems clearly reflected in the climactic motivedescribing references to Jesus› death, the first and the last:

> 5:18 For this reason the Jews sought all the more to kill him, be-cause . . . he was speaking of God as his own Father, thus making himself God's equal.

> 19:7 The Jews answered him [Pilate], "We have a law, and ac-cording to our law he ought to die, because he made himself the Son of God."[43]

And the same development is dramatically portrayed in relation to the death references in John 7.

3. An alteration of the Signs Gospel very nearly as obvious as the relocating of the Temple cleansing, and from a literary viewpoint its counterpart, is the sewing together of the Lazarus story and the porten-tious convening of the Sanhedrin. Again, John's editing is multifaceted. Consider one facet. In the Signs Gospel, the Lazarus story ended with the optimistic note characteristic of the signs in that document: "those who came to Mary and who saw what he did believed in him." Typi-cally, John accepts this positive reference to believers; but he then turns immediately to speak of others who show themselves to be informers against Jesus. Recall the healed paralytic and his action in chapter 5:

5:15	11:46
ἀπῆλθεν ὁ ἄνθρωπος καὶ ἀνήγγειλεν τοῖς Ἰουδαίοις ὅτι Ἰησοῦς ἐστιν ὁ ποιήσας αὐτὸν ὑγιῆ.	τινὲς δὲ ἐξ αὐτῶν ἀπῆλθον πρὸς τοὺς Φαρισαίους καὶ εἶπαν αὐτοῖς ἃ ἐποίησεν Ἰησοῦς.

This parallelism, plus the notes struck somewhat obliquely in 12:10–11 and 19, point to the same conclusion: the experience of martyrdom on

43. Which law is this? I suppose the reference—as in the case of 5:18—is to Deuter-onomy 13:5 and 9, as this law was interpreted and developed in Rabbinic tradition.

the part of highly successful Jewish-Christian evangelists has strongly colored John's presentation of the death motif in the first half of his Gospel. In light of the developments since the writing of the Signs Gospel, it is important for the one who thus dies to know that, like Lazarus, he has already passed from death to life by Jesus' word.

But I suspect that the experience of martyrdom is reflected also in the passion narrative itself. For the same motif, in the form True Mosaic Prophet/False Beguiling Prophet, plays an important role in the trial scenes, as Meeks has shown. And the key verses in this regard appear to be John's additions to the Signs Gospel. This may be one of those junctures at which *religionsgeschichtlichen* research intersects source criticism in such a way as to modify slightly the latter's results. I have in mind John 18:19. Fortna gives this verse to the Signs Gospel with some reservations, expressed by enclosing it in parentheses (p. 242). In his discussion of it (p. 120) he calls it "very likely pre-Johannine, showing none of the signs of John's characteristic dialogues."

Against its stemming from the Signs Gospel is the fact that there is no prior reference to Jesus' διδαχὴ in that document. Correspondingly, in favor of viewing it as John's own addition are factors recently mentioned by Meeks. At the parallel point in synoptic tradition, the High Priest asks Jesus whether he is ὁ χριστός. This question would have been well-suited to the Signs Gospel; perhaps it originally stood in the Signs Gospel at this point, though that can be no more than a guess. In any case it would have been in character for John to substitute for some such question the picture of the High Priest querying Jesus about his διδαχὴ and his μαθηταί. For

> of the false prophet it is required to determine whether he teaches words which have not come from God (Deuteronomy 18:20) and whether he has "led astray" others (Deut 13:1–6).[44]

---

44. Meeks, *The Prophet-King*, 6of. Dodd reaches a similar conclusion by a somewhat different route in his *Historical Tradition in the Fourth Gospel* (Cambridge: Cambridge University Press, 1963), 95, as Meeks notes.

(Perhaps a similar confluence of source criticism and *Religionsgeschichte* would lead one to delete ἦν δὲ ὁ Βαραββᾶς λῃστής [18:40] from the Signs Gospel. See Meeks, *The Prophet-King*, pp. 67f.).

From the foregoing, it will be obvious that with Bornkamm[45] and Meeks[46] I find some of the statements Käsemann has recently made about John's attitude toward the passion less than convincing. But they are also far from being entirely wide of the mark. If comparison with the Signs Gospel shows that John carefully introduced quite a number of remarks that point ahead to the passion (contra *Testament*, p. 7), thus supplying a distinct motive for the adversaries' deeds, an equally important and well-known pattern is revealed by a linear reading of the Fourth Gospel itself, especially if one bears in mind the synoptic tradition of Jesus' passion predictions: there is a distinct line pointing from such verbs as ἀποκτεῖναι to such verbs as ὑπάγειν. Such a pattern did not escape Bultmann's notice, of course,[47] and it is clearly this pattern that Käsemann has firmly in mind.[48] Käsemann's mistake lies, I think, in his assumption that the ἀποκτεῖναι references are traditional and more or less excess baggage, while "the comprehensive and, for John, characteristic description of Jesus death is given with the verb *hypagein*."[49] If Fortna's source analysis is essentially correct, both sets of references are largely Johannine.

But so is the pattern which leads from the one to the other and which makes abundantly clear that the Jesus

> who walks on the water and through closed doors, who cannot be captured by his enemies, . . . [who] debates with them from the vantage point of the infinite difference between heaven and earth.[50]

45. Bornkamm, 1968 review, 113–14.

46. Meeks's review is mentioned in note 1, above. See particularly p. 419.

47. Rudolf Bultmann, *Theology of the New Testament*, Vol. 2, translated by Robert Morgan (New York: Scribner, 1955), 53.

48. *Testament*, 17ff.

49. Ibid.

50. *Testament*, 9.

is not snatched away and killed. On the contrary, he goes away in an
entirely sovereign manner. Why does John employ so emphatically the
verbs ὑπάγειν, ἀναβαίνειν etc?

A full answer to this question may not be attainable. I close with it
primarily in order to point up the complex character of the *religionsge-
schichtlicher* factors that are involved in the transition from the Signs Gospel to the Fourth Gospel. On the one side, it should be clear that, in part,
the pattern ἀποκτεῖναι → ὑπάγειν / ἀναβαίνειν is polemically related to the
opponents' claims regarding Moses' ascent.[51] But the more obvious and
more often commented-upon pattern ἀναβαίνειν-καταβαίνειν is scarcely
to be viewed in such a manner. The Moses traditions provide no parallel.
Indeed the notion of a descending and, therefore, pre-earthly-existent figure is not "at home" either in Jewish apocalyptic or in Jewish mysticism.[52]
And while it is true that Wisdom descends, her descent is nowhere tied
to a victorious and redemptive ascent. In short, the descent/ascent pattern "has been and remains the strongest support for the hypothesis that
Johannine Christology is connected with gnostic mythology."[53] At this
point—and it is a very important point for John's theology—comparing
the Fourth Gospel with the Signs Gospel supports Haenchen's suggestion:

> Die gnostische Terminologie . . . muss daraufhin untersucht
> werden, ob sie der Wunder-Quelle oder nur dem Evst ange-
> hört. Ich vermute das Zweite.[54]

51. See Meeks, *The Prophet-King*, 297-301.

52. See, e.g., H. Odeberg. *The Fourth Gospel: Interpreted in its Relation to Contemporaneous Religious Currents in Palestine and the Hellenistic-Oriental World* (Amsterdam: B.
R. Grüner, 1929), 73; R. Schnackenburg, *The Gospel according to St. John*, I (1968), 551;
also R. Schnackenburg, *Present and Future: Modern Aspects of New Testament Theology*
(Notre Dame: University of Notre Dame Press, 1966), 176f.

53. Meeks, *The Prophet-King*, 297.

54. Haenchen, in a letter to J. M. Robinson, Spring, 1966 (English: "The Gnostic
terminology . . . must be investigated to see if it is source of the miracles or only the
Evangelist. I suspect the second.")

III. A Sketch of a Sketch

1. Source Criticism and Religionsgeschichte

This sketch—I accent again its partial character—suggests that a significant portion of the developments transpiring between the Signs Gospel and the Fourth Gospel arises from the side of Jewish opponents. There is a synagogue which, having expelled the messianic believers, now stands opposite John's church; its complex and varied response to Christian propaganda, including and, I suppose, centering in the Signs Gospel, is reflected in the Fourth Gospel, dominantly in non-Signs Gospel passages. Moreover, one of John's concerns as he reshapes the Signs Gospel is to correct those of its deficiencies that the intervening debate has brought to light.

If one is convinced of this much, the next question is: What kind of a synagogue stands opposite John's church? Two points are clear: (1) The Jewish community of John's city follows, at least in large part, the lead of Jamnia (ἀποσυνάγωγος γένηται is related to the reworded *Birkat Haminim*). The local Gerousia is through and through Pharisaic. (2) At least some of the Jewish opponents know and treasure exotic traditions about Moses as the one who ascended into heaven, receiving the secrets.[55] But this sort of speculation was very widespread (see Meeks). Its presence, therefore, cannot serve to draw narrow limits for the type of Jewish community in question. The possibility is certainly not to be excluded that some of the opponents represent a form of Jewish gnosis, although it is also possible that elements of *gnosis* are introduced into the picture by actors other than these opponents. One may recall with

---

55. It would be intriguing to see what would be shown by putting Fortna and Meeks together regarding the portraits of Moses and of Jesus as Kings. For example, Fortna gives 6:14 to the Signs Gospel and 6:15 to the Evangelist. Is the tradition of Moses as King unknown or unimportant to the author of the Signs Gospel? I have had insufficient time to explore this question and others that might similarly arise.

uncommon interest the remarks with which Odeberg forty years ago concluded his comments on John 5:19–29:

> (1) With regard to language, terms, expressions used, or problems treated, it may safely be stated that, on the whole, John 5:24–30 is most akin to Jewish, early Rabbinic, terminology. The section, it is true, makes use of two single terms which are foreign to the Rabbinic terminology, as far as it is known,[56] viz. those of the "voice" and the "Son of God" terms, which are familiar to other circles. Yet, there is no doubt but that the large proportion of terms used and the contiguity of the statements best fit in with Rabbinic modes of reasoning and assertion.

> (2) With regard to the inner meaning (roughly speaking: the doctrine) conveyed, on the other hand, it must be urged that John moves in a sphere far removed from the Rabbinic world of ideas. The situation in this respect might perhaps be best pictured by one of the two suppositions following viz. 1. either that John himself completely familiar with, brought up in, Rabbinic Jewish learning and schools of thought, tries to convey to Rabbinic readers, by using their terms and language, a doctrine, yea, a spiritual reality altogether different from their world of thought 2. or else that John addresses himself to readers who, although sharing the terms and language of Rabbinic religious thought, belong to a circle different from normative Rabbinic Judaism.

> . . . If, then, we call the religious atmosphere of John "the Johannine (Christian) salvation-mysticism" it might be said that the Johannine salvation-mysticism uses an idiom that is most nearly related to the Rabbinic style and terminology.

> It is significant 1. that in the scanty sources of early Samaritan and Jewish Mysticism or Gnosticism we meet with a similar salvation mysticism, 2. that we are actually able to demonstrate that there existed already in the first and second centuries A.D., in the Judaism that moved within the folds of

---

56. This is one of Odeberg's careful statements that would now have to be changed.

Rabbinic tradition, several circles of a salvation-mystical character, and 3. that some of these, in ideas and expressions, were more closely bound up with Mandaean mysticism than with any other known mystical religious formation outside Judaism. Certainly John cannot be maintained to be identical with or to have developed from any of these and still less from Rabbinic circles, but the sources in question afford parallel phenomena to John and make it possible to discern the approximate position of John in relation to Palestinian mysticism.[57]

In short, *religionsgeschichtliche* developments behind the Fourth Gospel are complex. Accepting the Signs Gospel as a working hypothesis promises to bring the complexity into sharper focus, if not to render it more readily understandable, and that fact speaks in favor of the hypothesis.

2. Source Criticism, Religionsgeschichte, and Theologiegeschichte

With respect to the problem of finding John's place in the history of Christian thought, the sketch leads to at least one conclusion: John belongs in a dominantly Jewish-Christian milieu. Bultmann suggested something similar about the setting of the Semeia-Quelle.[58] But if the lines of thought pursued above are essentially correct, the same must be said about the Gospel itself. As one views the growth of the tradition from the Signs Gospel to the Fourth Gospel, overt concerns with Jewish questions become more, not less, central.[59]

Although I have given no preparation for it in the body of the paper, let me underline this conclusion by appending a note on John and Luke.

57. H. Odeberg, *The Fourth Gospel*, 214ff.

58. See Moody Smith, Composition, 37f, and Bultmann, Johannes, 76 n. 6 and 78 n. 4. On the basis of Yoma 29a (Strack and Billerbeck, Vol. 2, 409f.) Bultmann ponders whether already in Judaism the OT miracles had been numbered and placed in a series.

59. Again, one should be warned, of course, that much turns on the precise contours of the Signs Gospel.

One thinks of comparing these two theologians because F. C. Baur placed both of them at or near the emergence of early Catholicism, and because in his own way Käsemann has revived Baur's thesis in our time. Without suggesting that the thesis is entirely erroneous, I want simply to point out one significant difference between Luke and John.

Centrally characteristic of Luke's stance is the replacing of the old frontier, the synagogue, by the new frontier, the marketplace of Greco-Roman culture. Luke's church views the Jewish mission as thoroughly closed. The horizon is occupied by a gentile church that is expanding into the gentile world. Luke must remind this church of its Old Testament roots, but even as he does just that, he emphasizes that the synagogue frontier is closed.

The author of the Signs Gospel is of quite a different view. He pens "a textbook for potential Jewish converts."[60] And John himself, in spite of the bitter Jewish opposition and persecution, holds that frontier still to be at least partially open.

> Yet there may have been one group of Jews that the Gospel
> addressed with a certain hopefulness; namely, the small group
> of Jews who believed in Jesus but as yet had not severed their
> relationship with the Synagogue. In the 80's and 90's of the 1st
> century these Jewish Christians were going through a crisis.[61]

In short, John precisely does not substitute one frontier for another. If he belongs to a sectarian milieu, as Käsemann has proposed, I wonder whether that milieu may not be considerably more Jewish-Christian than most interpreters have thought.[62]

60. Fortna, 234.

61. Brown, LXXIV.

62. I do not mean to suggest that John's own church is Ebionite in any proper sense of that term, but I am still struck with the natural way in which Johannine references crop up so often in H. J. Schoeps' *Theologie und Geschichte des Judenchristentums* (Tübingen: J. C. B. Mohr, 1949). There is surely something to it. Unfortunately an article by Jürgen Becker appeared too late for reference here, "Wunder und Christologie, zum literarkritischen und christologischen Problem der Wunder im Johannesevangelium," *NTS* 16 (1969-70): 130-48.

CHAPTER 5

A Gentile Mission that Replaced an Earlier Jewish Mission?

I

ALTHOUGH DIFFERENT FROM ONE another in numerous and important regards, the Johannine labors of Ernst Käsemann, Wayne Meeks, and myself converge in one shared conviction: The Gospel of John originated in a local church—or group of churches—markedly distinct from the types of Christianity that were developing during the same period into the Great Church.[1]

---

1. First published in *Exploring the Gospel of John: In Honor of D. Moody Smith*, ed. R. Alan Culpepper and C. Clifton Black (Louisville: Westminster John Knox, 1996), 124–44. Regarding the "place" of the Johannine community, Meeks's interest—to some degree like my own—is primarily focused on John and Judaism. Hence, when he introduced the term "sect" into the present-day discussion of that community, he meant, and continues to mean, a sect of Judaism. He has also said things about this sect, however, that bear on the question of its place in early Christian life and thought. (See note 7 below.) In this chapter, "the Gospel of John" refers to the document we have, less chapter 21 and a few other parts of the text that were also added by a redactor. Regarding the literary history of the Gospel, see esp. D. Moody Smith, *The Composition and Order of the Fourth Gospel: Bultmann's Literary Theory*, Johannine Monograph Series 3 (1965, Eugene, OR: Wipf & Stock, 2015); idem, *Johannine Christianity: Essays on Its Setting, Sources, and Theology* (Columbia: University of South Carolina Press, 1984), passim; Rudolf Schnackenburg, *The Gospel according to St John* (New York: Crossroad, 1982), 1.72–74; Raymond E. Brown, *The Gospel according to John (i-xii)*, AB 29

Käsemann's first serious plunge into the Johannine waters came in his inaugural lecture at the University of Göttingen in 1951.[2] A decade and a half later, with some changes, he used the Schaffer lectures at Yale to continue his search for the place of the Fourth Gospel in the history of early Christian thought and life.[3] The major result can be stated in two sentences: To compare John's theology with theologies in other strains of early Christian tradition is to see that the Evangelist was heir to the kind of naively docetic, highly enthusiastic strain of Christian thought combatted both by Paul (1 Cor 4:8–13; 15:12) and by the author of 2 Timothy (2:18). The church in which John lived, then, was a sort of conventicle shoved off into a corner, quite distinct from the emerging catholic church, indeed, in some regards hostile to it.[4]

(Garden City: Doubleday, 1966), xxxiv–xxxix; Robert Tomson Fortna, *The Gospel of Signs: A Reconstruction of the Narrative Source Underlying the Fourth Gospel*, SNTSMS 11 (Cambridge: Cambridge University Press, 1970); idem, *The Fourth Gospel and Its Predecessor: From Narrative Source to Present Gospel* (Philadelphia: Fortress, 1988).

2. Ernst Käsemann, "Ketzer und Zeuge: Zum johanneischen Verfasserproblem," *ZTK* 48 (1951) 292–311 = *Exegetische Versuche und Besinnungen*, 2 vols. (Göttingen: Vandenhoeck & Ruprecht, 1960, 1964) 168–87.

3. ERNST KÄSEMANN, *The Testament of Jesus: A Study of John in the Light of Chapter 17*, translated by Gerhard Krodel, Johannine Monograph Series 6 (1968 [German original, 1966], Eugene, OR: Wipf & Stock, 2017). Between "Ketzer und Zeuge" and *Testament* Kasemann published a productively provocative study of the Johannine prologue, "Aufbau und Anliegen des johanneischen Prologs," in *Exegetische Versuche und Besinnungen*, 1.155–80 (= "The Structure and Purpose of the Prologue to John's Gospel," in Ernst Käsemann, *New Testament Questions of Today* [London: SCM, 1969] 138–67).

4. Käsemann, *The Testament of Jesus*, 75–76. Among the numerous reviews of Käsemann's *Testament*, see Günther Bornkamm, "Towards the Interpretation of John's Gospel: A Discussion of *The Testament of Jesus* by Ernst Käsemann," in *The Interpretation of John*, edited by John Ashton, IRT 9 (London: SPCK, 1986), 79–98; and Wayne A. Meeks in *USQR* 24 (1969) 414–21. See also now the critique of Käsemann's work at numerous points in Udo Schnelle, *Antidocetic Christology in the Gospel of John: An Investigation of the Place of the Fourth Gospel in the Johannine School* (Minneapolis: Fortress, 1992 [German original, 1989]).

I myself approached the question of the place of the Johannine church in the history of early Christianity by first investigating that community's relations with its parent synagogue, a line of approach quite different from the one followed by Käsemann.[5] In one regard, however, my work led to a picture of Johannine Christianity similar to that of Käsemann. Convinced that the history of the Johannine community, from its origin through the period of its life in which the Fourth Gospel was composed, forms to no small extent a chapter in the history of *Jewish Christianity*, I concluded that this community stood at some remove not only from the parent synagogue—from which it had been excommunicated—but also from the emerging Great Church.[6]

Bringing to the study of the Johannine question both a penetrating *religionsgeschichtliche* analysis—focused largely on Jewish and Samaritan speculation about Moses as prophet and King—and an admirable sensitivity to what we might call the in-group nature of Johannine language, Wayne Meeks also concluded, following his own path, that what the church reflected in the Fourth Gospel was a "special group of former Jews" in which "we have the very model

5. J. Louis Martyn, "The Salvation-History Perspective in The Fourth Gospel" (PhD diss., Yale University, 1957); idem, *History and Theology in the Fourth Gospel* (1968, 1978, third edition, Louisville: Westminster John Knox, 2003). See also in the present volume, idem, "Source Criticism and *Religionsgeschichte* in the Fourth Gospel;" "We Have Found Elijah;" "Persecution and Martyrdom" (a shorter version of his earlier treatment of *Clementine Recognitions* 1.33–71);" "Glimpses into the History of the Johannine Community."

6. Martyn, "Source Criticism and *Religionsgeschichte* in the Fourth Gospel" and "Glimpses into the History of the Johannine Community," 120–21. The kernel of the present essay—doubt that the Johannine community had a discrete mission to gentiles at the time of the Gospel—was a major motif in a paper I presented at the 1979 meeting of SBL. The case for locating the Johannine community in the history of Jewish Christianity has now been both broadened and deepened in a fascinating and instructive essay by Martinus C. de Boer, "*L'Évangile de Jean et le christianisme juif (nazoréen),*" in *Le déchirement: Juifs et chrétiens au premier siècle,* edited by Daniel Marguerat (Geneva: Labor et Fides, 1996) 179–202.

of a sectarian consciousness."[7] Thus, from 1972 onwards, Meeks has repeatedly referred to the Johannine church as a sect, a practice that has elicited sharp disagreement in some quarters.[8]

7. Wayne A. Meeks, "Equal to God," in *The Conversation Continues: Studies in Paul and John in Honor of J. Louis Martyn*, edited by Robert T. Fortna and Beverly R. Gaventa (Nashville: Abingdon, 1990), 309–21 (quotation, 319). This conclusion is already present in Meeks's earlier works. See the classic study in which he successfully introduced the use of the term "sect" into present-day discussion of John: "The Man From Heaven in Johannine Sectarianism," *JBL* 91 (1972) 44–72 = *The Interpretation of John*, edited by Ashton, 141–73. See, further, Meeks, "'Am I a Jew?'—Johannine Christianity and Judaism," in *Christianity, Judaism and Other Greco-Roman Cults: Studies for Morton Smith at Sixty*, edited by Jacob Neusner, 4 pts., SJLA 12 (Leiden: Brill, 1975), 1.163–86; Meeks, "The Divine Agent and His Counterfeit in Philo and the Fourth Gospel," in *Aspects of Religious Propaganda in Judaism and Early Christianity*, edited by Elisabeth Schüssler Fiorenza (Notre Dame: University of Notre Dame Press, 1976), 43–67; Meeks, "Breaking Away: Three New Testament Pictures of Christianity's Separation from the Jewish Communities," in *"To See Ourselves as Others See Us": Christians, Jews, "Others" in Late Antiquity*, edited by Jacob Neusner and Ernest S. Frerichs, Scholars Press Studies in the Humanities (Chico: Scholars, 1985), 93–115 (esp. 103). As I have said above (note 1), Meeks's work—to some degree, like my own—has been focused primarily on the place of the Johannine church in its Jewish context. Prior to its exclusion from the synagogue, this church had been a sect "of Judaism," something socially true of none of the Pauline churches (Meeks, "Breaking Away," 94, 106). Meeks also says, however, that in John there is "hardly a hint of a specifically gentile mission" ("Breaking Away," 97). This statement alone suffices to show that Meeks's sociological use of the word "sect" has implications for the place of John in early Christian thought and life, as Raymond E. Brown correctly senses (*The Community of the Beloved Disciple* [New York: Paulist, 1979], 14 n. 8; see also Meeks, "Breaking Away," 114). Regarding Jewish-Christian sects that were as far removed from the emerging Great Church as they were from emerging rabbinism—something true of the Johannine community, I think, but by no means true of the church reflected in the upper strata of Matthew—see, for instance, Joan E. Taylor, "The Phenomenon of Early Jewish-Christianity: Reality or Scholarly Invention?," *VC* 44 (1990) 313–34.

8. See, for example, Brown, *The Community of the Beloved Disciple*, 14 n. 8. I will turn, below, to the recent works of Brown and Martin Hengel, the latter of whom writes on the Fourth Gospel without making any reference to the Johannine labors of Wayne Meeks later than *The Prophet-King: Moses Traditions and the Johannine Christology*, Johannine Monograph Series 5 (1967, Eugene, OR: Wipf & Stock, 2017). Is it because of Moody Smith's irenic approach to the question of John's place in early Christianity

that his labors have kindled no such disagreement (note the comment of Brown in the reference, given above)? I think it wise not to bring Smith directly into the debate at this juncture (see below, the discussion of John 12:37–50), but several of his comments should be cited, not least because he has himself applied the adjective "sectarian" to the Johannine church. In an essay titled "Johannine Christianity: Some Reflections on Its Character and Delineation" (*NTS* 21 [1976] 222–48 = Smith, *Johannine Christianity*, 1–36), Smith speaks of what he himself dubs the Johannine *Eigenart* ["distinctiveness"]:

> It can probably be agreed that on any reading of the Gospel and Epistles there appears a sectarian consciousness, a sense of exclusiveness, a sharp delineation of the community from the world. . . . If this sectarian or quasi-sectarian self-consciousness is not a matter of dispute, its roots, causes, and social matrix nevertheless are. What thereby comes to expression? A Christian sense of alienation or separation from the world generally? From the synagogue? From developing ecclesiastical orthodoxy? (*Johannine Christianity*, 2–4)

Later in the same essay, he begins to give at least a partial answer to these questions by speaking of the place of John in early Christian history:

> The relative isolation and independence of the Johannine material in language and conceptuality may militate against the traditional viewpoint [that it originated in Ephesus, although its final form may have been published there]. . . . John's relative isolation from other streams of tradition in the New Testament seems to bear witness to a place of origin somewhat off the beaten track. . . . If the Johannine Gospel or tradition actually originated in a relatively remote corner of the Christian map, its distinctive character as well as its difficulty in finding acceptance in the emerging catholic church become more intelligible. Nor is such an origin incompatible with John's Gospel's having rather early made friends among Christians later branded heretical." (22)

Note the reference to these comments of Smith in Klaus Wengst, *Bedrängte Gemeinde und verherrlichter Christus: Ein Versuch über das Johannesevangelium* (Neukirchen Vluyn: Neukirchener, 1981), 93; 3rd ed. (Munich: Kaiser, 1990), 178–79. Note also Robert Kysar, *John, the Maverick Gospel* (Atlanta: John Knox, 1976); Fernando F. Segovia, "The Love and Hatred of Jesus and Johannine Sectarianism," *CBQ* 43 (1981) 258–72; and the comment by John Ashton in *Understanding the Fourth Gospel* (Oxford: Clarendon, 1991), 173: "Finding itself alone and confronting persecution, [the Johannine group] had two choices. It could either look for support else where

II

Largely in response to the works of Käsemann, Meeks, and myself, there have been recent attempts—notably by Raymond E. Brown and Martin Hengel—to show that the Fourth Gospel, far from being the maverick product of an essentially sectarian church, originated in or near the streams that flowed together to become the Great Church.[9] As Käsemann,

---

or huddle self-protectively in a small knot. Perhaps it did both these things, but the evidence is stronger for the latter" (see also 173 n. 23).

9. See Brown, *The Community of the Beloved Disciple*; Martin Hengel, *The Johannine Question* (London: SCM, 1989). As Brown and Hengel are very far from understanding themselves to be, in any significant sense, heirs of Ferdinand Christian Baur, there is perhaps some irony in the fact that—in regard to the issue of the present chapter—the results of their labors largely coincide with the conclusion reached a century and a half ago by the Tübingen giant, for Baur thought the Fourth Gospel to be, along with Luke's volumes, a prime witness to the emergence of the Great Church. See F. C. Baur, *Geschichte der christlichen Kirche*, 3rd ed., 5 vols. (Tübingen: Fues, 1863), 1.172: "Auf diesen beiden Punkten [sc. die romische Kirche und das johanneische Evangelium] hat das christliche Bewusstsein in seiner freieren Entwicklung dasselbe Ziel im Auge, die Realisierung der Idee der katholischen Kirche" ("With respect to both [the Roman church and the Johannine Gospel], Christian consciousness in its unimpeded development has the same aim in view: the realization of the idea of the catholic church"). To the books of Brown and Hengel, one can add some elements in the work of Schnelle, *Antidocetic Christology in the Gospel of John*. In his conclusion, Schnelle says,

> The labeling of Johannine Christianity as a marginal group, which one so often reads, is probably not accurate, for sectarian flight from the world is far from the intention of the evangelist (see only 17:15, 18, 20; 20:21–22). Moreover, the high level of its theological reflection, as well as its connections to the Synoptics and especially to Pauline Christianity, make the Fourth Gospel appear rather to be located *at the center of the theological history of earliest Christianity*, at a point at which important currents in developing Christian theology converged. (236, emphasis added)

A brief assessment of Schnelle's work has been given by M. J. J. Menken, "The Christology of the Fourth Gospel: A Survey of Recent Research," in *From Jesus to John: Essays on Jesus and New Testament Christology in Honour of Marinus de Jonge*, edited by Martinus C. de Boer, JSNTSup 84 (Sheffield: JSOT, 1993), 292–320 (see esp. 307–8).

Meeks, and I have ourselves argued the sectarian case in quite different and sometimes mutually contradictory ways,[10] one is not surprised to see that Brown and Hengel have formulated a number of different counter-arguments.[11] They share, however, one very important claim: A major mark of the essentially orthodox character of the Johannine community lies in its understanding of its mission. With slight variations from one another, Brown and Hengel hold that, like the emerging Great Church, the Johannine community considered the gentile world to constitute its mission frontier. Indeed, in Brown's view, the Johannine community that

---

10. As stated earlier, Käsemann argued by making comparisons among lines of Christian tradition, and his portrait is that of a highly hellenized church, presumably one that was pursuing a gentile mission.

11. Indeed, Brown and Hengel differ in a number of ways. One notes, for example, that, whereas Brown speaks of the Johannine community as a church drawn both from Jews and from gentiles (*The Community of the Beloved Disciple*, 82), Hengel finds the founder of the Johannine school (although himself a Jewish Christian) to be "working in a Gentile-Christian milieu," for that founder "presupposes the Gentile mission and the solution of the question of the Law" (*The Johannine Question*, 123). That difference is related to the fact that, whereas Brown accepts the quest for the history of the Johannine community, Hengel does not: "Nowadays we already have all too many attempts to reconstruct a 'history of the Johannine community.' They are all doomed to failure, because we know nothing of a real history which even goes back to Palestine, and conjectures about it are idle" (*The Johannine Question*, 205 n. 85). Brown thinks that when the Gospel was written, the Johannine community had its mission frontier from Jews to gentiles (*The Community of the Beloved Disciple*, 55), whereas Hengel, as noted, thinks the founder himself presupposed the (sic!) gentile mission. Readers conversant with my own work will not be surprised to hear that, on the whole, I find Brown's argument much more finely nuanced than that of Hengel. Moreover, Brown is admirably willing to note factors that militate against his major argument. One notes, for example, "there is much in Johannine theology that would relativize the importance of institution and office at the very time when that importance was being accentuated in other Christian communities (including those who spoke of apostolic foundation)" (*The Community of the Beloved Disciple*, 87; also see 183–98). See, further, Martinus C. de Boer, "John 4:27—Women (and Men) in the Gospel and Community of John," in *Women in the Biblical Tradition*, edited by. George J. Brooke, Studies in Women and Religion 31 (Lewiston: Mellen, 1992), 208–30.

is reflected in the Gospel had substituted the gentile mission for its earlier mission to the Jews, as had the Great Church.[12]

We have, then, a question of some importance in our quest to discern the place of John in early Christian thought and life. What can we say about the history of the Johannine community's vision of the ecclesiological future? Specifically, at the time of the Gospel, had the Johannine community shifted its mission frontier from Jews to gentiles?

III

We can be confident, I think, that the community was born when Christian evangelists preached their gospel in the synagogue(s) of John's city.[13] With that event, a group of Christian Jews was born in the synagogue. During the immediately following period, members of this group continued what we may call a mission to Jews, preaching the good news of Jesus' messiahship to their fellows in the synagogue.[14]

12. Brown, *The Community of the Beloved Disciple*, 55. The nature of the communities reflected in the Johannine epistles is a matter left aside in the present chapter.

13 This view is not held by every Johannine critic, but it is fair to say that it is widespread in contemporary studies. See Robert Kysar, *The Fourth Evangelist and His Gospel: An Examination of Contemporary Scholarship* (Minneapolis: Augsburg, 1975), 147–72; idem, "The Fourth Gospel: A Report on Recent Research," *ANRW* 2.25.3 (1985) 2389–480; idem, "The Gospel of John," *ABD* 3 (1992) 912–31; Smith, Johannine Christianity, 62–79 and passim; Teresa Okure, *The Johannine Approach to Mission: A Contextual Study of John 4:1–42*, WUNT 2/31 (Tübingen: Mohr Siebeck, 1988), 13; R. Alan Culpepper, "John," in *The Books of the Bible: The Apocrypha and the New Testament*, edited by. Bernhard W. Anderson (New York: Scribner's, 1989), 2.203–28; John Painter, *The Quest for the Messiah: The History, Literature and Theology of the Johannine Community* (Edinburgh: T. & T. Clark, 1991; 2nd ed., Nashville: Abingdon, 1993), passim; Ashton, *Understanding the Fourth Gospel*, 109 and passim; John Riches, *A Century of New Testament Study* (Cambridge: Lutterworth, 1993), 180–97; Klaus Wengst, *Bedrängte Gemeinde und verherrlichter Christus* (1990), 75–104. The dominance of this view is also reflected in certain plaintive remarks of Schnelle and Hengel.

14. On the theory of a signs-source or Signs-Gospel, and on the closely related hypothesis that that source or Gospel played a role in the evangelization of Jews, see esp. Smith, *The Composition and Order of the Fourth Gospel*, 34–44 (Bultmann's analysis); Fortna, *The Gospel of Signs*; idem, *The Fourth Gospel and Its Predecessor*.

In time, several factors—not least the conversion of large numbers of synagogue members (12:11, 19)—led the Jewish authorities to expel this innersynagogue group (9:22; 12:42; 16:2).[15] Suffering the deep pain of being separated from their social and theological cosmos, the group of Christian Jews became a discrete community of Jewish Christians, with a common history of suffering and with a shared language system reflecting that history.[16]

One considers seriously the possibility, then, that the Gospel might also reflect a shift in mission frontier corresponding to the pain of ex-communication. That is to say, such a painful separation from the parent synagogue might have led members of the Johannine community to shake the Jewish dust off their sandals. In abandoning their Jewish mission, they might have turned to the gentiles, thus showing that, in this regard, their community found itself in the midst of the stream that flowed into the emerging Great Church.[17] Do the pertinent data in the Fourth Gospel reflect that development?

15. Whether this expulsion was in some way connected with the *Birkat Hamimim* is a question that can be left aside in this chapter (see Meeks, "Breaking Away," 102–3). See now the carefully nuanced discussion in de Boer, "L'Évangile de Jean et le christianisme juif (nazoréen)," and the literature cited therein, notably Philip S. Alexander, "'The Parting of the Ways' from the Perspective of Rabbinic Judaism," in *Jews and Christians: The Parting of the Ways A. D. 70 to 135*, edited by. James D. G. Dunn (Tübingen: Mohr Siebeck, 1993), 1–25. The thesis that the Johannine group experienced a painful exclusion from its parent synagogue is as close to a simple fact as one can come, whatever the instrument or process by which the leaders of that synagogue effected it. Moreover, seventy-five years of study of the Synoptic Gospels should suffice to teach us that one is obliged to date a given motif at or very near the time of the author of the document in which it is found, unless one can show it to have a significantly earlier origin—something accomplished, with regard to John 9:22; 12:42; and 16:2, neither by Ulrich Luz (with Rudolf Smend, *Gesetz*, Biblische Konfrontationen/Kohlhammer Taschenbücher 1015 [Stuttgart: Kohlhammer, 1981], 125), nor by Schnelle (*Antidocetic Christology in the Gospel of John*, 25–31, 120–21), nor by Hengel (*The Johannine Question*, 114–15).

16. One can compare John 16:2 with 1 Thessalonians 2:14–15 but not with 2:16a. See Paul S. Minear, *John: The Martyr's Gospel* (New York: Pilgrim, 1984). Regarding a shared language system, see note 20 below.

17. See, for example, P. Maurice Casey, *From Jewish Prophet to Gentile God: The*

IV

Explanations of Jewish Holy Times

> After this there was a festival of the Jews . . . (John 5:1)
> Now the Passover, the festival of the Jews, was near. (6:4)
> Now the Jewish festival of Booths was near. (7:2)[18]

These and similar explanatory notes have been taken by some to indicate that the Evangelist was addressing his work to gentiles, for it seems that only gentiles would need to be told that Passover and Booths are festivals of the Jews.[19] We have here, however, an instance in which modern interpreters can easily go astray if they do not trouble themselves to enter into the strange and linguistically dialectic world of the Johannine community.[20] To read through the whole of the Gospel is to see that the expression, "Passover, the festival of the Jews," begs for comparison with the Evangelist's numerous references to "the Jews," and even more with the expression, "their Law" (15:25; cf. 8:17; 10:34; 18:31; 19:7), both being locutions stemming,

---

Origins and Development of New Testament Christology (Louisville: Westminster John Knox, 1991), 27–31 and passim. See also the review of Casey's work by Leander E. Keck, *Interpretation* 47 (1993) 413–14; and Thomas L. Brodie, *The Gospel According to John: A Literary and Theological Commentary* (New York and Oxford: Oxford University Press, 1993), 164–65.

18. To this list one might add John 2:13; 4:45; 18:28; 19:14, 40.

19. See, for example, J. W. Bowker, "The Origin and Purpose of St. John's Gospel," *NTS* 11 (1964–65) 398–408 (408 n. 1); cf. R. Alan Culpepper, *Anatomy of the Fourth Gospel: A Study in Literary Design*, FFNT (Philadelphia: Fortress, 1983), 219–27 (but see the nuanced statements on 225). Schnelle takes these explanations and the translations, listed below, to show the great distance between the Gospel of John and Judaism (*Antidocetic Christology in the Gospel of John*, 34).

20. The Johannine language is admirably penetrated in the classic study of Meeks, "The Man from Heaven in Johannine Sectarianism." See also Meeks, "Equal to God" (above, note 7), and Martinus C. de Boer, "Narrative Criticism, Historical Criticism, and the Gospel of John," *JSNT* 47 (1992) 35–48.

probably without exception, from the Evangelist himself.[21] From that comparison one returns to the work of Meeks, thus recognizing that, given the sociolinguistic world of the Johannine community, these locutions reflect a group made up of former Jews, not of gentiles.[22] In short, the first words of 6:4 can be paraphrased, "Passover, the feast of the Jews who celebrate it, in distinction from the members of our community, who do not do so, being no longer [to] 'Jews' in the sense in which we ourselves use that term."[23]

Translations of Jewish Terms and Names

> They said to him, "*Rabbi*" (which translated means Teacher). (John 1:38)

> "We have found the Messiah" (which is translated Anointed [χριστός]). (1:41)

21. Fortna, *The Fourth Gospel and Its Predecessor*, 311. On "the Jews" in John, see, recently, Ashton, *Understanding the Fourth Gospel*, 131–59. On the expression "their Law" (and similar locutions), see Severino Pancaro, *The Law in the Fourth Gospel: The Torah and the Gospel, Moses and Jesus, Judaism and Christianity according to John*, NovTSup 42 (Leiden: Brill, 1975), 517–22; and de Boer's discussion of "your Torah" in 'Abodah 'Zara 16b–17a ("L'Évangilede Jean et le christianisme juif (nazoréen)").

22. See note 20 above, *pace* Hengel, *The Johannine Question*, 119. Note also the remark of Ashton about recognizing in the Gospel's "hot-tempered exchanges the type of family row in which the participants face one another across the room of a house which all have shared and all [to some degree still] call home" (*Understanding the Fourth Gospel*, 151, modified).

23. Meeks ("Equal to God," passim) is right to suggest that the modem exegete of the Gospel render numerous instances of "the Jews" by the expression "the other Jews," for ethnically, the members of the Johannine community were no less Jews than were the persons who remained in the synagogue. As Meeks knows very well, however, members of the separated community did not refer to themselves as Jews. And, as de Boer has shown, that is a point that invites one to compare the Johannine community with the Nazoreans: "Both communities reject the name 'Jews' to describe themselves" ("L'Évangile de Jean et le christianisme juif (nazoréen)").

"You are Simon, son of John. You are to be called *Cēphas*" (which is translated Peter). (1:42)

"I know that Messiah is coming" (who is called Christ [χριστός]). (4:25)

"Go, wash in the pool of Siloam" (which means Sent). (9:7)
"*Rabbouni*" (which means Teacher). (20:16)[24]

In these passages we have parenthetical, explanatory translations of a sort that would be needed, one may suppose, only by gentiles. Regarding them, Brown has commented, "The fact that such explanations are clearly parenthetical indicates that this effort towards comprehensibility for non-Jews was made in the last preGospel period of Johannine life."[25] More probable is the suggestion of John Painter, that these explanations are glosses, added to the body of the Gospel by the redactor responsible for John 21.[26] That chapter reflects the redactor's concern to baptize the Johannine community and its Gospel into the emerging Great Church by bringing both community and Gospel into an essentially positive relationship with the Petrine line of Christianity.[27] And, since the Great

24. One might add John 11:16 and 20:24, but they are in some regards different from simple translations; note also instances of translation in the other direction: 19:13 ("Gabbatha") and 19:17 ("Golgotha").

25. Brown, *The Community of the Beloved Disciple*, 55.

26. Painter, *The Quest for the Messiah* (2nd ed.), 131. Suggesting a line of interpretation that is surely possible, Painter includes in his list of these glosses the passages I have treated above.

27. Regarding the intentions of the redactor in adding John 21, see Rudolf Bultmann, *The Gospel of John: A Commentary* Johannine Monograph Series 1 (1941, Eugene, OR: 2014), 706-18 (*pace* Smith, *The Composition and Order of the Fourth Gospel*, 237), and the cogent comments of Brown: "The themes of Peter's rehabilitation, his role as shepherd of the sheep, his death as martyr, the role of the Beloved Disciple, his death, its relation to the second coming—*these are questions that affected the relation of the Johannine community to the Church at large*" (*The Gospel According to John (xiii–xxi)*, AB 29A (Garden City: Doubleday, 1970), 1082 (emphasis added). Did the redactor do his work after the Johannine community moved from the east, to Ephesus? Regarding the hypothesis of such a move, see Brown, *The Community of the Beloved Disciple*, 56 n. 103, 178–79 (on

Church lived on the gentile mission frontier, and since the Johannine redactor was intent on making the Gospel of his church compatible with the interests and makeup of that Great Church, he would have had ample reason for adding the instances of translation that are found in the body of the Gospel. On this reading, then, those parenthetical translations are post-Johannine glosses that tell us nothing about the makeup and missionary passions of the Johannine community when the Gospel itself was written.

A Reference to Teaching "Greeks"

> The Pharisees heard the crowd muttering such things about him, and the chief priests and Pharisees sent temple police to arrest him. Jesus then said, "I will be with you a little while longer, and then I am going to him who sent me. You will search for me, but you will not find me; and where I am you cannot come." The Jews said to one another, "Where does this man intend to go that we will not find him? Does he intend to go to the Dispersion among the Greeks [τὴν διασπορὰν τῶν Ἑλλήνων] and teach the Greeks [καὶ διδάσκειν τοὺς Ἕλληνας]? What does he mean by saying, 'You will search for me and you will not find me' and 'where I am you cannot come'?" (John 7:32–36).

The major thrust of this passage has to do with Christ's return to the Father. Allowing the Jews to misunderstand that reference, however, John refers to the possibility that Jesus will leave the Jewish homeland, go into the diaspora, and teach there.[28] And whom might he teach?

Marie-Émile Boismard). In light of the arguments advanced later in this chapter, one might also see the parenthetical translations as aids provided for God-fearers who, of their own volition, came to meetings of the Johannine community after it had moved.

28. On the rhetorical use of ironic riddles and misunderstanding in the Fourth Gospel, see especially Herbert Leroy, *Rätsel und Missverständnis: Ein Beitrag zur Formgeschichte des Johannesevangeliums*, BBB 30 (Bonn: Hanstein, 1968).

Linguistic analysis suggests two major possibilities for translating the expression, τὴν διασπορὰν τῶν Ἑλλήνων, the locution that provides the antecedent for τοὺς Ἕλληνας. John could mean "the Diaspora that consists of Greek-speaking Jews" (an explanatory genitive). On this reading, the prospect is that Jesus (through the Johannine community) might go away from Palestine to the diaspora of Greek-speaking Jews in order to teach those Jews. This interpretation was advanced in 1959 by J. A. T. Robinson.[29] It has also been questioned, often by saying that, had John intended to refer to Greek-speaking Jews, he would have spoken of Ἑλληνισταί ("Hellenists") rather than of Ἕλληναι ("Greeks").[30]

Alternatively, John could mean "the Diaspora of Jews who live among the Greeks" (a genitive of direction), in which case the prospect is that going abroad into the Jewish Diaspora, Jesus (through the Johannine community) would teach gentiles. A large number of interpreters have elected this reading.[31]

---

29. John A. T. Robinson, "The Destination and Purpose of St. John's Gospel," *NTS* 6 (1959–60) 117–31; cf. Painter, *Quest for the Messiah* (2nd ed.), 300 n. 45. A recent comment of Meeks's is worth noting. Having cautiously suggested that "there is hardly a hint of a specifically gentile mission in. John," he echoes Robinson, saying that in 7:35 and 12:20 John refers to Greek-speaking Jews. He then adds in a footnote: "In any case, if the *hellēnes* in John were meant to refer to a mission to gentiles, the passages in question are a strangely muted way to say so" ("Breaking Away," 97 and n. 10; see also 101).

30. Thus, in effect, Walter Bauer, *Das Johannesevangelium*, HNT 6 (Tübingen: Mohr Siebeck, 1933), 112; BAGD. In 1935, Hans Windisch also argued for gentiles in John 7:35 ("Ἕλλην, κ. τ. λ." *TDNT* 2 [1964] 509–10), but, as Meeks has pointed out, only after noting that Ἕλληναι sometimes refers to "Hellenized Orientals" (Meeks, "Breaking Away," 97 n. 10). On the one hand, then, the assumption that John would have drawn a hard-and-fast distinction between Ἕλληναι and Ἑλληνισταί may be an instance of rushing to judgment (see Meeks, ibid.; and note the comments on John's Greek in K. Beyer, *Semitische Syntax im Neuen Testament* [Göttingen: Vandenhoeck & Ruprecht, 1962], 17, 297–99). On the other hand, the criticism of Robinson's interpretation by C. K. Barrett is to be taken seriously: *The Gospel of John and Judaism* (London: SPCK, 1975), 11–19.

31. See, for example, Brown, *The Gospel according to John (i–xii)*, 29.314; idem, *The Community of the Beloved Disciple*, 57.

A third possibility emerges, however, when one compares 7:35 with 12:20, for the latter is the only other text in which John uses the word,Ἕλληνες ("Greeks"). There, as we will see below, he employs that word to refer neither to Greek-speaking Jews nor to gentiles, but rather to non-Jews who have attached themselves to the synagogue and who are, therefore, scarcely typical gentiles.[32] Thus, one may see 7:35 itself as a reference to a development subsequent to the Johannine community's move away from Palestine. God-fearers come not only to synagogues in the neighborhood of the Johannine community, but also to meetings of that community itself:[33] "Does he intend to go to the Diaspora of Jews who live among the (numerous) God-fearers [τὴν διασπορὰν τῶν Ἑλλήνων; genitive of direction] and there teach the God-fearers [τοὺς Ἕλληνας]?" On that reading, this text tells us nothing about a mission to gentiles themselves.

Weighing all three readings of John 7:35, one sees that this rather opaque text may reflect some kind of openness to non-Jews who have already begun to worship the God of Israel. It scarcely tells us that at the time of the Gospel the Johannine community had a discrete mission to gentiles. And it certainly does not indicate that the community had shifted its mission frontier from Jews to gentiles.

32. Josephus uses the word Ἕλλην to speak of God-fearers (θεοσέβής), "the multitudes of Greeks" (πολὺ πλῆθος Ἑλλήνων) who attached themselves to the Jewish community in Antioch (J. W. 7.45). Similarly, in Acts 17:4 (and also other passages) Luke refers to "a great many of the devout Greeks" (τῶν τε σεβομένων Ἑλλήνων πλῆθος πολὺ). About John 12:20 Windisch said that the addition of the clause, "in order to worship at the feast," "definitely excludes the sense of Gentiles" Ἕλλην, κ. τ. λ." TDNT 2 [1964] 509).

33. See esp. Martinus C. de Boer, "God-Fearers in Luke-Acts," in Luke's Literary Achievement: Collected Essays, edited by Christopher M. Tuckett (JSNTSup 116; Sheffield: JSOT, 1995), 50–71. See also John MacRay, "Greece," ABD 2 (1992) 1092–98, especially 1093: "Luke probably reserves the term 'Greeks' [Ἕλληναι] for non-Jews who worship the one true God (Acts 14:1; 16:1, 3; 17:4, 12; 19:17) [because they are God-fearers] . . . and designates as 'Gentiles' [ἔθνη] those who are polytheistic pagans (4:25, 27; 9:15; 18:6; etc.)."

"Other Sheep"

> I have other sheep that do not belong to this fold. I must
> bring them also, and they will listen to my voice. So there
> will be one flock, one shepherd (John 10:16).[34]

In chapter 10, John employs the word "sheep" fifteen times, using it in
ways that reveal both the history of the Johannine community and the
community's hopes for the future.[35] Leaving aside for a moment John's
reference to "other sheep," we attend both to the parable of 10:1–6 and
to its interpretation in 10:7–10 and in 10:11–18.

Noting that 10:1 follows on from 9:41, one sees that the sheep who
hear the voice of the Good Shepherd have already been portrayed in the
blind man of 9:1–39. He has heard Jesus' voice and has followed him,
while refusing to hear the voice of strangers (the synagogue authorities
who attempted to snatch him out of Jesus' hands). Thus, just as the blind
man of John 9 is the prototypical member of the Johannine community,
so the sheep of John 10 stand for that community in four ways:

a. It is they who hear the Good Shepherd's voice, who follow him,
and whom he calls by name (10:3, 4, 27).

b. It is they who flee from alternative shepherds and who refuse to
listen to them, because they do not recognize the voices of those
shepherds (10:5).

---

34. Using the word "gather" rather than "lead," I have given a translation that follows P66 and Clement of Alexandria. That reading is suggested not only by 11:52, but
also by 10:12.

35. The following paragraphs present in amplified and somewhat revised form the
interpretation of John 10:16 that I offered in "Glimpses into the History of the Johannine Community" (1975), 170–74 (= *The Gospel of John in Christian History*, 115–19).
Regarding the interpretation offered there, my colleague and steady friend Raymond
Brown proved his usual accuracy by means of an exception. In *The Community of the
Beloved Disciple* (1979), he credited me with the view that in 10:16 John refers to the
group Brown himself calls "the apostolic Christians" (90).

c. It is they whose lives are threatened by the wolf when he comes to snatch them away (ἁρπάζω) and to scatter them (σκορπίζω 10:12; see also ἁρπάζω in 10:28, 29; cf. 16:2). And it is they who, when they are thus endangered, are abandoned by the hired hand, who chooses to protect himself rather than to risk his life for the sheep (10:12; cf. 12:42).

d. And finally, it is they—the members of the Johannine community—who receive the absolute assurance from the Good Shepherd that however threatened they may be, no one will ever be able to actually snatch them out of his hand or out of the hand of the Father (10:28–29).

Clearly, then, the parable and its interpretation constitute an allegory, in the reading of which those who were initiates by virtue of sharing both a common history and a language reflecting that history—that is to say, the members of the Johannine community—would easily recognize the following four representations:

a. The sheep stand, as said above, for the Johannine community.

b. Strangers, thieves, robbers, and the wolf stand for the Jewish authorities ("the Pharisees" of John 9), who kill, destroy, snatch away, and scatter members of the Johannine community (16:2).

c. The hireling probably stands for the secretly believing "rulers" (12:42), who avoid the possibility of their own excommunication and death by abandoning the Johannine community when it is endangered.

d. The Good Shepherd stands for Jesus, as he is active through Johannine evangelists who are prepared—in his pattern—to face the most severe forms of persecution for the community, and who both receive and transmit the absolute assurance that, however threatening the Jewish authorities may become, they shall never be able to snatch any member of the community out of the hands of Jesus and the Father.

In light of this reading, who are the "other sheep" of John 10:16? Authors of commentaries are virtually unanimous in the opinion that these other sheep are gentiles who will be evangelized in what is universally called, "the [sic!] gentile mission." There are good reasons, however, to swim directly against the stream in this instance.[36]

In the reading of 10:16 itself, one notes several points. These other sheep already exist, as Jesus' sheep. Moreover, like "the dispersed children of God" (11:52; see below), they do not need to be evangelized. Being altogether trusted by the Johannine community—they are other sheep of Jesus—these persons presumably share with that community a history of persecution at the hands of synagogue authorities. They need to be comforted and assured, then, no less than the Johannine group itself. That shared need is sensitively described by H. B. Kossen:

> These people, whose belief was so severely tested because of their expulsion from the Jewish community, had to be confirmed in their conviction that it was precisely their belief in Jesus as the Christ, the Son of God, which gave them eternal life in his name (John 10:31). They must be assured that—like Nathanael who was told by Jesus: "Behold an Israelite indeed, in whom is no guile!" (1:47)—they [were not severed from Israel. They needed to be assured that, on the contrary, they] belonged to the true Israel, that they belonged to Jesus' sheep. "The Jews" did not belong to Jesus' sheep because they did not believe in him as the Messiah (10:24–26). But they—the readers of this gospel—could apply Jesus' word to themselves: "My sheep hear my voice, and I know them, and they follow me: and I give them eternal

36. In 1964, Hans Joachim Schoeps suggested that John 10:16 refers to "the existence of separate Jewish Christian communities" (*Jewish Christianity: Factional Disputes in the Early Church* [Philadelphia: Fortress, 1969], 131 [German edition, 1964]). Without being influenced by Schoeps's suggestion, H. B. Kossen proposed a similar reading in "Who Were the Greeks of John xii 20?" in *Studies in John Presented to Professor Dr. J. N. Sevenster*, NovTSup 24 (Leiden: Brill, 1970), 97–110. For Kossen, the "other sheep" are "the Christians among [the Jews of the Diaspora] to whom this gospel is particularly addressed" (107).

life; and they shall never perish, and no one shall snatch them out of my hand" (10:27–28).[37]

In John 10:16, the Evangelist informs his community that there are other Jewish Christian communities, whose members need the same comfort and assurance needed by their own. He then adds that these other communities also need to be gathered. Apparently considering his own community to be a sort of mother church to other Jewish-Christian churches, the Evangelist looks forward to a unity—one flock, one shepherd—that will ensue when these others are gathered into his church. On this reading, John 10:16 is very far indeed from reflecting a gentile mission. The ecclesiological future portrayed that there is not the result of a mission of any sort, properly speaking. That future will come with the unification of several Jewish-Christian communities, all of which have an essentially common history of persecution by Jewish authorities.[38]

---

37. Kossen, "Who Were the Greeks of John xii 20?," 102–3, slightly altered for clarity.

38. If space is permitted, we should also consider in detail the fact that after speaking of the hope for one flock and one shepherd, John interprets the picture of the shepherd and the sheep by means of a disputation (10:22–39) that was developed in the conflict his community continued to have with the synagogue (see especially Painter, *The Quest for the Messiah* [2nd ed.], 361, and Meeks, "Equal to God," 314). One finds the note of assurance, mentioned above: Jesus' sheep are secure from all threats, because it is impossible for someone to snatch them either out of his hand or out of the hand of the Father (vv. 28–29). One finds also the christological claim that "I and the Father are one" (v. 30). Sensing blasphemy in this claim, the Jews threaten to stone Jesus, for "you, though only a human being, are making yourself God" (v. 33). Jesus finally responds with another and more complicated assertion of his relation to the Father: "I am God's Son . . . the Father is in me and I am in the Father" (vv. 36–38). All of the terms of this disputation are Jewish, producing a text focused on the question of whether the Johannine community is in violation of monotheism, an issue bearing no relationship to a gentile mission or even to the putative presence of gentiles in the Johannine community. See further, Mark L. Appold, *The Oneness Motif in the Fourth Gospel: Motif Analysis and Exegetical Probe into the Theology of John*, WUNT 2/1 (Tübingen: Mohr Siebeck, 1976), 263.

The Prophecy of Caiaphas

> But one of them, Caiaphas, who was high priest that year,
> said to them, "You know nothing at all! You do not under-
> stand that it is better for you to have one man die for the
> people than to have the whole nation destroyed." He did
> not say this on his own, but being high priest that year he
> prophesied that Jesus was about to die for the nation, and
> not for the nation only, but to gather into one the dispersed
> children of God. (John 11:49–52)

Brown points out the carefulness of Severino Pancaro's exegesis, according to which John hears in Caiaphas's prophecy a reference to "all those
(whether Jew or Gentile) who would be united into this new People by
the death of Christ."[39] In several regards, such as the analysis of pertinent
expressions in the Septuagint, I should agree. As an exegesis of John's text,
however, Pancaro's treatment leaves much to be desired. In his conclusion, this usually perceptive scholar says, "[Jesus'] death makes children
of men [presumably, Pancaro means "makes men children of God"], and
it is because they are made children that they are united, but John wishes
to insist more on the 'gathering into one' than on the act of becoming a
child of God."[40] But in 11:52 John utters not a word about persons being
made children of God. He speaks, rather, of the gathering of persons who
were children of God before they were scattered.

From this observation, one returns first to 1:12–13, and second,
to 10:16. John 1:12–13 is the only other passage in which the Evangelist
speaks of children of God. There one learns that, in the Evangelist's

---

39. Severino Pancaro, "'People of God' in St John's Gospel?," *NTS* 16 (1969–70)
114–29 (here, 129); Brown, *The Community of the Beloved Disciple*, 56. Contrast the
comment of Meeks: "Now because the context makes it clear that these children include more than the *ethnos* of the Judeans, the reader may jump to the conclusion that
Gentiles are included" ("Breaking Away," 97).

40. Pancaro, "'People of God' in St John's Gospel?" Pancaro's book, *The Law in the
Fourth Gospel* (see above, note 21), is a significant contribution to Johannine studies.

view, neither Jews nor gentiles are children of God. That identity is given by God only to those who receive Jesus as the Logos.[41] In 11:52, John speaks of the gathering into one of persons who are already Christians.

And which Christians, specifically, does he have in mind? That question brings us back to 10:16. Taking one's bearings from that passage, one sees that in 11:52 John is using the prophecy of the high priest Caiaphas to formulate a reinterpretation of the widespread and classic motif pertaining both to the Jewish diaspora and to its being gathered in. In John's setting the children of God who have been scattered are the other Jewish-Christian conventicles we have seen reflected in 10:16. In 11:52, John again speaks to his own community about those other conventicles, adding the assurance that the high priest himself "had unwittingly prophesied the redeeming significance of Jesus' death especially for them."[42]

Again, then, we have a passage that fails to reflect a gentile mission.[43]

"Greeks" Who Have Come to Worship at the Feast Seek Jesus

Now among those who went up to worship at the festival [Passover] were some Greeks [Ἑλληνές]. They came

41. So, rightly, Brown, *The Community of the Beloved Disciple*, 56. Thus, Pancaro is surely correct in saying, "The 'children of God', mentioned in John xi.52, are—contrary to what has been traditionally held—neither the Gentiles nor the Jews of the dispersion as such" ("'People of God' in St John's Gospel?," 129).

42. Kossen, "Who Were the Greeks of John xii 20?," 107. See also, therein, 106, n, 2; and Martyn, *The Gospel of John in Christian History*, 119. It should be noted that the conclusion to which Kossen comes is different from the one reached in the present chapter: for Kossen, John wrote his Gospel for Christian Jews in the Greek-speaking diaspora of Asia Minor in order to assure them that they still belonged to the Messiah of Israel, but also in order to call them to fulfill the Messiah's mission by preaching to the gentiles among whom they lived (110).

43. It is the note of *assurance*, the motif of *gathering the scattered*, and the resultant *unification* that bind John 11:52 and 10:16 to one another, both containing echoes of Zechariah 13:7.

> to Philip . . . and said to him, "Sir, we wish to see Je-
> sus." . . . [Then] Andrew and Philip went and told Jesus. Jesus
> answered them, "The hour has come for the Son of Man to
> be glorified. Very truly, I tell you, unless a grain of wheat
> falls into the ground and dies, it remains just a single grain;
> but if it dies, it bears much fruit." (John 12:20–24)

In an admirable essay, Kyoshi Tsuchido begins by noting that this paragraph shows Johannine style at numerous points, indicating it to be "an
editorial creation, freely composed by the Evangelist." To be sure, in
his composition, John "used some pre-Johannine fragments," but in the
text as it stands one finds that he "describes the sayings and the works
of Jesus and simultaneously reflects his own *Sitz im Leben*."[44]

In John's own setting, who are these "Greeks"? Since they are identified not only as Ἕλληνές, but also as persons who regularly come to
Jerusalem in order to worship at the time of Passover, they are surely
gentiles who—like the Ethiopian eunuch of Acts 8—had become attached to Judaism before expressing interest in Jesus.[45] Their attach-
ment to Judaism is hardly a matter in which John has no interest.
Scarcely typical gentiles, they worship the God of Israel by observing
Passover, ignorant of Jesus' having replaced that feast.[46] Given that
characteristic, their coming on the scene is, in John's view, a development of considerable import. Jesus responds by saying that the hour

---

44. Kyoshi Tsuchida, "Ἕλλην in the Gospel of John: Tradition and Redaction in John
12:20–24," in *The Conversation Continues*, 348–56 (esp. 350, 352, 353; see also Tsuchido,
Tradition and Redaction in the Fourth Gospel [in Japanese; Tokyo: Sobunsha, 1994]). In
addition to providing a comprehensive catalogue of the opinions of other scholars, Tsuchida has penned his own strong argument for finding a reference to gentiles in John
12:20. I must confess, however, that I am not persuaded.

45. The participle ἀναβαινόντων ("those who went up") is surely rendered correctly by Walter Bauer as a reference to those "die hinaufzugehen pflegten, um am
Fest *anzubeten*" ("who customarily went up there, *in order to worship* at the Festival";
Das Johannesevangelium, 160, emphasis added). Note also the comment of Windisch,
given in note 32 above.

46. See esp. John 1:29; 19:36.

has arrived for his glorification, an event that will bear much fruit (John 12:24), demonstrating, among other things, Jesus' replacement of the Jewish feasts.

But if John refers here to God-fearers—persons who are Jewish to the extent of regularly praying to the God of Israel—and if their desire to see Jesus is a move of their own volition, on what reading of the text can one say that it has pertinence to the question of a discrete mission *to pagan gentiles*? A number of interpreters would answer by saying that John considers these God-fearers to be representatives of the gentile world.[47] One might endorse that reading if one had already found secure references to gentiles in 7:35, 10:16, and 11:52. And if one had found references to gentiles in those earlier texts, one could find further reflections of a gentile mission in such references as "the savior of the world" (4:42) and "all people" (12:32), clear indications of some kind of theological universalism.[48] Jesus' statement about drawing "all people" to himself would then be particularly revealing, coming as it does shortly after the reference to the God-fearers' request to see him. That is to say, one could read 12:20 as a text in which John—like Luke, the author of Acts—views inquisitiveness on the part of God-fearers as an intermediate step in the direction of a discrete mission to gentiles.

47. Referring to proselytes rather than to God-fearers, C. H. Dodd remarked, "In the dramatic situation we may suppose [the Ἕλληνες of 12:20] to be proselytes, but in the intention of the Evangelist they stand for the great world at large; primarily for *the Hellenistic world which is his own mission field*" (*The Interpretation of the Fourth Gospel* [Cambridge: Cambridge University Press, 1953], 371, emphasis added).

48. On John 4:42 see especially Craig R. Koester, "'The Savior of the World' (John 4:42)," *JBL* 109 (1990) 665-80, who reaches there and in *Symbolism in the Fourth Gospel: Meaning, Mystery, Community* (Minneapolis: Fortress, 1995) conclusions counter to those given at the end of the present study. Koester sees reflections of a shift in mission frontier in several instances of the Gospel's symbolism, not least that of the three-language sign above the cross. See also Okure (note 13 above) and Miguel Rodríguez Ruiz, *Der Missionsgedanke des Johannesevangeliums: Ein Beitrag zur johanneischen Soteriologie und Ekklesiologie*, FB 55 (Würzburg: Echter, 1987).

That last interpretation is especially to be resisted, however, because reading an aspect of Luke's *Weltanschauung* into John is precisely the move to be avoided in pursuing our question (see further, below). Moreover, as we have seen, the case for finding pagan gentiles in John 7:35 is scarcely convincing, while in 10:16 and 11:52 that case is excluded.

There is also a striking congruity between John 12:20–21, 32, and Isaiah 2:2–3: In each case, the motif is that of people *coming* to the established group, rather than that of missioners *going out to* those people. Thus, the interpreter who wishes to see in John 12:20 the reflection of a discrete mission to gentiles must accept the burden of proof.

Jesus' statements about much fruit (12:24) and about drawing all people to himself (12:32) remain indications of an ultimate, theological universalism comparable to that of Isaiah 2:2–3, until they are followed by a story in which—on the contemporary level—a Johannine missioner reaches out to and brings in at least one God-fearer. And on John's landscape, the God-fearers of 12:20 vanish without a trace.

Pondering that fact, one recalls the care with which John included stories in which members of his community could find reflections of themselves. In 9:1–38, he included a dramatic representation of Jews who had been brought into the community from the synagogue. In 1:29–51, he provided an engaging portrait of followers of the Baptist who had been led to make their entry. And in 4:5–42, John furnished the Samaritans in his church with an account of their journey.[49] If, then, there were other members of his community who had been brought into it as the result of a mission to pagan gentiles—especially if that mission was of such importance to the community as to have replaced the earlier mission to the Jews—one should certainly expect the Evangelist to have provided these persons with an account of their journey.[50]

49. See Leroy, Rätsel und Missverständnis, 88–99; Kikuo Matsunaga, "The Galileans in the Fourth Gospel," *AJBI* 2 (1976) 139–58; Brown, *The Community of the Beloved Disciple*, 36–40.

50. On characterization in John, see Culpepper, *Anatomy of the Fourth Gospel*, 105–48; idem, "L'application de la narratologie à l'étude de l'évangile de Jean," in *La*

Striking is the fact that a representation of persons being brought into the Johannine community from the pagan gentile world is found nowhere in the Gospel. Indeed, except for Pilate, whose presence is demanded by the passion tradition, the Gospel has no compelling gentile actor at all.[51] In reading 12:20, 12:24, and 12:32, then, we are left with a reference to a certain inquisitiveness on the part of some God-fearers who regularly pray to the God of Israel, with a reference to Jesus' death as the event that will bear much fruit—among God-fearers who at one time observed the Jewish feasts?—and with a theologically universalistic statement. Is the result a sequence of texts that reflects the undertaking of a discrete mission to gentiles, substituting that gentile mission for the earlier mission to Jews?

Failure to Believe, in Spite of Many Signs

> Although he had performed so many signs in their presence, they did not believe in him. This was to fulfill the word spoken by the prophet Isaiah: "Lord, who has believed our message, and to whom has the arm of the Lord been revealed?" And so they could not believe, because Isaiah also said, "He has blinded their eyes and hardened their heart, so that they might not look with their eyes, and understand with their heart and turn—and I would heal them."
>
> Isaiah said this because he saw his glory and spoke about him. Nevertheless, many, even of the authorities, believed in him. But because of the Pharisees they did not confess it, for fear that they would be put out of the synagogue,

---

Communauté johannique et son Histoire: La trajectoire de l'évangile de Jean aux deux premier siècles, edited by Jean-Daniel Kaestli, Jean-Michel Poffet, and Jean Zumstein, Monde de la Bible (Geneva: Labor et Fides, 1990), 97–120.

51. Cf. Hengel, *The Johannine Question*, 168 n. 48. On the "royal official" of John 4:46, see Brown, *The Gospel according to John (i–xii)*, 29, cxliv. Meeks is right to note that "the boundaries of [John's] story are the boundaries of Israel" ("Breaking Away," 97).

for they loved human glory more than the glory that comes
from God.

    Jesus then cried aloud: "Whoever believes in me be-
lieves not in me but in him who sent me . . . for I have not
spoken on my own, but the Father who sent me has himself
given me a commandment about what to say and what to
speak. And I know that his commandment is eternal life.
What I speak, therefore, I speak just as the Father has told
me." (John 12:37–50)

Moody Smith has given us fundamental guidance for the reading of
this passage.[52] Following him, we can suppose two pre-Gospel stages.
(1) Materials attesting to Jesus' mighty signs were probably collected
by Jews—the nascent Johannine community—who used that collection
to win other Jews to belief in Jesus as the Messiah. At the same time,
persons in this community collected passion traditions into a coherent
form, so that the community had a collection of signs and a primitive
passion story, both probably formed in large part for the same audience—Jews who were the objects of the community's mission. (2) As
some of those other Jews proved extremely resistant to the Johannine
mission, raising in time very sharp questions and objections, members
of the nascent community found that neither of their traditions was effective without the other. In response to this development (and perhaps
to inner-church factors as well), someone combined these two traditions in the manner proposed by Robert Fortna in *The Gospel of Signs*,
forming a primitive gospel by stitching these two traditions together
with the threads that we now have as John 12:37–40.[53]

---

52. Smith, *Johannine Christianity*, 80–93.

53. See esp. Smith, ibid., 93. It is encouraging to see the mutual enrichment resulting from the interchanges between Fortna and Smith; see, for example, Fortna, *The
Fourth Gospel and Its Predecessor*, 137 n. 304, 207 n. 492. The argument that lack of
detailed agreement among source and tradition critics vitiates their work is well answered in de Boer, "Narrative Criticism, Historical Criticism, and the Gospel of John."

Since Smith assigns the material beginning in 12:41 (or 12:42) to the Evangelist, we can speak of a third stage in which the Evangelist made his own contribution, expanding on the earlier transition by means of 12:41–50. This analysis leads, then, to the crucial question: Interpreting 12:37–40 by means of his own composition in 12:41–50, does the Evangelist leave indications that, faced with Jewish unbelief, his community has substituted a gentile mission for its earlier mission to its fellow Jews?

There are no convincing grounds for answering that question in the affirmative.[54] Quite the contrary. Having noted the massive Jewish unbelief that played such a painful role in the history of his community, the Evangelist does not find a measure of relief by referring to the encouraging development of a gentile mission. One notes with some amazement that after mentioning massive Jewish unbelief, he leads his reader right back into the synagogue, so to speak. And there he finds authoritative persons who do believe (John 12:42; cf. 7:48), although they are afraid to confess their faith openly. We are doubtless right to sense here a profound ambivalence. On the one hand, these secret believers elicit from John a certain amount of scorn (cf. 12:43 with the portrait of the hireling in 10:12–13). On the other hand, however, John sees them as persons who may yet be drawn (by God; 6:44) fully into his own community.[55] It is for that reason that in 12:44–50 he provides members of his community with arguments by which they can lessen Jewish fears that to join their community is to stand in violation of monotheism (a matter of no general concern to the gentile world).[56]

---

54. Brown answers in the affirmative, but he argues as though John's interpretation of 12:37–40 were given in 12:20–22 rather than in 12:41–50 (*The Community of the Beloved Disciple*, 55).

55. So, rightly, Brown, *The Gospel according to John (i–xii)*, 29, lxxiv.

56. See again Meeks, "Equal to God," passim.

V

This redaction-critical interpretation of John 12:37–50 may not be the *coup de grâce* to the suggestion that, at the time of the Gospel, the Johannine community had embraced an openness of some kind to some kind of gentiles: to God-fearers, that is, who on their own volition seek Jesus (12:21). Taken together, however, with the readings of other texts offered earlier (including some degree of uncertainty about 7:35), this interpretation seems to me to virtually rule out the thesis that the community had already substituted a gentile mission for a Jewish one. Moreover, in this reading of 12:37–50, we come to sense the large and significant distance—in regard to mission frontier—between John and Luke-Acts, the major New Testament witness to the emergence of the early catholic church. For a Christian community maintaining a Jewish mission into the closing years of the first century is neither portrayed nor forecast on Luke's canvas.

Brown is right to recall that Isaiah's prophecy about the blinding of eyes and the numbing of minds was used by some early Christians "as an explanation of the Jewish failure to accept Jesus and as the rationale for turning to the Gentiles (Acts 28:25–28; see Matt 13:13–15)."[57] But when one notes that John has interpreted Isaiah's prophecy by means of the motifs struck in 12:41–50, and when one compares the result with the final scene in Acts, one is doubly impressed with the gulf between Luke-Acts and John, as regards mission frontier. That final scene in Acts is artfully constructed:

> After [the leaders of the Jews in Rome] had set a day to meet with [Paul], they came to him at his lodging . . . Paul made one further statement: "The Holy Spirit was right in saying to your ancestors through the prophet Isaiah, 'Go to this people and say, You will indeed listen, but never understand, and you will indeed look, but never perceive. For this people's heart has grown dull, and their ears are hard of hearing, and they have shut their eyes, so that they might not look

57. Brown, *The Community of the Beloved Disciple*, 55.

> with their eyes, and listen with their ears, and understand
> with their heart and tum-and I would heal them.' Let it be
> known to you then that this salvation of God has been sent
> to the Gentiles; they will listen." (Acts 28:25-29)

It is also a scene without parallel in the Gospel of John.

Was the Johannine community, then, a sect in the sense of being not only distinct from the synagogue, but also far removed from the streams that issued into the emerging Great Church? That question has not been fully answered in the present chapter. We have simply found that the community's sense of mission—at the time of the Gospel—was significantly different from the sense of mission characteristic of the Great Church. We can add, however, one weighty observation. From a host of early Christian witnesses, we know that no aspect of life was more important to the self-understanding of first-century churches than the definition of mission frontier.[58]

---

58. See, notably, Gal 2:7, 9; Mark 12:9; 13:10; Matt 21:43; Acts 28:29. Cf. Justin, *Dial.* 47; and Ferdinand Hahn, *Mission in the New Testament*, SBT 47 (London: SCM, 1963).

CHAPTER 6

The Johannine Community among Jewish and Other Early Christian Communities

BECAUSE RESPONDING TO TOM Thatcher's gracious invitation to participate in this volume necessarily involves a bit of reminiscence, we find ourselves briefly at Yale University in the 1950s. To a large extent, the period was marked in Protestant American Biblical Studies by a concentration on issues handed across the Atlantic, so to speak, from Germany and Switzerland. We knew that there was genuine learning in England and Scotland, but the interpretive work that exercised our minds came our way largely from the continent. So when the time arrived for proposing a dissertation topic (1954), I thought in European terms without noticing it. I turned first to Johannine matters, partly because Rudolf Bultmann's commentary on John seemed to me both enormously impressive—it is still worth reading!—and seriously inadequate. I found it impossible to avoid ambivalence while paying close attention to the writings of this scholar, a true giant and also imperfect.[1]

---

1. This essay was published in *What We Have Heard From the Beginning*, edited by Tom Thatcher (Waco: Baylor University Press, 2007), 183–90.

Timeless and Placeless Reading of the Fourth Gospel in the Post-Enlightenment Western University

As I reflected on Bultmann's work, I saw, on the one hand, that there was an uncanny congeniality (*Verwandtschaft*) between the first-century Johannine Evangelist and this twentieth-century interpreter. At juncture after juncture, one came to a deeper understanding of a passage after pondering and wrestling with Bultmann's comments on it. On the other hand, there were what impressed me as direct and unqualified reflections of the philosophy of Martin Heidegger. Noting earlier a linguistic habit of Bultmann—equally evident in his books and articles on Jesus, Paul, and John—I had concocted a humorous story for the amusement of my fellow doctoral students. Bultmann's publisher, I said, had ordered a special typesetting machine for the production of his works: the depression of a single key brought up the word *Möglichkeit* ("possibility"); the depression of another produced the term *Entscheidung* ("decision"). But were possibility and decision actually central categories in the teaching of Jesus, in the theological systems of Paul and John, and in the thinking of many other early Christian authors as well? Or were those categories borrowed from Heidegger and imposed on the ancient texts? I noted, for example, in John 6:44 that the Evangelist puts the verb ἑλκύω ("to draw") in Jesus' mouth in a way that seems emphatically to deny the human capacity of autonomous decision: "No one can come to me unless drawn by the Father who sent me" (cf. 12:32). There was no doubt that the Gospel of John evidences patterns of dualistic thought; but did Bultmann's expression "decision dualism" really stem from that document itself? Those seemed to me weighty questions.

Wide reading in the critical literature soon caused me to be further puzzled. To be sure, Clement of Alexandria had dubbed John the "spiritual Gospel" in the late-second century. Why, however, did post-Enlightenment biblical interpreters so seldom apply old-fashioned historical analysis to the Fourth Gospel, thereby leaving this ancient text to timeless, placeless interpretation in the hands of scholars whose antecedent loyalties lay with Plato and Philo, and now with twentieth-century, existentialist, thoroughly individualistic philosophers? We all knew, to be sure, that Leopold von Ranke was naïve in saying that the historian's task was to reconstruct a given ancient picture as it actually was: *wie es eigentlich gewesen war*. We read with great interest Wilhelm Dilthey, thereby outgrowing von Ranke by learning that even the historical exegete is to understand ancient texts "empathetically." But had Dilthey's insights legitimately eclipsed the need for hard-headed historiography? Had I known at that time the writings of Leo Beck, I would have found an ally in my concern that we should learn some things from Dilthey while maintaining our von Rankean interest in everyday history. Beck wrote his dissertation under the direction of Dilthey, thereby savoring what Hugo von Hofmannsthal characterized as Dilthey's ability to convince his students of their own involvement in the exegetical task by stimulating around himself an atmosphere of "impassioned conversation, impassioned listening." In Beck's case, however, empathetic understanding of ancient texts was not purchased at the cost of historical accuracy, as one learns in reading his thoroughly candid response to Adolf von Harnack's *What Is Christianity?* Noting the astonishing extent of Harnack's ignorance of Jewish matters, such as the high value placed on poetic homily by the rabbis, Beck wastes no time with artificial politeness: "Whoever reaches judgments like those of Mr. Harnack knows nothing of a vast area of Jewish life *as it actually existed* in the time of Jesus and the early church; or he compels himself to know nothing of it."[2]

Giving special attention to Jewish sources as I prepared for general examinations, I noted that, like Harnack, Bultmann had a truly skimpy knowledge of Judaism, while being remarkably learned in non-Jewish materials of the Hellenistic era. Formulating a dissertation topic, I now began to ask whether this imbalance was taking a toll on his

2. J. Louis Martyn, *Theological Issues in the Letters of Paul* (Nashville: Abingdon, 1997), quote 51, emphasis added.

interpretation of the Fourth Gospel. Had he leapt over the old-fashioned requirements placed on the *wissenschaftlich* historian, in order—however unconsciously—to make use of the Fourth Gospel in his devotion to the timeless and thoroughly individualistic existentialism of Heidegger? Had the time (the post-Enlightenment period) and the place (the Western university) paradoxically facilitated a timeless, placeless reading of an ancient document (John) as though it had fallen from heaven into the lap of Bultmann (cf. the work of a fellow old-Marburger, Hans Georg Gadamer)? In the case of the Gospel of John, I thought both questions were to be answered in the affirmative, mainly because that document had not been consistently and rigorously subjected to historical analysis by reading it in relation to Second Temple Judaism.

An Attempt to Read the Fourth Gospel in Its Own Setting

In my dissertation, then, two matters claimed major attention: the Evangelist's repeated references to οἱ Ἰουδαῖοι ("the Jews"? "the Judeans"?) and the attention he gives to the matter of scriptural interpretation.[3] I attempted to provide a sober and fundamental exegetical analysis of both, leading to the conclusion that, for John, the term "the Jews" is more than a disembodied symbol for the unbelieving world, but instead often refers to real flesh-and-blood Jewish authorities in John's city. And a third focus accompanied those two: because it seemed to me imperative to wrest the Gospel out of the hands of timeless, placeless, philosophical interpreters, I ventured away from the ivy-covered study that is the normal habitat of those of us who labor as lonely, "individual" interpreters. From the beginning of my own work, both in my 1957 dissertation and in *History and Theology in the Fourth Gospel* (essentially written in 1964, published in 1968), I referred to "the Johannine

---

3. C. K. Barrett, "The Old Testament in the Fourth Gospel," *JTS* 48 (1947) 155–69; Francis J. Moloney, "The Gospel of John as Scripture," *CBQ* 67 (2005) 454–68.

community," the "corporate" setting in which the Evangelist penned his Gospel and the one in which that Gospel was first interpreted. When I transformed the dissertation, using it as a third of *History and Theology*, the Johannine community assumed even greater importance.[4]

> Our first task . . . is to say something specific about the actual circumstances in which John wrote his Gospel. How are we to picture daily life in John's church? Have elements of its peculiar daily experiences left their stamp on the Gospel penned by one of its members? May one sense even in its exalted cadences the voice of a Christian theologian who writes in response to contemporary events and issues which concern, or should concern, all members of the Christian community in which he lives? [A positive answer necessitates our making] every effort to take up temporary residence in the *Johannine community*. We must see with the eyes and hear with the ears of that community. We must sense at least some of the crises which helped to shape the lives of its members. And we must listen carefully to the kind of conversations in which all of its members found themselves engaged. Only in the midst of this endeavor will we be able to hear the Fourth Evangelist speak in his own terms, rather than in words we moderns merely want to hear from his mouth. And initially it is only in his own terms that he can speak to our own time.

New to *History and Theology*, vis-à-vis the dissertation, were (a) the suggestion that the peculiar Johannine locutions ἀποσυνάγωγος γένηται ("be put out of the synagogue," John 9:22; 12:42) and ἀποσυνάγωγους ποιήσουσιν ὑμᾶς ("you will be made outcasts from the synagogue," 16:2) were probably related to the Twelfth Benediction (the *Birkat Haminim*), and (b) a more developed emphasis on the thoroughly theological nature of the Fourth Gospel as a "two-level drama," one that to some extent told the story of the Johannine community while narrating

---

4. J. Louis Martyn, *History and Theology in the Fourth Gospel*, NTL (1968, 1978, 3rd ed., Louisville: Westminster John Knox, 2003), 29, emphasis added.

the story of Jesus of Nazareth *because* in the work of the Paraclete the risen Lord continues to determine the life of his new community.

The reviews of and references to *History and Theology* over the decades since its initial publication require no rehearsal here beyond my saying that the extensive enthusiasm was genuinely surprising to me. To become in some degree a part of the establishment by publishing a work written somewhat in opposition to the (earlier) establishment can throw one a bit off balance; but that was a matter of merely personal concern. I must admit that I have sometimes been reminded, as recently as last year, of a friend's *bon mot*: "The highest compliment to a person's labors is not imitation, but rather mild larceny."[5] Scholars having a far greater rabbinic expertise than my own expressed skepticism about directly connecting the ἀποσυνάγωγος references in John's Gospel to the Twelfth Benediction. Wayne Meeks identified that part of my work as a red herring (it did indeed prove to be a pink one), and Moody Smith called it a tactical error in the sense that a few Johannine interpreters were taking the work of Kimelman and Katz as proof against the larger thesis that the Fourth Gospel is a two-level drama shaped in part by the experience of a group of Christian Jews who had suffered—against their wills—the trauma of being severed from their undisturbed membership in their synagogue.

The history of the *Birkat Haminim* is, to be sure, a somewhat uncertain matter inviting debate—I say only "somewhat uncertain" partly because of the work of William Horbury.[6] The word ἀποσυνάγωγος,

---

5. I was sobered by the works of Reuven Kimelman, "*Birkat Haminim* and the Lack of Evidence for an Anti-Christian Prayer in Late Antiquity," *Jewish and Christian Self-Definition*, Vol. 2, edited by E. P. Sanders, A. I. Baumgarten, and Alan Mendelson (Philadelphia: Fortress, 1981), 226–44, 391–403; Steven T. Katz, "Issues in the Separation of Judaism and Christianity After 70 C.E.: A Reconstruction," *JBL* 103 (1984) 43–76; Pieter W. van der Horst, "The *Birkat ha-minim* in Recent Research," *ExpT* 105 (1994) 363–68; and Daniel Boyarin, *Border Lines: The Partition of Judeo-Christianity* (Philadelphia: University of Pennsylvania Press, 2004).

6. William Horbury, "The Benediction of the *Minim* and Early Jewish-Christian Controversy," *JTS* 32 (1982) 19–61.

on the other hand, is there in the text, and it was not coined in an individual's private fit of paranoia: the occurrences of this term are communal references to a communal experience. Further, we have similar data in the Pseudo-Clementine literature.[7] And as odious as we find the Nazi-like thesis that Christian persecution of Jews is "'justified' by the theory that Jews did the first persecuting [Paul, for example]," I still contend that "modern relations between Jews and Christians are not helped by an anti-historical interpretation of biblical texts."[8] I remain thoroughly convinced on two matters. First, working chronologically backward and forward from the ἀποσυνάγωγος references, it is possible to sketch the history of the Johannine community "from its origin through the period of its life in which the Fourth Gospel was composed." Second, so sketched, that history "forms to no small extent a chapter in the history of *Jewish Christianity*."[9]

Reading the Fourth Gospel in Two Settings

Given the work of Kimelman and Katz on the *Birkat*—work I found instructive in some regards, to be sure—there was now the danger, I thought, that parts of the discourse between Jewish and Christian

---

7. J. Louis Martyn, *The Gospel of John in Christian History: Essays for Interpreters* (New York: Paulist, 1979), ch. 2; Hans-Josef Klauck, "Community, History, and Text(s)," *Life in Abundance: Studies of John's Gospel in Tribute to Raymond Brown, S.S.*, edited by John R. Donahue (Collegeville: Liturgical, 2005), 82–90.

8. Martyn, *The Gospel of John in Christian History*, 56.

9. Martyn, *The Gospel of John in Christian History*, 121; D. Moody Smith, *John* (Nashville: Abingdon, 1999); Harold W. Attridge, "Johannine Community," *Origins to Constantine*, edited by Margaret M. Mitchell and Francis M. Young (Cambridge: Cambridge University Press, 2006), 125–43. Regarding the Johannine community and Jewish Christianity, see now the weighty study of M. Theobald, "Das Johannesevangelium—Zeugnis eines synagogalen 'Judentenchristentum'?" *Paulus und Johannes: Exegetische Studien zur paulinischen und johanneischen Theologie und Literatur*, edited by Daniel Sänger and Ulrich Mell, WUNT 197 (Tübingen: Mohr Siebeck, 2006), 107–58. If there was a Signs Gospel—as Fortna has successfully argued—it too belongs to the history of Jewish Christianity.

scholars might take a tumble into pure apologetics, all participants being then the poorer.[10] There are significant differences between indulging in apologetics and being truly sensitive to the Other, notably when the Other is a sibling. Especially when focused on the matter of Christians persecuting Jews and Jews persecuting Christians—Christian Jews—juvenility is as unhelpful as are ad hominem and inaccurate reports of personal conversations, both being forms of childishness that, easily falling into anachronistic readings, dishonor the Other. What liberates us from the *Tendenzen* of our exegetical conversation partner is not our own *Tendenzen*, but rather the text. In short, the relationship between John's community and its parent synagogue(s) was certainly somewhat complex. It was, however, fundamentally different from the relationship between the mighty post-Constantinian church and the synagogue of its era. Dispassionate historical analysis clearly tells us that, at the time of the Fourth Gospel's origin, the later pattern was to some degree reversed. At its origin, the Johannine community was a small conventicle faced with a truly more powerful parent in the local Jewish establishment (e.g., John 19:38; 20:19; cf. Matt 10:17).

Even so, the question remains: Are there passages in the Gospel produced in this separated and threatened community that cause us justly to identify that document itself as "anti-Judaic"? It is an important question. It is also one that cannot be answered in precisely the same way by every person, in every time, and in every place. I myself cannot pose it without recalling the time in the 1960s when Abraham Joshua Heschel took a leave of absence from the faculty of Jewish Theological Seminary to cross the street and join for a year our faculty at Union Seminary (the board of directors temporarily changed the Trinitarian elements in the professorial induction ceremony). In addition to his classroom teaching, Heschel organized a small discussion group, drawing three members from each

---

10. I was amused when, upon the appearance of the pertinent works of Kimelman and Katz, some Christian scholars assumed that, whereas Christian interpreters have *Tendenzen*, Jewish interpreters, being totally objective, have none.

of the two faculties. The book we were to produce, each writing a chapter (mine on Romans 9–11), never came to fruition—for it was to begin with a manifesto signed by all, and there were always sentences to which one member or another could not agree. In our discussions, however, there was much valuable fruit, not least in our various stories. Heschel, markedly reserved about scholarship for its own sake, was a master at eliciting frank and candid narratives from us about earlier periods in our lives. We sometimes had as much *haggadah* as *halacha*.

Here I was provided with my first sustained exposure to the possibility that, in the New Testament itself, there are *sustained* strains of rhetoric and thought that can be correctly identified with the expression "anti-Judaic." At Yale, I had paid some attention to the odious use of the Fourth Gospel by the *Deutsche Christen*, the Nazi-sponsored, anti-Semitic German Christian Church (a possible dissertation subject, I thought), but I had not before asked myself whether in important regards some of the church's foundational documents were *themselves*, and in a sustained manner, anti-Judaic. Formulated that way, the question had occurred to me neither in writing my dissertation nor in my later attempt to produce an exegetically *wissenschaftliches* monograph. Now, however, partly because of some of Heschel's stories, that question arose. He spoke, quite simply and without personal heroics, of his early youth in Warsaw, mentioning, for example, his mother's dispatching him to fetch the day's bread. He had to travel a roundabout route to the baker, he said, to avoid walking by the huge cathedral. Why? Because simply finding himself in its shadow produced uncontrollable trembling. Why? Because, literally overshadowed by that giant monolith, he inevitably recalled stories about one or another of his rabbinic forebears who had been summoned there for a disputation, the outcome of which would fundamentally affect for some time the life of the Jewish community. It was for me a highly affective and truly effective introduction to the degree to which the power of the Christian church hovered menacingly over the life of the largely powerless Jewish community in Warsaw and elsewhere. And, trying to see through the eyes of the frightened little boy, I had to ask myself whether the monolithic nature of that power—so well represented by the literal monolith of the cathedral's structure—was truly separable from its various parts. Was the glorious church music implicated: the scriptural oratorios of Handel and Felix Mendelssohn? Did the Christian Scriptures themselves play a role in the persecutory shadow of the cathedral? Heschel suggested no such thing, but this question occurred to me when I visualized the little boy in short pants trembling in the shadow of a towering edifice, which should have been for all human beings a secure place of refuge.

And, that question takes us back to the Gospel of John and the matter of anti-Judaism. Would it be salutary to focus the anti-Judaic question on the setting in which the Fourth Gospel had its origin, before carrying it farther?

From its birth, the Johannine community was conscious of its existence as a conventicle with its own fund of images and its own language, as Wayne Meeks insisted.[11] It was not, however, a monolith. We can be confident that one of its subgroups consisted of ἀποσυνάγωγοι with deeply loved kinfolk who remained in the synagogue. What would members of this subgroup have heard as the Fourth Gospel was read aloud in the community? They would presumably have warmed their hands over John 4:22, in which Jesus says to the Samaritan woman, "You worship what you do not know; we worship what we know, for salvation is from the Jews." But how would they have heard 8:31–59, and especially 8:44, "You [Jews] are of your father the devil"?[12] I suppose they would have regretted that verse. They would surely have heard the words of life in the Christology of the entire passage, while

11. Wayne Meeks, "Man from Heaven in Johannine Sectarianism," *In Search of the Early Christians: Selected Essays*, edited by Allen R. Hilton and H. Gregory Snyder (New Haven: Yale University Press, 2002), 55–90.

12. The odious potential of this verse reached a crescendo when Hitler's mentor Dietrich Eckart quoted it in his *Der Bolschewismus von Moses bis Lenin: Zwiegespräch zwischen Adolf Hitler und mir* (1924), 18.

feeling, perhaps, that it goes too far with the specific application of its uncompromising dualism to their flesh-and-blood kinfolk. It was, of course, the Johannine community's peculiar history applied to the absolute nature of its dualism and its equally absolute Christology that produced such passages. And, because the result is not greatly different from the absolute dualism of Qumran, we inevitably ask ourselves why that passage should present us with an intensified form of the regret experienced by those members of the Johannine community who had beloved kinfolk in the local synagogue. The answer lies, one hardly needs to say, with the subsequent history of the church and the Jewish people.[13] There was no Qumran cathedral in Warsaw.

But, precisely in thinking of that history, we are reminded of the fact that the church we know has never lived—and cannot live—solely on the basis of John 8:44. As Brevard Childs has taught us, some form of canonical criticism has to bind the modern Christian interpreter to all of the church's foundational documents, and that means that John 8—indeed the whole of John's Gospel—is always read and preached together with, for example, Romans 9–11.[14] For when we imaginatively find ourselves in the company of Johannine community members whose beloved kinfolk remain firmly in the synagogue, we can remind ourselves that some members of Paul's churches—and especially members of the church in Rome—were similarly situated (perhaps even Paul himself). Here, then, we cannot resist the impulse to read to ourselves—and imaginatively to these special forebears of ours—the whole of our canon, interpreting John on the basis of Paul and Paul on the basis of John, thereby honoring both.

---

13. Philip Alexander, "The Church and the Jewish People: the Past, the Present, and the Future," Lectures to the School of Fellowship in Alderley Edge, Cheshire (Fall Term, 2001).

14. Roy A. Harrisville and Walter Sundberg, *The Bible in Modern Culture: Baruch Spinoza to Brevard Childs*, 2nd ed. (Grand Rapids: Eerdmans, 2002), 304–28.

CHAPTER 7

Listening to John and Paul on the Subject of Gospel and Scripture[1]

I. Reading as Listening

LET ME BEGIN BY inviting you to take a brief trip, chronologically back in time, a third of a century to 1957, geographically across the Atlantic to the delightfully low-key university town of Göttingen. For me it was a Fulbright year, and the main attraction of Göttingen was the presence there of two very different New Testament scholars: Joachim Jeremias and Ernst Käsemann. The year left indelible marks on me from both men.

At the moment, however, thinking about the year 1957–58 takes me back to two other *Neutestamentler*, Walter Bauer and Ferdinand Christian Baur. And, pondering aspects of the work of the two Bau(e)rs leads me, in turn, to two observations about the learning process that has claimed my allegiance over the third of a century since 1957, and that, more than anything else, has led to several changes of mind.

The first of these observations has to do with Walter Bauer. He had been in Göttingen when Jeremias arrived from Greifswald in 1935. In

1. This essay is a revision of an address presented by J. Louis Martyn at the annual Society of Biblical Literature meetings in New Orleans in 1990. Responses were given by Beverly Roberts Gaventa and Paul W. Meyer, to which Martyn responds at the end. It was first published in *Word and World* 12.2 (1992) 68–81.

1957, this grand old man, then eighty years of age, was still living there, in retirement, and the multiple aspects of his legacy were much in evidence. The one that became most important to me is not to be found in any of his writings, so far as I know. It was a piece of circulating oral tradition, which had it that Bauer had propounded a hermeneutical rule to be used in interpreting early Christian documents:

> On the way toward ascertaining the intention of an early Christian author, the interpreter is first to ask how the original readers of the author's document understood what he had said in it.

It is, at the minimum, an intriguing suggestion. In formulating it, Bauer presupposed, of course, that a thoughtful reader of a document in the New Testament would be concerned to learn everything possible about the author's intention, a clear indication that the famous essay of Wimsatt and Beardsley on the intentional fallacy had not yet made its way across the Atlantic.[2] For Walter Bauer, however, one begins one's reading not by inquiring after the author's intention, but rather, by asking how the author's text was understood by those who first read it.

I should admit that when I initially heard this rule, I was not uncontrollably enamored of it, having developed a certain allergy to discussions of hermeneutics. In retrospect, I can see that it eventually got past my anti-hermeneutical bastion because of a striking experience one had while sitting in a seminar offered by Jeremias. Others will remember, as I do, one's amazement the first time one saw Jeremias stride to the blackboard, open his New Testament to the Gospel of Mark, and, holding it in one hand, begin with the other hand to write the text in Aramaic, as though having given it no thought beforehand. Instant translation, or as he thought, instant *re*translation.

---

2. The essay of Wimsatt and Beardsley is itself widely misconstrued in our time, as Richard B. Hays has recently remarked, *Echoes of Scripture in the Letters of Paul* (New Haven: Yale, 1989), 201 n. 90. Cf. W. Wimsatt Jr. and M. Beardsley, "The Intentional Fallacy," *The Verbal Icon: Studies in the Meaning of Poetry* (Lexington: University of Kentucky Press, 1954).

To one who had struggled with Aramaic under the genial tute-lage of Marvin Pope, it was an amazing feat. Before long, however, I began to sense a head-on collision between Jeremias's act of instant translation and Bauer's rule, and I had no great difficulty in sorting the matter out. The exegetical stance of Jeremias clearly involved an act of interpretive hubris, for in that stance, the first hearers of the Gospel of Mark received no attention at all: the hearers, namely, whom Mark had in mind when he wrote his tome in the Greek language. It seemed no accident, in fact, that the initial hearers of Mark's Gospel and the Evangelist himself disappeared simultaneously.

Thinking of Bauer and Jeremias, one could say, on the pedestrian level, that one colleague was having a mighty brief affair with a Greek lexicon, on which another colleague had spent a large portion of his lifetime. At a deeper level, much more was involved: namely, the question whether, both initially and fundamentally, the New Testament interpreter necessarily has a responsibility that somehow involves the original hearers, *in order* to be able to discharge his responsibility to the author who had those hearers in mind as he wrote. An affirmative answer seems to me to be demanded. Bauer's rule is one of the chief things I have learned and tried to practice over the years; it has more than once led to a change of mind. The second observation from 1957 is focused on the labors of an earlier Baur, the one without the "e," Ferdinand Christian. I had already read fairly widely in Ferdinand Christian Baur's writings, but the year in Göttingen drove me back to his work in a decisive and unexpected way. That happened primarily as a result of truly formative—and very enjoyable—debates with Ernst Käsemann about the Gospel of John. We found ourselves in considerable disagreement, but the disagreement was focused on a question we agreed to be crucial: Where does the document we are reading belong in the strains and stresses characteristic of early Christian history? With regard to every early Christian document, that was one of the chief questions for Ferdinand Christian Baur; during the Göttingen year, it became a truly burning question for me.

What needs to be added is the fact that the period in Göttingen also led—with the passing of time—to a conscious confluence of the hermeneutical rule of Walter Bauer with the historically dynamic, interpretive framework of Ferdinand Christian Baur. The confluence is not hard to explain. First, one thinks again for a moment of the rule of Walter Bauer.

On its face, Bauer's rule may seem quite simple, even simplistic. Pursued both rigorously and poetically, however, the rule proves to be highly complex and immensely rich. For it involves all of the imagination and all of the disciplines necessary for a modern interpreter to take a seat in an early Christian congregation, intent on borrowing the ears of the early Christian neighbors in order to hear the text as they heard it. To mention only a few of these disciplines, the exercise of Bauer's rule involves:

1. Resurrecting the hearers' vocabulary, as it is similar to and as it is different from the vocabulary of the author;

2. Straining to hear the links between the hearer's vocabulary and their social and cultural world, as those links are strengthened and assailed by the author's words;

3. Ferreting out the way in which certain literary and rhetorical forms are likely to have worked on the first listeners' sensibilities;

4. Trying to match the first listeners' ability to hear a fine interplay between figure and narrative, and on and on.

But how, then, does Walter Bauer's rule lead one back to the labors of Ferdinand Christian Baur? If the interpreter's initial step is the attempt to hear an early Christian document with the ears of its first hearers, it follows necessarily that, in addition to the partial list just given, one will have to hear the text as it sounded in the midst of the strains and stresses in early Christian theology that were of major concern to those first hearers.

One listens to an early Christian writing, as far as possible, with the ears of the original hearers; and, listening with those ears, one hears not only the voice of the theologian who authored the document in question, and not only the voices of, say, various itinerant teachers in rural Palestine, and of various street preachers and artisan—philosophers in this or that essentially Greek city—but also one hears the voices of other Christian theologians who prove, more often than not, to be saying rather different things, and in some instances to be saying those different things quite effectively. If one does not hear the chorus of these other voices, one does not really hear the voice of the author as his first hearers heard him.

I mention Göttingen, the year 1957, Walter Bauer, and Ferdinand Christian Baur in order to confess that the interpretive confluence I have just sketched goes a long way toward defining the location and the passion of my own exegetical labors through the years. And, as I have already said, it is that interpretive confluence that has more than once changed my mind, that is to say, has taught me something.

I do know that there are other ways of reading early Christian texts, and some of those ways are, I think, helpful. I have learned—even in my old age—from scholars whose exegetical stance is different from my own. At the moment, however, I am concerned simply to point out that lying in wait for every interpreter is the omnipresent and dangerously unconscious tendency to domesticate the text, to cage the wild tiger. Every serious interpreter, therefore, is looking for an antidote to that domesticating tendency. In my judgment, a truly powerful antidote has been given to us in the heritage that has come our way from Walter Bauer and from Ferdinand Christian Baur.

II. Two Examples of Trying to Listen

Let me now offer very briefly two examples that may illustrate the way in which the interpretive confluence I have just sketched has changed my mind. The general issue to be addressed is that of *Scripture* and *gospel*, and the two examples arise when we interview John and Paul with that issue in mind. How do John and Paul see the relationship between Scripture and gospel? I hardly need to say that the area to which this question points is massive and highly complex. Having been approached in the main by asking how Paul and John interpret Scripture, it is also an area much studied.[3]

Something a bit different might emerge, however, when we ask not how these first-century theologians interpret Scripture, but rather how they see the *relationship* between Scripture and gospel, a distinguishable even if closely related question. Moreover, we will interview them by imaginatively taking up residence in their circles, in order first of all to try to listen to their writings with the ears of their first hearers. And finally, we will mount a galloping horse, in order to see whether attending to both John and Paul in a single essay may enable us to sense an aspect of early Christian theology we may have missed on more pedestrian sorties. Two terms fix the focus of our inquiry, then: Scripture and gospel. And the issue is one of relationship.

A. Scripture and Gospel in John

When we take up temporary residence in the Johannine community, what do we hear? The first thing we note is that without exception John's references to Scripture are references to the Law, the Prophets, and the Writings. When, therefore, he relates Scripture to gospel, he is relating the Law, the Prophets, and the Writings to the gospel of Jesus Christ.

The second thing we sense, as we listen, is that a number of John's references to these ancient Scriptures are couched in a distinctly

---

3. See recently D.-A. Koch, *Die Schrift als Zeuge des Evangeliums* (Tübingen: Mohr/ Siebeck, 1986); Donald Juel, *Messianic Exegesis* (Philadelphia: Fortress, 1988); and Hays, *Echoes of Scripture.*

polemical tone of voice. To take just one example, Jesus says to the crowd of people who have seen him raise the paralytic:

> You search the scriptures, because you think that in them you
> have eternal life; and it is they that bear witness to me; yet you
> refuse to come to me that you may have life. (John 5:39–40)

When John is speaking about or quoting Scripture, his voice often has an edge to it. In part, that edginess is doubtless a rhetorical stratagem, but with Ferdinand Christian Baur at one's elbow, one may also think that this stratagem is designed to play a role in a rather tense setting in the history of early Christian thought and life.

Further listening may convince one, then, that there have been— and probably still are at the time of John's writing his Gospel—theologians both in and around John's community whose understanding of the relationship between gospel and Scripture is not only different from that of John, but is also an understanding of gospel and Scripture that sets his teeth on edge. In order to hear the Gospel of John with the ears of its original listeners, we must try very hard to hear in the background the voices of these other theologians. For the sake of ease of reference, I will refer to these other persons as "the simple-exegetical theologians in John's setting." And, let me repeat that they seem to be located both in and around John's community.[4] How do *they* view Scripture and gospel?

In a word, "simply." Both the exegetical theologians who accept Jesus as God's Son, and those who do not, share one fundamental conviction: They believe that whenever God acts newly, he does so in a way that is demonstrably in accordance with Scripture. Thus, all of these exegetical theologians prefigure C. H. Dodd's book on the subject,[5] by agreeing that the Scriptures form the substructure of true theology.

---

4. Some of these theologians have elected to remain in the synagogue; others are in John's group. With regard to the relationship between Scripture and gospel, they are essentially of one mind.

5. C. H. Dodd, *According to the Scriptures* (London: Nisbet & Co., 1953).

We can be still more specific. These exegetical theologians presuppose a clear trajectory *from* the scriptural expectations connected with various "messianic" figures *to* the figure of the Messiah. They believe, in turn, that all theological issues—including ones having specifically to do with Christology—are *subject to exegetical discussion*.

Now, tuning our ears for John's own voice brings surprises. For when we do that, while hearing the voices of the simple-exegetical theologians ringing in the background, we notice that John's theology is radically different from theirs. To be sure, there is some common ground, and that common ground is important. Like the simple-exegetical theologians, John gives considerable attention to the interpretation of Scripture; and he several times speaks explicitly about the exegetical process itself, making clear that exegesis of Scripture is part of the totality of preaching the gospel.

For John, however, the *relationship* between Scripture and gospel is anything but simple and innocent. He is sure, in fact, that exegesis of Scripture can blind the blind and deafen the deaf. There is, accordingly, a striking subtlety and even, as we will see, a radicality to John's understanding of gospel and Scripture. Three major points stand out.

1. First, John finds that the story of Jesus contains numerous geological faults (*Verwerfungen*), radical disjunctures that cause the gospel story to be a landscape over which it is impossible for human beings to walk.[6] Again and again, the hearer of this gospel senses the motif of the impossibility of human movement. Again and again, the Evangelist hears Jesus say, in effect, "You cannot get *here* from *there*" (see, for example, John 6:44 and 6:65). One does not walk into the community of the redeemed across the terrain that reaches from the past into the present, for there seem to be no bridges that

---

6. For a suggestive use of the term *Verwerfung* in the sense of a geological fault, see G. Bornkamm's critique of Käsemann's "Jesu Letzter Wille Nach Johannes 17" in *Evangelische Theologie* (1968) 8–25; see John Ashton, *The Interpretation of John* (Philadelphia: Fortress, 1986), 91.

reach over the geological fault created by the advent of Christ, the Stranger from Heaven.[7]

2. Second, in the Evangelist's opinion, the impassable geological faults are nowhere more evident than in the relationship of Scripture to Jesus Christ, for that relationship is as riddly and elusive as are Jesus' words, themselves. Contrary to the opinion of the simple-exegetical theologians, exegetical discussion does not offer a route beyond the geological faults. It is thus a fundamental error to think that, if one will only persevere with one's interpretation of Scripture, one can leap over the geological faults from this side.[8]

Does John believe, then, that Scripture has lost its voice altogether? Hardly! The Evangelist several times speaks of *memory* in order explicitly to address the issue of the relation between the proclamation of the gospel and the exegesis of Scripture. When we pause in order to listen with Johannine ears to John's use of the verb μιμνῄσκομαι (bring to remembrance), we sense one of John's basic convictions; and it is a conviction that all members of John's community will have recognized as polemical with respect to the views of the simple-exegetical theologians: Only after Jesus' resurrection/glorification were his disciples given the power of a memory that could believe *both* Scripture *and* Jesus' words (cf. notably John 2:22 and 5:46–47).[9]

The connecting link, then, between Scripture and gospel is a matter of great importance, but for John that link is given by the gospel story itself, a fact that tells us two things: first, that the gospel story has to do with the same God who granted to Isaiah a vision of Jesus' glory

---

7. See Wayne A. Meeks, "The Man from Heaven in Johannine Sectarianism," *JBL Literature* 91 (1972) 44–72; reprinted in Ashton, *The Interpretation of John*; M. de Jonge, *Jesus: Stranger from Heaven and Son of God* (Missoula: Scholars, 1977).

8. For John, Jesus' own lack of education, for example, is a clear warning, showing that his identity cannot be perceived on the basis of exegetical exertion (John 7:15).

9. Those who do not believe Jesus show *thereby* that they do not believe Moses. On "believing in Moses," cf. Wayne Meeks, *The Prophet-King* (Leiden: Brill, 1967), 295.

(John 12:41) and who allowed Abraham to see Jesus' day (John 8:56); and second, that the fundamental arrow in the link joining Scripture and gospel points from the gospel story to Scripture, and not from Scripture to the gospel story.

In a word, with Jesus' glorification, belief in Scripture *comes into being* by acquiring an indelible link to belief in Jesus' words and deeds.[10]

3. Third, while we can do little more here than mention it, John's acknowledgement of the geological faults also produces a radicality in the matter of origins, and thus a view of history that must have been as strange to the simple-exegetical theologians as was his view of the relation of Scripture to gospel. Here the question is not whether John can speak positively of the Jews and of Israel. Clearly he can, and he does. The question is whether for him Scripture points to a *linear* entity that in a linear fashion prepares the way for, and leads up to, the incarnation of the *Logos*. In this regard, we have simply to note in the Gospel of John the absence of even an embryonic *Heilsgeschichte*, a linear sacred history that flows *out of* Scripture *into* the gospel story.[11]

Indeed the *heilsgeschichtliche* perspective is more than absent; it is a perspective against which John is waging a battle. In his gospel, *the* origin, *the* beginning, *the* point of departure for the doing of theology is not to be found in the linear development of a linear history. In the very beginning with God, there was the *Logos*, the Word. He has no precedent in any history, for nothing and no one anteceded him. The *Logos*

10. In Luke 24:6 and 8, a similar motif involves the use of the verb, μιμνῄσκομαι. What is absent in Luke is a sense for the gospel-created geological faults, and thus a theological allergy to the naïve promise-fulfillment hermeneutic.

11. In the scenes presented in John 1:35–51, disciples of the Baptist confess Jesus to be the Messiah, him of whom Moses wrote, Son of God, and King of Israel, thus seeming to make their way *from* scriptural expectations *to* Jesus. I take this material to be tradition that John accepts only because he can enclose it in a gospel that proves overall to be *anti-heilsgeschichtlich*. See R. T. Fortna, *The Fourth Gospel and Its Predecessor* (Philadelphia: Fortress, 1988), 15–47. See also, however, the response below by Professor Gaventa.

alone has been with God. It follows that he alone is the exegete of the Father (1:18), and thus, that nothing and no one can provide the criterion against which he is to be measured, not even Scripture.

B. Scripture and Gospel in Paul

When we turn to Paul's letters, asking about Scripture and gospel, 1 Thessalonians brings us a jolt. That letter contains not one exegetical paragraph. It is both true and important, as Richard Hays has recently argued, that the voice of Scripture is more weighty to Paul himself than one would think, on the basis of his explicit exegeses.[12] Still, the absence of even one of these in 1 Thessalonians is impressive. If we had only that letter, we would have no reason for thinking that Paul ever caused his gentile converts to trouble their minds over the relationship between the gospel and Scripture.

Things change dramatically when we come to Galatians, where we encounter two finely crafted exegetical sections that address quite directly the matter of Scripture and gospel. Indeed, in one of these, Paul speaks in a single sentence of both gospel and Scripture, saying in the main two things: first, that Scripture foresaw a development which is transpiring in the current scene, namely God's present activity in rectifying the gentiles by faith; and second, that, foreseeing this development, Scripture preached the *gospel* ahead of time to Abraham (Gal 3:8; cf. Rom 1:1–2). Thus, the exegetical sections of Galatians offer rich possibilities for the pursuit of our question. Before we look at one of these, however, we will find it profitable to sharpen the issue by a brief detour into 1 Corinthians.

In an arresting paragraph in the first chapter of 1 Corinthians, Paul speaks thematically of the gospel, identifying it as the preaching of the cross. Trying to listen to that paragraph with the ears of the Corinthians, we hear most sharply an utterly outrageous affirmation.

12. See Hays, *Echoes of Scripture*.

Specifically, in 1 Corinthians 1:18, Paul is saying that the gospel of the crucified Christ is not subject, and cannot be made subject, to criteria of perception that have been developed apart from it.[13] To bring this outrageous affirmation into sharp focus, we need to return to the two Bau(e)rs, asking how this affirmation is likely to have been heard by the various factions in the Corinthian Church.

Members of the church for whom the Scriptures were of central importance will have foreshadowed Eusebius and numerous other theologians by holding that God did in fact provide some preparation for the gospel. They will have thought, moreover, that with regard to that preparation, a clear distinction is to be drawn between the scriptural traditions of Israel and the traditions of other peoples. One can imagine a comment from some good, solid exegetical theologian in the Corinthian church:

> Paul may be quite right to say that the gospel is not subject to criteria of perception that have been developed apart from it—among the gentiles! Surely the same does not apply to perceptive criteria embedded in the Scriptures. We have noted that Paul himself quotes from Scripture, and that he does so immediately after insisting that the gospel is not subject to extragospel criteria of perception.

As if to anticipate this line of thought, Paul is shockingly evenhanded when he speaks of the difficulties created by the gospel's refusal to be subject to previously crafted criteria of perception. The gospel of the crucified Christ is foolishness to the gentiles, as one might expect; but that gospel proves, with equal clarity, to be an offensive scandal to the Jews (1 Cor 1:23).[14] No one, and no one's way of understanding the

13. The exegetical arguments given in Martyn, "Paul and His Jewish-Christian Interpreters," *Union Seminary Quarterly Review* 42 (1988) 1–15.

14. W. Schrage, "'. . . den Juden ein Skandalon'? Der Anstoss des Kreuzes nach 1 Kor 1,23," *Gottes Augapfel*, edited by E. Brocke and J. Seim, 2nd ed. (Neukirchen-Vluyn: Neukirchener, 1988), 59–76.

world, is exempted from the geological fault created by God's foolish and scandalous act in the cross of Christ (cf. Rom 3:9).

For our present concern, the point is the explosive implication for the relationship between gospel and Scripture. Obviously, Paul grants to Scripture a role he does not give to any other body of tradition. Yet he is both consistent and comprehensive in his insistence that the gospel cannot be made subject to perceptive criteria developed apart from it. How can Paul have it both ways?

As a hypothesis, one could suggest that, like the Fourth Evangelist, Paul sees no route from Scripture to gospel, while seeing very clearly a route from gospel to Scripture.[15] We might explicate this hypothesis by returning finally to the letter to the Galatians, for the exegetical sections in that letter are indeed produced by the radical hermeneutic we see in the first chapter of 1 Corinthians. Consider, for example, Galatians 4:21—5:1, which features Paul's exegesis of the stories in Genesis 15–21 about Abraham, Sarah, Hagar, Ishmael, and Isaac. When we listen to Paul's exegesis of the Genesis text with the ears of the Galatians, we notice several things.

First, we are immediately thrown back into the company of the two Bau(e)rs, for the form of Paul's exegesis in Galatians 4:21—5:1 shows us that, if we really take our seat in the Galatian churches, we hear not only Paul's words, but also the words of the teachers who invaded those churches.[16] It was in the teachers' sermons, in fact, that we Galatian gentiles *first* heard about Abraham, Sarah, Hagar, Ishmael, and Isaac. And, in the interpretation given by these exegetical theologians, we have noted three major accents, all having to do with the term "covenant":

15. Ph. Vielhauer, "Paulus und das Alte Testament," in *Studien zur Geschichte und Theologie der Reformation: Festschrift für Ernst Bizer*, edited by L. Abramowski et al. (Neukirchen-Vluyn: Neukirchner, 1969), 33–62.

16. On the nomenclature, "the teachers," see J. Louis Martyn, "A Law-Observant Mission to the Gentiles: The Background of Galatians," *Scottish Journal of Theology* 38 (1985) 307–24.

1. God's covenant with Abraham commenced a covenantal line that extended through Isaac to God's people, Israel;

2. God provided a specific definition of his covenant: that covenant is the commandment of circumcision, observed repeatedly in generation after generation (Genesis 17);

3. At the present time, via the good news streaming out from the Jerusalem church, the covenantal line is being extended to gentiles; for, through the Messiah Jesus, gentiles are now invited to enter the line of the Abrahamic covenant by observing the commandment of circumcision.

Second, now we turn with our other ear, so to speak, to listen to Paul's exegesis of Genesis 15–21, and doing that, we find a radically different picture:

1. In his exegesis of Genesis 15–21, Paul gives to the term "covenant" an emphasis at least equal to that given to this term by the teachers;

2. But, departing radically from the plain sense of Genesis 15–21, Paul affirms *two* covenants, diametrically opposed to one another, something not at all to be found in the text itself;

3. Paul is totally silent about the fact that, in the Genesis stories, God specifically defines his one covenant as his commandment of circumcision; Paul is equally silent about there being in his Scripture no covenant attached to Hagar and her son Ishmael.[17]

Of two things we can be confident. First, we can say that, when Paul's messenger had finished reading aloud this exegetical section of Galatians, both the teachers who had invaded Paul's Galatian churches and their followers must have risen to their feet, vociferously condemning it as one of the most arbitrary and unfaithful interpretations one can

17. Cf. J. L. Martyn, "The Covenants of Hagar and Sarah," *Faith and History: Essays in Honor of Paul W. Meyer,* edited by John T. Carroll et al. (Atlanta: Scholars, 1991), 160–92.

imagine.[18] Second, we can be equally sure, though, that when Paul had finished dictating this paragraph, he was certain that, by providing *this* exegesis of Scripture, he had preached the *gospel* once again, and specifically the gospel that was "in accordance with the Scriptures," the gospel, indeed, that had been preached ahead of time to Abraham by Scripture, itself.

Pause now for a moment, and allow yourself the fantasy of being able to raise with Paul the matter of ancient texts often being subjected to eisegetical domestication. And, since you are indulging in a fantasy, you might as well go ahead by suggesting to Paul that Galatians 4:21—5:1 is a prime instance of such eisegetical domestication. If you have enough imagination to do all of that, then you also have enough imagination to hear Paul's response:

> Whether in interpreting the stories in Genesis 15–21 I have used the gospel to domesticate the voice of Scripture is a question that can be answered only on the basis of the gospel.[19]

One hardly needs to add that, with that response, Paul takes us back to the radical hermeneutic of the first chapter of 1 Corinthians, and we are thus faced with some of the specific dimensions of Paul's understanding of the relationship between gospel and Scripture.

If the gospel is significantly related to Scripture—and for Paul it is—and if the gospel of the crucified Christ nevertheless brings its own criteria of perception, then in the case of Paul, as in the case of John,

---

18. Jewish scholars of our time have understandably characterized it in similar terms; see, e.g., Schalom Ben-Chorin, *Paulus, der Völkerapostel in jüdischer Sicht* (Munich: Taschenbuch Verlag, 1980), 132: "eine völlige Umdrehung der Vätersage."

19. It is imperative to note that Paul believes Scripture actually says exactly what he hears it saying. He is not constructing what some rabbis of the Middle Ages called *pilpul*, an exegesis one knows not to correspond to the original meaning. In fact, Paul does not think of one meaning back then and a second and debatable meaning now. For him, the scriptural stories in Genesis 15–21 do in fact speak about the two gentile missions: one law-observant and one law-free, thus uttering the gospel ahead of time (cf. 1 Cor 10:11).

it is misleading to speak of an even-handed dialectical relationship between Scripture and gospel.[20] That much should be clear from the fact that, for Paul, the text of Scripture no longer reads as it did before the advent of the gospel.[21] When one needs to do so—and most of Paul's formal exegetical exercises are polemical[22]—one *can* find in Scripture a voice that testifies to the gospel. But, one finds this testifying voice—the voice of God in Scripture—only because one already hears God's voice in the gospel, that is to say, in the story of the cross: the story that brings its own criteria of perception, the story, therefore, that brings its own criteria of exegesis.

20. Note Ph. Vielhauer's critique of statements by U. Wilckens: "So gewiss 'das Christusgeschehen ... nicht als isoliertes Faktum in seinem universal-eschatologischen *Heils*sinne erkannt und verstanden werden (kann)', so wenig ist die Behauptung begründet: 'es bedarf des Zeugnisses der Geschichte, deren Erfüllung es ist'. . . ; denn so gewiss Abraham für Paulus von hoher theologischen Bedeutung und so gewiss die Verheissung dem Gesetz vorgeordnet ist, so gewiss gibt der Text von Röm 4 und Gal 3 die Folgerung auf eine ' *Erwählungsgeschichte*' nicht her . . . . Die Geschichte Israels als Ablauf interessiert den Apostel überhaupt nicht." Ph. Vielhauer, *Oikodome. Aufsätze zum Neuen Testament*, Vol. 1 (Munich: Kaiser, 1979), 217–18.

21. Hays, *Echoes of Scripture*, 149: "This means, ultimately, that Scripture becomes—in Paul's reading—a metaphor, a vast trope that signifies and illuminates the gospel of Jesus Christ."

22. Regarding the thesis that Paul's exegetical efforts are mostly polemical, see A. von Harnack, "Das Alte Testament in den Paulinischen Briefen und in den Paulinischen Gemeinden," *Sitzungsberichte der Preussischen Akademie der Wissenschaften* (Berlin: Akademie der Wissenschaften, 1928), 124–41. From the work of E. Grässer, *Der Alte Bund im Neuen* (Tübingen: Mohr Siebeck, 1985), it seems clear that all of the crucial διαθήκη passages in Paul's letters (Gal 3; 4; 2 Cor 3) are exegeses formulated by Paul in an explicitly polemical form because of opponents in Galatia and in Corinth who are speaking *scripturally* to his churches about the term διαθήκη. Paul is an exegetically active "covenantal theologian" only when compelled to be.

III. A Few Provisional Conclusions

To listen to John and Paul with ears borrowed from members of their own circles is, at least in my experience, to have one's mind repeatedly changed by noting several things.

1. To a considerable extent, the earliest history of Christian thought and life can be profitably analyzed as the history of various struggles over a single issue: Is the gospel of the crucifixion and resurrection of Jesus Christ subject to criteria of perception that have been developed apart from it? And with regard to this issue, Paul and John share a number of convictions, not least the belief that, prior to the event of the gospel, the human being does not possess adequate powers of perception any more than he or she possesses freedom of will. One hardly needs to add that the issue of perceptive criteria became truly thorny when one was asking whether the gospel was subject to criteria of perception one had inherited *in Scripture.* For, to take one's bearings again from Paul and John, one would say that the human being cannot find these adequate powers of perception even in the Scriptures themselves.

2. When we analyze early Christian history in the light of this issue, listening to the multitude of voices that were directed to it, we see that, more often than we should like to admit, we have attributed a motif to John or Paul, when in actuality that motif is characteristic of theologians against whom these authors were waging a significant battle.[23]

3. Why have we often done that? In part, I think, because we have been unconsciously afraid that, if Paul and John should prove to be *anti-heilsgeschichtlich* theologians, they would also prove to

---

23. An example lies before us, I think, in the chart E. P. Sanders presents in *Paul, the Law, and the Jewish People* (Philadelphia: Fortress, 1983), 7. To speak of the human being transferring from sin to righteousness is characteristic of the teachers who invaded Paul's Galatian churches, not of Paul himself.

have applied to Scripture an anti-Judaic hermeneutic. That fear is unfounded. Theologically, it is important to note that neither Paul nor John was an absolute innovator. In Scripture itself, there is ancient tradition for theology oriented to the geological fault. Consider two examples: Psalm 78 and Second Isaiah. The prophet, you will recall, several times calls on his fellow exiles to remember the things of old—to remember the exodus—in the sure hope of the new exodus, and so on. One time, however, he reflects on the ways in which tradition can blind eyes and stop ears. Thus he hears God say with emphasis:

> Do *not* remember the former things, nor remember the things of old. Behold I am doing a new thing; now it springs forth; do you not perceive it? (Isa 43:18–19)

4. Even the similar note in the Second Isaiah cannot forestall, however, a final question: Did Paul and John unwittingly prepare the way for Marcion? In the present context, this question has to be posed for two reasons.

First, the battle that raged around Marcion was focused, to no small degree, on the issue to which we have been directing our attention: that of the relationship between Scripture and gospel. Second, when the emerging great church identified Marcion's theology as heretical, it did so in part by adopting a view of the relationship between Scripture and gospel that in general terms looks rather similar to the view of the simple-exegetical theologians against whom Paul and John struggled in the first century (Justin Martyr; Rhodo; Irenaeus). Had the orthodox theologians of the great church had an accurate sense for the faulty theology of Paul and John, would they not have been compelled to draw some degree of analogy between those two and Marcion, thus raising some doubts as to the complete orthodoxy precisely of Paul and John, themselves?[24]

The raising of the question can lead us to a closing point. If one of the most virulent heresies of the second century emerged in connection with the matter of gospel and Scripture, may it not be that the same is true of the first century, except that, as one passes from one century to the other, the identities of orthodoxy and heresy undergo a remarkable reversal?

If one listens to Paul and John, and if, at least tentatively, one takes one's view of heresy from them (note the term *anathema* in Galatians 1:8–9), then one could be led to ponder the possibility that, while the problem of relating Scripture to gospel did in fact produce several heresies, the earliest of these wore a very un-Marcionite hat, being the cross-avoiding, simpleminded, exegetical view of Scripture and gospel that flourished in some circles almost from the beginning. It is the author of the letter to the Galatians, at any rate, who is the theologian of the cross, whereas the teachers are theologians of an incipient *Heilsgeschichte*.

Could it be, then, that thinking in a Pauline-Johannine mode would lead one to identify as the *earliest Christian heresy* precisely the embryonic *Heilsgeschichte* characteristic of the simple-theologians? And, would one then trace as heretical the heritage from those theologians that made its way through the centuries to the full-blown *Heilsge-schichte* of Eusebius, J. C. K. von Hofmann, Tobias Beck, and others?

However those questions are to be answered, it seems that Paul and John, in their respective settings, perceived it to be an essential part of their vocation to struggle against an incipiently *heilsgeschich-tlich* reading of the relationship between Scripture and gospel. And, positively put, they carried out that struggle, precisely in order to bear witness to the true identity of the God of Abraham by speaking of him

---

24. As the Gospel of John won its place in the canon only with difficulty, that development has rightly been said to have occurred "through man's error and God's providence." E. Käsemann, *The Testament of Jesus*, Johannine Monograph Series 6 (1968, Eugene, OR: Wipf & Stock, 2017), 75.

as the Father of Jesus Christ. By his deed in the crucified Christ, this God is announcing who he is, and thus showing who he always was: the one who rectifies the ungodly. It follows that this God is sovereign, even over traditions celebrating his own earlier deeds.

The struggle of Paul and John is thus one that Second Isaiah would have understood.

Critical Responses

In her critique, Beverly Gaventa expressed a measure of agreement as regards Paul and some serious reservations with respect to John. In her remarks, I heard two major points: (a) The location of inadequacy to assess the gospel. Does it lie with Scripture or with human beings? (b) The role of Scripture is making the gospel intelligible. What is signified by the line that runs from gospel to Scripture?

Regarding John:

> The target [of John's polemic in 5:39–47] is not the adequacy of Scripture to reveal Jesus Christ. The target . . . is the adequacy of human beings, who read Scripture—which does testify on behalf of Jesus—without seeing what it says. [Thus,] while John practices an interpretation that reads Scripture by means of the gospel and not the other way around, he nevertheless perceives a line . . . [that] begins with God and the Logos, . . . contains the history of Israel and, with it, Scripture, and then culminates in the gospel. The *Logos* thus precedes Scripture, but Scripture in turn points toward the advent of Jesus [note particularly John 1:35–51].

Regarding Paul:

> [The apostle holds as a major conviction] the inadequacy
> of human beings to assess the gospel, [but] this conviction
> comes to expression in terms drawn from Scripture (e.g. 1
> Cor 1:19–31). [Paul does not reason from Scripture to the
> cross, but—even in 1 Thessalonians—the words and echoes
> of Scripture] provide the language with which Paul articu-
> lates the meaning of the gospel. [That is so because] the
> gospel . . . remains unintelligible apart from the language of
> Scripture and the story of Israel. [In short, for Paul] Scrip-
> ture is not only a convenient mode for interpretation but a
> vital requirement.

This is, I think, a constructive critique. Both John and Paul focus the
polemic I have discussed against other *interpreters* of Scripture, while
being able themselves, beginning with the gospel, to hear God's voice in
Scripture itself. But what is one to make of Gaventa's use of the expression, "the story of Israel"? If, in Galatians, Paul understands Abraham
to be a point rather than the beginning of a line, and if our word "story"
indicates a narrative always possessing some sort of linearity, then can we
say that Paul articulates the gospel by drawing not only on the language
of Scripture, but also on the story of Israel? It is a service of Gaventa to
express herself in a way that calls for further substantive discussion.

    In contrast to Beverly Gaventa, and perhaps as much to her sur-
prise as to mine, Paul Meyer professed basic agreement with my remarks about John, while expressing a significant degree of skepticism
about my reading of Paul.

Regarding John

> This gospel avoids making Jesus as Messiah dependent upon
> the Hebrew Scriptures or any tradition of their interpretation.
> In John's theology, the Son is so carefully aligned with the

Father who sent him, so completely transparent to the presence and reality of the God who confronts the world in him, that there is no possibility of any independent access to God to establish the credentials of the Son.

Regarding Paul,

[For Paul, Scripture is far too important to be left in the hands of] those who are intent on domesticating the gospel to their own criteria of perception. It provides access not just to the continuities of Israel but to the God of Israel, who is the "antecedent" of the gospel as well as its *ex post facto* authorizer, indeed who cannot be the latter without being the former, without whom the gospel too would have no validity.

The appeal to Abraham does provide to Paul, in his own hands of course, a confirmation to his preaching of the gospel . . . that parallels the confirmation that God himself provided when he . . . "raised Jesus our Lord from the dead." Without this authentication from Scripture, i.e., from God's side, Paul's argument would no more be believed and trusted than could the dead Jesus of Nazareth apart from his authentication from God's side. It is not just criteria of perception that are at stake in the relationship of gospel and Scripture. It is also a matter of categories of interpretation . . . and above all, within the historically concrete process of a life-and-death argument about God, a way of reaching beyond the tools of argument to a truth and reality that argument alone cannot establish or adjudicate. It requires a Scripture that is more than a product of Paul's hermeneutic, one in which God speaks before human beings interpret. [The issue is] fundamentally the relationship between the Father of Jesus Christ and the God of Abraham, Isaac, and Jacob.

Like Gaventa, Meyer has provided a critique that is constructive by raising in one's mind further questions. Let me mention two: (a) Granted that Paul was in every instance concerned to search for a way of reaching beyond the tools of argument, can we say that he was success-ful in this search? And if he was, can we identify the result? Is further conversation perhaps needed with regard to the relationship between Scripture and the event of apocalypse? (b) Granted also that the God who sent his Son is the God who uttered his promise to Abraham. Both of these deeds are deeds of the same God; thus the expression "God's steadfast identity" is altogether crucial, especially in light of the continuing influence of a Marcionite type of thought in the modem church. Could it be, however, that Paul compels us to use the terms "identity," "identical," and "identify" in several ways? Gaventa, Meyer, and I should surely agree that Romans 9–11 shows us a theologian who is thoroughly convinced that the God who elected Abraham is identical with the God who sent his Son. Is this theologian also concerned to say that, in sending his Son, this one God is *newly identifying himself* as the one who rectifies the ungodly? And if so, is this dual use of the root *idem* something that was missed (to make theology of linguistics) both by Marcion and by many of those who read Marcion out of the church? With hearty thanks to Beverly Gaventa and to Paul Meyer, let me say that the discussion is to be continued.